War and Trade with the Pharaohs

War and Trade with the Pharaohs

An Archaeological Study of Ancient Egypt's Foreign Relations

By
Garry J. Shaw

PEN & SWORD
ARCHAEOLOGY

First published in Great Britain in 2017 by
Pen & Sword Archaeology
An imprint of
Pen & Sword Books Ltd
47 Church Street
Barnsley
South Yorkshire
S70 2AS

ISBN 978 1 78303 046 0

A CIP catalogue record for this book is
available from the British Library.

Printed and bound in Malta
By Gutenberg Press Ltd.

Pen & Sword Books Ltd incorporates the Imprints of Pen & Sword Books
Archaeology, Atlas, Aviation, Battleground, Discovery, Family History, History,
Maritime, Military, Naval, Politics, Railways, Select, Transport, True Crime,
Fiction, Frontline Books, Leo Cooper, Praetorian Press, Seaforth Publishing,
Wharncliffe and White Owl.

For a complete list of Pen & Sword titles please contact
PEN & SWORD BOOKS LIMITED
47 Church Street, Barnsley, South Yorkshire, S70 2AS, England
E-mail: enquiries@pen-and-sword.co.uk
Website: www.pen-and-sword.co.uk

Contents

Maps

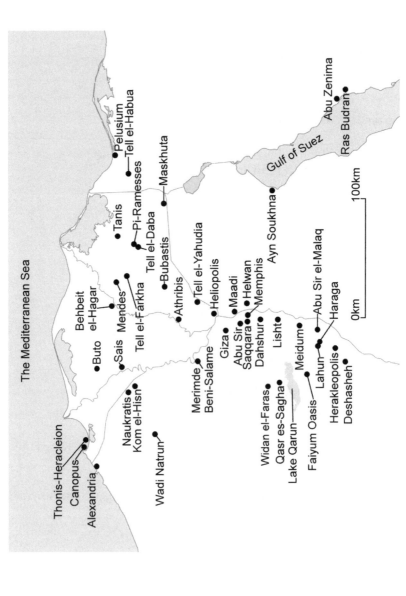

Map 1: Lower Egypt. Adapted by the author from a map made with Natural Earth.

Map 2: Middle and Upper Egypt. Adapted by the author from a map made with Natural Earth.

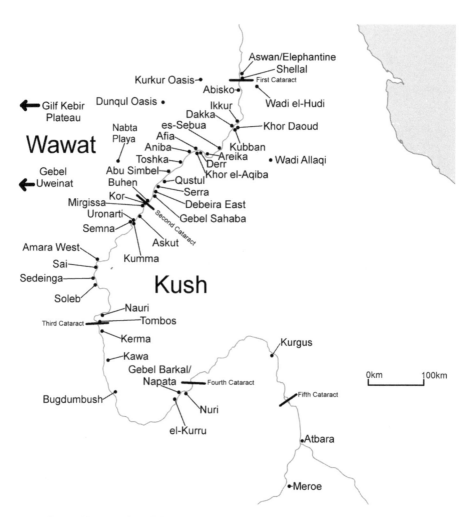

Map 3: Nubia. Made with Natural Earth.

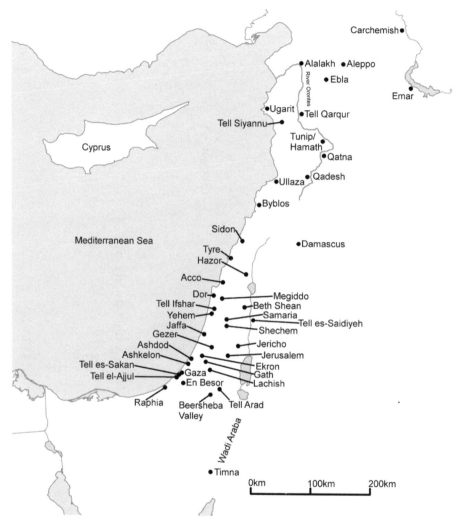

Map 4: The Levant. Adapted by the author from a map made with Natural Earth.

Map 5: The Eastern Mediterranean and Mesopotamia. Made with Natural Earth.

Acknowledgements

I'd like to thank Julie Patenaude for reading and commenting on the initial drafts of my manuscript (and for providing photographs), and Henning Franzmeier of the Qantir-Piramesse Project, for giving me permission to include photographs from the team's excavations, as well as one of his own photographs. I'm also grateful to everyone at Pen and Sword for giving me the opportunity to write, what I hope, is a readable and useful introduction to Ancient Egypt's foreign relations. Finally, many thanks to my students at the Bloomsbury Summer School 2015, who took my course 'Pharaoh's Friends and Foes: Diplomacy, Trade, Travel, and Warfare' – your questions and comments helped a great deal during the writing of this book.

This book is dedicated to my brother, Peter Shaw.

Preface: Crossroads

When we look at a map of Ancient Egypt, its limits create the illusion of a country separated from the rest of the world – a place of isolation and borders – a thin strip of green in an unforgiving sea of yellow. Introductions to Ancient Egypt also tend to emphasize the country's natural barriers: the Mediterranean Sea to the north; the Eastern and Western Deserts; the difficult to navigate Nile Cataracts in the south. But how true is this idea of an isolated Egypt? How connected were the Ancient Egyptians with their neighbours? If they were so isolated, how did they trade? And how did they interact with foreigners in times of war and peace?

Let's start again with a different approach: rather than regarding Egypt as an isolated piece of north-east Africa – a fertile anomaly in the desert – what if we view it as a gateway? A hub, connected to the Mediterranean Sea and the world beyond, to Asia via the Sinai, and south – along the Nile, the Red Sea, and desert routes – further into Africa. Throughout ancient history, boats arrived on Egypt's northern coast and sailed along the Delta's tributaries to reach the Nile; traders from all directions crossed desert tracks into the Nile Valley; and Egyptians left their homeland to visit neighbouring cultures, trading goods, sharing knowledge, and sometimes waging war. Many of the boundaries said to isolate the Egyptians were no such thing: Egypt was, in fact, a crossroads. What follows is a story of interactions: of warfare, trade, immigration, and emigration.

Just as Egypt's isolation is a popular misconception, its unchanging character is too. Throughout Egyptian history, there were political changes, technological advancements, and religious developments. An Old Kingdom Egyptian might recognize a Late Period Egyptian as one of his fellow countrymen, but they would probably find it hard to relate to one another – too much had happened in the 2,000 years that separated them. Egypt's interactions with the wider world changed over time too: foreign civilizations emerged and crumbled, empires rose and fell, and periods of warfare gave way to times of friendship. Slowly, but continuously, the Egyptians were changed by their interactions. Nothing happens in a vacuum – we are each the products of decisions taken by people we will never know or meet, many long dead, and the Egyptians were no different. Their society was not isolated, and far from static.

The Egyptians saw their land as crossing a great disc, the fertile land and the River Nile at its centre representing order, balance, and justice, a concept known to them as *maat*. Surrounding them were foreign lands, representative of disorder (*isfet*), and above were the gods, distant in the sky. The Egyptians also saw duality everywhere, an interest that probably stems from the prominent divisions in the environment around them: the marked difference between the marshy Delta and the thin path of the Nile Valley to its south led them to separate Lower Egypt (the north) from Upper Egypt (the south). While *kemet*, the black fertile soil that flanks the Nile, found its opposite in *djeseret* – 'the red land' – the dangerous desert beyond.

Egypt, as a geographic entity, expanded and contracted as the centuries passed. The Sinai was not always under Pharaonic influence, neither was the desert west beyond the Nile Valley. Sometimes the pharaoh's control ended at the First Cataract, at others it pushed towards the Fourth. The Egyptians had two concepts of 'borders': cosmic borders, which could never be crossed, called *djer*, and physical borders, called *tash*, often marked by boundary stelae, which designated the political limits of control. But despite such strict terminology, for much of Egyptian history, rather than clear borders, there were 'borderlands' between the Egyptians and their neighbouring cultures, places where the ownership of the territory was in flux.

For the purposes of this book, we will regard 'Ancient Egypt' as the land stretching from the northern coast of the Delta south to Aswan at the Nile's First Cataract (the Nile having Six Cataracts – patches where the river is difficult to navigate due to rocks, rapids, or shallows). And to the east and west, I'll follow the modern definition: the eastern edge being just beyond the Sinai Peninsula, and the western edge just beyond Siwa Oasis.

Foreigners and Warfare

Throughout Egyptian history, and even in prehistory, the Egyptians came into frequent contact with their neighbours, who they referred to as *khastyu*, literally 'people from the hill countries,' but often simply translated as 'foreigners.' The Egyptians were intrigued by the geography of the world beyond the Nile Valley, seeing a place of hills and uneven terrain, quite different from the level-terrain of their home. They were also interested in the people of the world, dividing them into four groups: Egyptians, Nubians, Libyans, and Asiatics. These, including themselves, were depicted in standardized, stereotyped ways, making them immediately recognizable, as if they were hieroglyphs representing the people of Egypt, the south, west and east, irrespective of how they might appear in real life.

The people of Nubia – an area defined as lying between the First Cataract of the Nile and the Fifth Cataract – were known to the Ancient Egyptians as Nehesyu, and Nubia itself was subdivided into Lower Nubia, called Wawat – the area between the First Cataract and the Second Cataract – and Upper Nubia, called Kush, from the Second Cataract to the Fifth Cataract. People from the Levant – the strip of land running along the eastern side of the Mediterranean, comprising modern Palestine, Israel, Lebanon, and Syria – and those generally from the east, were called Aamu, translated normally as 'Asiatics.' Meanwhile, Libyans – effectively anyone from the west of Egypt – were called Tjehenu if they lived roughly west of the Delta, and Tjemehu if they lived further south (although the number of Libyan peoples known increases from the New Kingdom). Each 'people' of the world was subdivided into many other cultural groups, which we will encounter as we progress through this book. The Egyptians also identified foreign groups by their clothing or skills; Asiatics could be called 'shoulder-knot people' because of their distinctive clothing, and Nubians 'bowmen' because of their famed proficiency at archery.

Given the Egyptians' longstanding (and lucrative) contacts with people from all directions, even in Predynastic times, it is a curious aspect of their worldview that 'foreigners' came to be regarded as the ultimate representatives of disorder – the official antithesis of everything Egyptian. This view remained a key part of Egyptian royal ideology and presentation for over 3,000 years: whether a king fought a military campaign or not, he still had himself depicted smiting an assortment of foreign enemies, smashing their skulls in with his mace or axe; the underside of the pharaoh's sandals bore images of foreigners, so that with every step, he trampled his enemies; and the phrase 'nine bows' referred to the totality of Egypt's enemies, which as well as being represented as bows, could be shown in art as nine bound foreigners. Wars were presented on temple walls and royal stelae as times of glory, when the pharaohs speared, cut down, smote, and burned their enemies in the name of the gods. In such scenes, the king is often depicted on a massive scale, riding into battle, crushing his foes, who fall chaotically beneath the hooves of his horses and the wheels of his chariots. Captured enemies were ceremonially executed.

So far, so nasty. You'd think that the Ancient Egyptians hated everything foreign and wanted nothing to do with anyone from beyond their borders.

We must remember, however, that there was the reality of the Egyptians' daily interactions with foreigners, and the ideological fiction – repetitive themes used to promote Egypt's superiority – presented on temple walls and tombs. One moment, the king could be giving his artisans the go-ahead to carve a massive royal 'smiting scene' on his temple gateway – showing him as embodiment of order and destroyer of foreigners; the next, he could be drafting a diplomatic letter to one of his fellow 'great kings' elsewhere in the world, expressing brotherhood and friendship. Some kings were served by viziers, butlers, and chief craftsmen (among many other roles) of foreign origin, and foreigners even worked on the royal tombs, not as slaves, but as members of the artisan community.

Foreigners lived in Egyptian society at all levels, from slaves and mercenaries, to merchants and viziers. Travelling around Ancient Egypt, there'd be a good chance that you'd bump into someone of Libyan descent, or from Nubia. Similarly, in the Levant, you might meet Egyptians, perhaps traders or interpreters, soldiers, and diplomats. On a state level, foreigners were treated as enemies, disordered, wretched, and cowardly, but in daily life, the reality of interacting with non-Egyptians was quite different.

Nonetheless, most foreigners entered Egypt as slaves, having been traded or captured as prisoners of war (described as 'bound for life'); indeed, military raids in Nubia, Libya, and the Levant were sometimes conducted in order to abduct people for work on State projects. Treated as property, these foreign slaves were normally forced to work for households, temples, and building projects; they had no rights (though from the Ramesside Period, they could own property), and passed their status on to their children, but could be freed by their owners.

Ancient Egyptian Chronology

The 'Pharaonic Period' of Egyptian history stretches from around 3100 BCE to the arrival of Alexander the Great in 332 BCE. According to an Egyptian priest named Manetho, who lived in the third century BCE, thirty dynasties of kings ruled during this nearly 3,000 year span of time (later writers added a thirty-first for the final Persian occupation). Although each dynasty should really represent a single royal family line (a ruling house or single bloodline), Manetho also created a division when a major event occurred; so, for example, King Khasekhemwy, last king of the 2nd Dynasty is the father of King Djoser, first king of the 3rd Dynasty, but Manetho created a division because Djoser erected the first pyramid.

Though adapted to reflect current research, modern scholars still use Manetho's dynastic divisions, and have grouped them into longer chronological phases, defined by whether Egypt was unified and ruled by a single king ('kingdoms'), or had entered a period of political disunity, when multiple kings ruled simultaneously ('intermediate periods'). These are: the Early Dynastic Period, the Old Kingdom, the First Intermediate Period, the Middle Kingdom, the Second Intermediate Period, the New Kingdom, the Third Intermediate Period, and the Late Period. The phase before Egypt's unification under a single king is called the Predynastic Period. Taken together, the general divisions of Egyptian history can be broken down as follows (all dates until 664 BCE, are approximate):

Period	Dynasties	Dates
Predynastic Period		*ca*. 5000–3100 BCE
Early Dynastic Period	1–2	*ca*. 3100–2584 BCE
Old Kingdom	3–6	*ca*. 2584–2117 BCE
First Intermediate Period	7–11 (first half)	*ca*. 2117–2066 BCE
Middle Kingdom	11–12	*ca*. 2066–1781 BCE
Second Intermediate Period	13–17	*ca*. 1781–1549 BCE
New Kingdom	18–20	*ca*. 1549–1064 BCE
Third Intermediate Period	21–25	*ca*. 1064–664 BCE
Late Period	26–30	664–332 BCE

Approaching this Book

This book is aimed at interested readers with little to no previous knowledge of Ancient Egypt, and undergraduate students wanting to learn more about Egypt's foreign relations. Throughout, I've tried to strike a balance between the latest discoveries and the 'greatest hits' of Egyptian history (the Battle of Qadesh under Ramesses II, for example), with the aim of providing a readable, enjoyable, and accessible account of what is (to put it mildly) a very large subject. Presented chronologically, from the Predynastic Period through to the arrival of Alexander the Great, it is also a history of Ancient Egypt, viewed through the prism of Egyptian activity abroad and foreign activity in Egypt. Along the way, we'll examine warfare, diplomacy, trade, tourism, immigration, and emigration, always with an eye on the wider world and its interactions with Egypt. As much as possible, I've tried to provide the wider context, describing what was going on beyond Egypt's borders at any one time. This, I hope, will create a smoother understanding of historical events.

So, passports ready, bags (over)packed (do you really need all those socks?), guidebook at hand, chariot horses fed and watered, it's time to begin our journey through time: and our first stop is an Egypt quite unlike the one we usually imagine.

Chapter 1

Another World
(10000–2584 BCE)

Twelve thousand years ago, there was no Egypt and no Nubia, no borders or nations, just an expanse of land in north-east Africa, where people spent their lives hunting and gathering food. Their world consisted of the land along the banks of the Nile and, further west, the lakes and grasslands fed by sporadic torrential rains in what today is entirely desert. Wandering this savannah, in small groups, people hunted animals using weapons of stone, wood, and bone, fished, and gathered plants to eat. They moved with the seasons, covering great distances, and probably shared whatever food they gathered among the group. Lions, elephants, ostriches, and giraffes still roamed the vast plains. It had been this way for hundreds of thousands of years. The civilization of 'Ancient Egypt,' with its pharaohs, complex bureaucracy, and famous architecture, would not exist for several thousand years more. Its future existence could not have been predicted or even imagined. It was truly another world.

During the ninth millennium BCE, the people of south-west Asia learnt how to domesticate animals – sheep and goats, then cattle and pigs. Although exchange contacts existed between Egypt and the Levant from at least 11000 BCE, the Egyptians only adopted animal domestication sometime between 7000 and 5000 BCE. Still, better late than never, once they'd taken up breeding and herding sheep and goats – both species previously unknown in Egypt – as well as cattle, they never looked back to their hunter-gatherer ways. To the people of Nubia, south of Egypt, however, animal domestication was nothing new: archaeologists have found evidence for domesticated cattle in the region as early as 8400 BCE at Bir Kiseiba, and from 7750 BCE at Nabta Playa.

Life in Egypt might have continued this way indefinitely if climatic change hadn't intervened. From around 5300 BCE, the savannah west of the Nile started to become increasingly arid. The lakes dried up. People had to adapt. Some chose to move east and settle on the banks of the Nile. Others travelled south into Nubia, to live in the fertile zone around Kerma, near the Nile's Third Cataract. Established in their new environment, these early people of the Nile now adopted another south-west Asian innovation (one known there since the tenth millennium BCE): plant cultivation. With the introduction of domesticated grains – emmer wheat and barley – in around 5000 BCE, many Egyptians settled down to sedentary lives of farming. They founded settlements along the thin band of cultivable land flanking the Nile, following its course, causing these villages, despite their distance from one another, to become part of an interconnected chain. This brought challenges: notably, each village had to get on with its neighbours – there was really no way of avoiding them anymore. And if people couldn't get along peacefully – say, by refusing to share goods or by forbidding trade items to pass through their territory – the only option was violence.

Conflict must have occurred reasonably frequently among these early settlers along the Nile; this was certainly the case thousands of years earlier, in around 11000 BCE, when a similar period of climatic change forced northeast Africa's hunter-gatherers to temporarily live along the banks of the river. One group moved to Gebel Sahaba, just north of the Second Cataract, where, they probably imagined, there'd be plenty to hunt and gather. The problem was, every other tribe had come to the same conclusion. Competing tribes, previously spread out, now lived in close proximity, each vying for the same precious resources. Forsaking their traditional egalitarianism, violence erupted. Gebel Sahaba's men, women, and children became the targets of repeated raids, their bones shattered by invaders armed with maces, and pierced by arrows and spears. Of the bodies buried in the village cemetery – one of the earliest true cemeteries known – 45 per cent died from their wounds. Some were buried with arrows still puncturing their bodies. Others, wounded during the attacks, slowly healed and lived out their lives; beneath the skin, however, their skeletons still bore the marks of their violent experiences.

Let's All Meet Up in the Year 5000 (BCE)

By the fifth millennium BCE, the disparate tribes living along the Nile had merged to form distinct cultural groups, marking the start of a phase known as the Predynastic Period (i.e. a time before successive dynasties of kings came to rule the whole of Egypt). In northern Egypt alone, three separate cultures co-existed: one at Lake Qarun in the Faiyum Oasis; one on the western edge of the Delta, with a major settlement at Merimde Beni-Salame (where villagers buried their dead – particularly infants – within the settlement, rather than outside); and the third – today known as the el-Omari Culture – on the east bank of the Nile, just south of modern Cairo. Having each abandoned their hunter-gatherer lifestyles, these groups now cultivated crops, bred domesticated animals, and lived settled lives in small villages with grain silos. Each group also used their own unique tools, including items that other contemporary cultures hadn't developed, suggesting a lack of sharing, and a sense of 'us versus them.' Nonetheless, they still interacted with one another to some degree: a turquoise bead found at Lake Qarun, as well as a shark's tooth and seashells from the Red Sea, may indicate early contact between the Faiyumian Culture and people living in the Sinai. They also had access to diorite, a hard stone found in Nubia. Herringbone motifs – typical of the Levant – decorate Merimde Culture pottery; and certain pottery-manufacturing methods used by the el-Omari Culture are similar to those found in the Levant.

Further south, in Middle Egypt, another cultural group had developed in the region of modern el-Badari – referred to as 'Badarians' by scholars. From 4400 to 4000 BCE, Badarian material culture, including their distinctive pottery, could be found at sites dotted across Upper Egypt, south of their heartland. Archaeologists have also discovered Badarian stone arrowheads in the Faiyum, indicating some degree of contact with their northern neighbours. Unlike the Delta population at this time, however, the Badarians also had access to copper, which they hammered into shape (as opposed to casting), creating tools, beads, and decorative pins, among other items. They probably gained this copper directly from Levantine groups mining across the Red Sea in the Sinai; the Badarians placed Red Sea shells in their graves and sometimes buried their dead in the Wadi Hammamat – a route through the Eastern Desert, connecting the Nile Valley with the Red Sea – showing that they knew this region well; it was therefore probably somewhere along the Red Sea coast that they met and traded with these Levantine miners.

At the same time, the increasing aridity of the Western Desert continued to force people eastward, out of the dying savannah and into Middle Egypt; these settled among the Badarians, bringing along their own material culture, which the Badarians adopted. Nubians of the Abkan Culture (see below) travelled north too, and had a similarly strong influence on the Badarians; for one, the Badarians started producing black-topped pottery, characteristic of Nubian material culture, and adopted Abkan stone tools.

The Abkan Culture flourished in Nubia between the Nile's Second and Third Cataracts from the start of the fifth millennium BCE. They relied mainly on fishing and gathering to sustain themselves, and so built their settlements close to the Nile. They may have bred and raised goats on a small-scale too. Though producing their own distinctive pottery and stone tools, the Abkan Culture was connected with another Nubian group, who lived further south along the Nile: the people of the Khartoum Neolithic (*ca.* 4900–3800 BCE). Unlike the Abkan people, these kept domesticated cattle and grew crops.

As the years passed, each of these cultures continued to evolve, expanding their territory, merging, developing their technology, and influencing one another. In fact, by 4000 BCE, they had changed so radically that north-east Africa's cultural map had been rewritten. The various cultures of Egypt's north had by now coalesced into one dominant group: the Lower Egyptian Culture (also referred to by scholars as the Maadi-Buto Culture); in Middle Egypt and Upper Egypt, the Badarians had given way to the Naqada Culture (named after the settlement of Naqada); and in Lower Nubia, a Nubian culture called the A-Group lived concurrently with, and then replaced (or developed from), the Abkan Culture in the Second Cataract region. To the west, other distinct cultures continued to live in the oases and around the increasingly dry water sources of the expanding Sahara. Meanwhile, to the east, in the Levant, there were numerous farming villages, housing people who made high quality arts and crafts, tools and weapons, and already knew how to smelt copper. These mined in the Wadi Araba, on the modern border between Jordan and Israel, and procured turquoise from southern Sinai.

The Western Desert

With the slow transformation of northern Africa's savannah into a desert zone, various groups moved in search of better living conditions, and in particular, sources of water. One such group, the Libyan Culture, originally lived at Dunqul Oasis, near the First Cataract, but moved when conditions became drier in around 5000 BCE. At nearby Dakhla Oasis, a group known as the Bashendi Culture seasonally visited until around 3000 BCE, when they were replaced there by a sedentary group called the Sheikh Muftah Culture, primarily known by their pottery. The Sheikh Muftah Culture interacted with people along the Nile Valley, from whom they received pottery of Nile clay and copper objects brought from the Levant.

The Lower Egyptian Culture and the Levant

From as early as 4000 BCE, people from the southern Levant – already well-established in the wider trade network from the north and east – were crossing the Sinai into the Delta, bringing along their own possessions and sometimes leaving behind their distinctive pottery in Egypt. Seasonal camps even existed along the north Sinai coast, used by travellers who spent at least some of their time living in the region. Some Egyptians, although seemingly fewer in number, had similarly crossed eastwards into the southern Levant. Over the following centuries, not only were trade goods exchanged, but ideas too: Levantine traders may have introduced mud-brick construction techniques to the Delta, as well as beer production, better pottery production, metallurgy, and in particular, the increased use of copper.

One group of Levantine settlers, perhaps motivated by drought, moved to Buto in the Nile Delta early in the fourth millennium BCE; although these individuals initially made typically Levantine vessels from local clay, and for a time afterwards created hybrid vessels, uniting Egyptian and Levantine styles, they slowly acculturated to the Lower Egyptian Culture and were eventually totally absorbed. They even abandoned their wheel-turning method of making pottery vessels. Later, trade goods continued to arrive in Buto from the Levant through exchange, including pottery vessels, and items of flint and copper. Because of the presence of Syrian pottery at Buto, the settlement may also have had a seafaring connection with the northern Levant.

People from the Levant were also well-known at the village of Maadi – today a southern suburb of Cairo. Sometime between 4000 and 3500 BCE, the people of Maadi were met with a curious sight: not only had Levantine traders decided to settle down in the north of the village, but they were digging great pits in the ground, creating subterranean dwellings for themselves, following construction techniques similar to those found in the Beersheba Valley, just across the Sinai in modern Israel. Some were oval, although one was rectangular with a roof supported by a single column. Within these subterranean homes, the traders stored pottery vessels in the floor, and kept spindle whorls for weaving, as well as flint knives – everything that they might need while awaiting their next trip across the Sinai into the Levant.

Until losing importance in around 3500 BCE, Maadi prospered because of its control of trade routes. The villagers reared animals, including cattle, sheep, goats, and pigs, made pottery by hand, and stored their grain in silos. They sent some of this grain to the Levant to be traded for cast copper items (there's no evidence for a metallurgical workshop at the village), such as tools and ingots, which entered the village in great quantities. Mined just across the Sinai at Timna or at the Wadi Araba, and cast by expert craftsmen, these copper items are the first known in the Delta. Levantine traders brought oils, cedar, stone items, such as basalt discs and bowls, and high quality flint tools too. The 'foreign style' of imported Levantine vessels must have been attractive to the Maadi villagers, because they made their own copies. In return for such goods, as well as the previously mentioned grain, the villagers may have exported Nile catfish bones for use as arrowheads, for these have been found piled up within vessels. The Maadi villagers also traded with people from southern Egypt, normally referred to as Naqadans during this phase of Egyptian history (more about these below). Although the Naqadans had no permanent presence at Maadi, they did exchange their own goods at the village, including pottery vessels, cosmetic palettes (used for grinding up eye makeup) and mace-heads, seemingly in return for copper, obsidian, turquoise, and lapis lazuli. At the same time, the Maadi villagers imported Nubian goods, such as leopard skins and ivory.

Located in the central Delta region, another key Predynastic village was Tell el-Farkha. This replaced Maadi as the Delta's main trading centre with the south and east in around 3550 BCE. The villagers took full advantage of their wide-reaching trade connections (some gold beads may have even come from as far away as Jordan), using their newfound prosperity to develop their mud-brick architecture and beer brewing skills. In fact, under the Lower Egyptian Culture, the village boasted an extensive beer production area – apparently the earliest brewery in the world. If, as thought, they were sending this beer to the Levant, they can perhaps also claim to have created the world's first 'export beer.' Like their trading predecessors at Maadi, the people of Tell el-Farkha were similarly intrigued by the foreign vessels brought by traders to their village, to the extent that some kept imported vessels in their homes, and even created their own imitations.

The Rise of Naqada Culture and Its Connections with the A-Group

While the Lower Egyptian Culture was busy developing their relations with the Levant, in southern Egypt, around 4000 BCE, another distinct culture had developed, with major centres at Abydos, Naqada, and Hierakonpolis, and associated settlements a little further north and south; as a whole, this is referred to as the Naqada Culture. The Naqadans appear to have co-existed with the Badarians before absorbing their territory, and may even have been a related culture. Just like the Badarians, the early Naqadans continued to use copper, hammering it into shape to make harpoons and bracelets, among other objects, and sourced gold and electrum from Nubia and the Eastern

Desert. Their other trade connections were far more wide-reaching: the owner of Tomb 1863 at Naqada, from around 3600 BCE, was buried with a cylinder seal, probably from Mesopotamia, and a tomb dated from 4000–3500 BCE contained lapis lazuli from Afghanistan; these foreign prestige goods probably entered Egypt via Buto, brought on ships from the northern Levant. (Indeed, it is perhaps through this route that various Mesopotamian motifs entered the Naqadan artistic repertoire.) The Naqadans' fondness for luxury goods – and particularly foreign imports – led to their society becoming highly stratified by around 4000 BCE; basically, ownership of the right items flaunted your status for all to see, separating the haves from the have-nots. And in death, you made sure to take it with you.

Early in the fourth millennium BCE, the Naqadans shared many aspects of their culture with that of the A-Group, a Nubian people, living just north and south of the Nile's First Cataract. Culturally, however, the two slowly separated as the centuries passed: the A-Group moved south of the First Cataract, and eventually expanded down to the area around the Second Cataract (although some continued to live north of Aswan too). Living in a semi-nomadic and stratified society, A-Group Nubians travelled from campsite to campsite, and buried their dead in oval or rectangular graves, along with items reflecting their personal wealth: pottery, jewellery, female figurines, and Naqadan imports.

In exchange for Naqadan beer, wine, flint knives, cosmetic palettes, and stone vessels (among many other items), A-Group Nubians traded ebony and ivory, animal skins, ostrich eggs, and – perhaps most importantly – gold, sourcing many of their luxury goods from further south in Upper Nubia. To facilitate the movement of these items, the Egyptians and A-Group Nubians established trading outposts along the Nile, with one important outpost constructed at Elephantine in around 3300 BCE; this area would be closely associated with trade for the rest of Egyptian history (in fact, the Ancient Egyptian name for the nearby town of Aswan was *swenet*, meaning 'trade,' from which the modern name derives). Another outpost, active from around 3500 BCE, and for 500 years afterwards, was at Khor Daoud, close to the Wadi Allaqi in Nubia; this outpost had 578 storage pits, seemingly for oil, wine, and beer.

The Expansion of Naqada Culture: 3500 BCE

By around 3500 BCE, Naqadan culture had already spread across Upper Egypt and into Lower Nubia. Northern Egypt would be their next target. Probably motivated by the desire to control access to Levantine prestige items, over the following centuries the Naqadans came to be the dominant culture in the region. Lower Egyptian Culture vanished from existence, perhaps in part due to their peaceful acceptance and assimilation of southern material culture, and in part because of forceful domination. Although there's little evidence for warfare between the north and south, the Naqadans certainly enjoyed celebrating violence. Symbols of strength and power were an important aspect of Naqadan art: they produced ceremonial mace-heads, for example, and among the painted decoration of Tomb 100 at Hierakonpolis, there's an early scene of a man smiting an unfortunate victim (imagery known as 'smiting scenes').

The Naqadan expansion can be neatly illustrated by returning to Tell el-Farkha. After an increase in Naqadan goods – and thus interaction – by around 3300 BCE, the village was totally dominated by their southern neighbours. An extensive domestic area, including the massive brewery, was destroyed, and upon its ruins, the Naqadans built a huge residence and storage area – a complex that would often be rebuilt over the coming years. Levantine pottery, seal impressions, and tokens – all evidence of the building having a major role in trade between the east and south – were kept there. This building was eventually destroyed by fire, and replaced by an administrative-cultic centre; nevertheless, this new complex continued to serve as a storage area for Levantine imports.

The main imports from the Levant at Naqadan-controlled Tell el-Farkha were wine, olive oil, copper, and bitumen. In return, the Naqadans offered grain, meat, and probably also beer and pork. The only pig bones found by archaeologists at Tell el-Farkha were the parts with the least meat, suggesting that the Naqadans sent the meat-rich parts of the pigs elsewhere. The Naqadans may also have exported Nile fish to the Levant: archaeologists found copper harpoons at Tell el-Farkha, as well as other evidence for a fishing industry, but – curiously – no fish bones. Nile fish bones have, however, been discovered in the Levant, contemporary with this phase of Tell el-Farkha.

Interactions with Nubia and the Levant at Unification

Towards the end of the fourth millennium BCE, Egypt as a whole became politically and culturally unified under a single king. This marks the end of the Predynastic era and the first phase of Egypt's Pharaonic Period: the Early Dynastic Period, covering the 1st and 2nd Dynasties (*ca.* 3100–2584 BCE). However, it still isn't exactly clear when, and under whom, unification occurred, a matter further complicated by the identification of a number of obscure yet powerful 'proto-kings' that precede the traditional 1st Dynasty, referred to by Egyptologists as 'Dynasty 0.' Typically, however, Egypt's first true king is thought to be King Narmer, last ruler of Dynasty 0, with Hor Aha normally cited as the first king of the 1st Dynasty.

One Dynasty 0 'proto-king' was buried within Tomb U-j at Abydos, a large burial that contained a great number of imported goods, emphasizing its owner's importance: among them was a large obsidian bowl – the obsidian probably imported from Ethiopia – and 500 wine vessels, many possibly imported from the Levant. The tomb also contained the earliest known hieroglyphs, inscribed on small labels once attached to grave goods; although there's currently no consensus on how these labels should be read, it's possible that they refer to the royal estates from which the goods were sent.

While the Egyptians were consolidating their territory, a centralized kingdom was also developing in northern Nubia under the A-Group. By this time, A-Group Nubians had settled at Dakka and Afia, as well as at Qustul, near the Second Cataract of the Nile, where they built the largest and wealthiest graves in A-Group Nubia, either for rich members of the elite or for their kings. The graves of these late A-Group Nubians, and in particular those at Qustul, included large amounts of imported pottery and stone vessels from Egypt. Among the Egyptian imports unearthed at Qustul, for example, archaeologists found a breccia-mace head, a copper spearhead, cosmetic palettes, and maces with handles sheathed in gold. The A-Group also imported some items from the Levant, which probably passed through Egyptian traders. Markings made by the A-Group on official seals, placed on goods, might connect these items with individual Nubian chiefs, and so could represent the first steps towards a Nubian writing system.

At this point, late in the fourth millennium BCE, the Egyptians and the A-Group Nubians still enjoyed friendly relations. Egyptian and A-Group traders continued to meet at Elephantine to exchange goods, and the typically A-Group practice of cattle burial is attested at Hierakonpolis in Upper Egypt. Archaeologists have also excavated an A-Group grave at Abu Sir el-Malaq in Middle Egypt, showing that at least one Nubian lived and died far from home. Despite the increasing cultural separation between them, for the time being, ideas and goods continued to flow between Egypt and Nubia.

Meanwhile, in an unexpected move, the Egyptians decided to establish colonies among the villages of the southern Levant, enabling them to take greater control of the eastern trade route. Their main base of operations was at Tell es-Sakan, close to the Levant's Mediterranean coast, at the end of the northern Sinai trail from Egypt. Built in an entirely Egyptian architectural style on a previously untouched site (and with almost every object found there Egyptian too), this served as the administrative heart of this newly envisioned trading operation. Dated to Dynasty 0 (with the name of King Narmer found on one pottery sherd), its first incarnation was unfortified, but soon after a defensive wall was constructed with towers or bastions – the oldest fortification known to be built by the Ancient Egyptians (though representations of fortified walls are known in Predynastic art). During excavations, archaeologists found silos and ovens, Egyptian stone vessels, and clay jar sealings that bore impressions from Egyptian cylinder-seals. There were also a great many wine jars, suggesting that wine was the major export passing through this base into Egypt.

From Tell es-Sakan, the Egyptians managed various nearby satellite colonies. Among them was En Besor – much smaller than Tell es-Sakan – located close to a source of fresh water, where caravans could resupply. A typically Egyptian mud-brick construction, used as a storehouse for the movement of goods, within the building at En Besor, around twelve men placed Egyptian seals on goods passing through, 'registering' their presence, and ate using Egyptian kitchenware made from local clay. Other potential Egyptian 'colonies,' include Tel Ikhbeineh, Tel Erani, and Tel Maahaz, all close to Tell es-Sakan. Passing through these bases, Levantine wine, grain, copper, scented oils, bitumen, resins, wood, and perhaps even people, entered Egypt. And in return, the Egyptians sent luxury goods, such as stone vessels and jewellery.

Egyptians also lived further north, among the population of Levantine towns, perhaps acting as traders: some burials at Azor contained Egyptian goods, interred with Egyptians who died there. Other items have been found at Jericho, Gezer, and Megiddo, among many others. And at Nahal Tillah, about 35 km east of En Besor, archaeologists excavated an Egyptian-style burial – perhaps the body of a local person emulating Egyptian burial practices.

Symbolic and True Warfare

It's difficult to say whether the people of the Lower Egyptian Culture accepted the domination of the Naqadans without resistance. From violent scenes depicted on ceremonial items, such as commemorative palettes – slabs of stone, used as prestige items for display – Egyptologists once argued that the south had attacked the north, forcing unification upon them. The Battlefield Palette, for example, now in the British Museum, depicts a lion tearing into a hapless enemy, while fallen foes lie on the ground nearby, picked at by birds. The Bull Palette shows bulls trampling enemies and cities under attack. It's perhaps not going too far to suggest that the lion and bull motifs on these items represent the king defeating his enemies.

The most frequently cited proof of violent unification is the Narmer Palette, discovered at Hierakonpolis and now in the Egyptian Museum, Cairo. On one side, this piece depicts King Narmer of Dynasty 0 smiting an enemy, with fallen or fleeing enemies in the register below. On the reverse, the king walks in a procession before two rows of decapitated foes, their heads placed between their legs. In the register below, the necks of two fantastical creatures are tied, perhaps representing the unification of the Two Lands – the north and south. And in the final register at the bottom, a bull, perhaps representing the king, tramples an enemy and attacks a fortified town.

Although such imagery may suggest a violent invasion of the north, we must remember that scenes of animals, fighting, hunting, and execution are found across the Predynastic Period on a variety of objects. Rather than expressions of history, they could instead be expressions of ideology: the elimination of disorder and the establishment of *maat* – a fundamental concept in Egyptian philosophy, representing balance, order, justice, and correct action. These images, rather than being thinly veiled allusions to historical battles, could simply show that the Egyptian concept of *maat* was present from the very beginning of their civilization, representing the triumph of order over chaos.

Inventing Enemies

At the close of the fourth millennium BCE, the Egyptians suddenly developed a more aggressive attitude towards their neighbours to the south and east. Why this happened, we can only speculate, but it was perhaps a result of the Egyptians wanting to remove the 'middlemen' from the trade networks.

From the south, the Egyptians craved the exotic items of Upper (southern) Nubia and beyond, so they aggressively expanded their sphere of influence deeper and deeper into Lower Nubia, creating conflict with the A-Group. Glimpses of what happened next can be seen in two rock carvings at Gebel Sheikh Suleiman, just south of Abu Simbel: the first carving shows the *serekh* of an Egyptian king (a royal symbol, normally containing a king's name) holding a Nubian prisoner by the neck, while to the right, a further prisoner, with an arrow in his chest, is tied to a boat. Four drowned enemies are beneath. In the second carving, there's a large scorpion, probably representing an Egyptian king, and three figures: one bound, one holding a weapon, and the other holding a bow and arrow. As these carvings show, Egypt's friendly relationship with Lower Nubia had ended. Violent raids must have become common. In a desperate attempt to save themselves, the A-Group abandoned Qustul – the probable capital of their emerging kingdom that would never be – but it was a futile move: by 2800 BCE, the A-Group, as a distinct cultural entity, had disappeared from existence, leaving Lower Nubia depopulated for the next 400 years. The Egyptians and Nubians, up until this point culturally intertwined, now firmly parted ways.

The people of the southern Levant – the Egyptians' trading partners for many centuries – received equally hostile treatment; with most of Egypt's eastern trade imports now arriving directly by ship from the northern Levant, the Egyptians saw no reason to treat their former allies as friends: from now on, Egypt's kings would depict them as defeated enemies, bound as prisoners, worthy only of being crushed beneath their feet. King Qaa of the 1st Dynasty embellished a rod with a bound Asiatic. On an ivory label, King Den, also of the 1st Dynasty, smites an 'easterner,' his mace held high with one hand, while grasping the hair of his cowering victim with the other. King Sekhemib of the 2nd Dynasty called himself 'conqueror of a foreign land.' Just as they'd done with the A-Group in Nubia, the Egyptians had removed the pesky 'middleman' of the southern Levant.

The city of Byblos, in modern Lebanon, now became Egypt's most important trading contact in the Near East, to the extent that one Egyptian word for 'boat' is literally 'Byblos boat.' A major source of high quality Lebanese cedar, Byblos held a key position on the wider Mediterranean and Asian trade networks, enabling its traders to provide the Egyptians with many of the prestige goods they desired – goods that previously entered Egypt via the southern Levant. And so, with the land route across the Sinai into the Levant increasingly irrelevant, midway through the 1st Dynasty the Egyptians abandoned the administrative-cultic building at Tell el-Farkha in the Delta, followed by their colonial outposts in the southern Levant.

By the end of the Early Dynastic Period in around 2584 BCE, Egypt had already risen as a state, wiped out a unique Nubian culture, ruined relations with the southern Levant, solidified relations with Upper Nubia and the northern Levant, and had woven itself into the long distance trade networks of the then known world. Prestige items – commonly agreed symbols of status, marking the high from the low – flowed into Egypt from the south and east, feeding the insatiable hunger of the newborn state's developing elite for the exotic. The Egyptians had tasted power, invented enemies, and asserted themselves on the world stage. Their actions over the following centuries would expand and strengthen their growing State, develop their sense of identity, and ensure that their civilization would be remembered forever. Enter the Old Kingdom.

Chapter 2

Building Foreign Relations (and Pyramids)
(2584–2117 BCE)

The Old Kingdom begins with the reign of King Djoser, first ruler of the 3rd Dynasty and owner of the world's first pyramid: the Step Pyramid at Saqqara. It would not be the last. The need to manage projects as complex as pyramid-building led to the ongoing development of the Egyptian State, creating an increasingly complex bureaucracy. Over successive centuries, the government expanded, and non-royals began to be appointed to positions of importance. And just like the royals and elite of earlier times, this new elite vaunted their status through fabulous monuments, their proximity to the king, and their access to luxury goods, such as exotic, foreign imports. As the Old Kingdom progressed, high-level courtiers also began to decorate their tomb chapels with idealized autobiographies, highlighting their outstanding achievements in life, in order to 'wow' visitors into leaving offerings for their souls. One particular courtier, a man named Weni, left a detailed account of his life as a military leader, and describes the activities of the Old Kingdom army. To gain a flavour of this period, there's no better place to start.

The Adventures of Weni

In around 2265 BCE, an Egyptian noble named Weni was called upon by his king to assemble a vast army and lead a series of campaigns against Egypt's enemies; although undoubtedly an important honour, this may have come as some surprise to him, for his career up to that point had required no military leadership skills whatsoever. A privileged individual, Weni had grown up at court under King Teti of the 6th Dynasty, and began his career supervising a storehouse. Soon after, he'd been promoted to overseer of the robing-room of King Pepi I, a position that gave him the ear of the king and, we must assume, some level of influence (and fashion sense). From there, he rose to become senior warden of Nekhen, a judicial role (which saw him acting as sole judge in a probable case of attempted regicide, masterminded in the royal harem). So, from a quick glance at Weni's CV, a career in law or fashion might seem the best fit, not leading men on the battlefield.

Indeed, the idea of leading a military expedition had probably never entered Weni's head before that fateful day, when King Pepi I commanded him to launch a campaign against rebellious Asiatic 'sand-dwellers' – the Egyptian term for people living on the southern Levantine sea coast, who were blocking Egyptian ships from stopping in the natural harbours close to their fortified settlements. As reported in his autobiography, inscribed in his tomb at Abydos, Weni performed his royal duty admirably. His first step was to assemble an army of tens of thousands, gathered from across Egypt, as well as Nubian mercenaries from different regions – Yam, Wawat, Kaau – the Medjay-Nubians of the Eastern Desert, and Tjemehu-Libyans from the Western Desert. This was normal practice in the Old Kingdom because Egypt had no standing army: troops were called up as needed, their service treated as a form of taxation. Once assembled, the army was led by trusted royal advisors, men (like Weni) that the king could happily let wander through his domain with a huge, armed force. Loyalty and organizational experience were the main requisites for the job.

Weni led his army eastwards in the name of the king, followed on the march by an odd assortment of nobles: royal seal-bearers, palace officials, the chieftains and mayors of Upper and Lower Egypt, chief district officials, and the chief priests of Upper and Lower Egypt. In his account, Weni is quick to note that none among his troops seized a loaf of bread or stole sandals from a fellow traveller, and that no one took cloth from any town along the way. He also thought it worth mentioning that no soldier under his command took a goat from another person. Naturally, this implies that such events did occur during campaigns led by less trustworthy and able leaders (though you'd think that the guy with the extra goat would be easy to spot). There's no detail in Weni's account about the specific organization of his fighting force, and, owing to the general lack of military organization in the Old Kingdom, there's little terminology to aid a reconstruction. Troops were placed into battalions called *tjeset*, and military leaders were called overseers of the army (*imy-ra mesha*). There were also army scribes, who accompanied campaigns.

Despite Weni's lack of military training, his missions were successful. In his own words, he 'ravaged' and 'flattened' the land of the sand-dwellers, sacked their fortified settlements, cut down their figs and vines, burned down their homes, slew tens of thousands of their troops, and dragged many back to Egypt as captives. Of course, this is exactly what King Pepi I had hoped would happen, and upon Weni's return, the king praised the newly-minted war hero for his excellent leadership. So successful was Weni that the king sent him to lead the troops five times in total – effectively whenever the Asiatic 'sand-dwellers' were causing trouble. One particularly noteworthy event occurred at 'the land of the Nose of the Gazelle's Head' – an unknown location, though perhaps to be equated with the hill of Jaffa in the southern Levant – where Egypt's enemies had gathered. Weni marched half his troops by land, and sailed the other half north of the enemy position along the Levantine coast. Catching the Asiatics in a pincer movement, the Egyptian army slaughtered each and every one of them. Under Pepi's successor, King Merenre, Weni continued his career, acting as a chamberlain and sandal-bearer at the palace, roles that also involved watch and guard duties; though an unexpected move, Weni's role as war leader had a lasting influence on his career. He was a military man before military men existed.

Old and Middle Kingdom Military Technology

Just as Weni doesn't mention the organization of his army, he also fails to mention what weapons they carried. Nevertheless, as the technology of war changed little between the Old Kingdom and the close of the Second Intermediate Period, 1,000 years later, we can make some educated guesses.

For certain, there were archers among Weni's troops. The earliest depiction of archers on the march dates to the 4th Dynasty and shows a row of men, armed with bows; this was originally part of the decoration within the mortuary complex of either King Khufu or King Khafre, the builders of Egypt's two largest pyramids at Giza. The bows they carry – known as self bows – remained in use until the New Kingdom, and consisted of simple wooden staves with gut string wound around the ends; they probably had a maximum range of around 190 m. Arrowheads were often made from flint, bone, ebony, and, from the late Middle Kingdom, bronze.

Other troops among Weni's army would have been armed with stone daggers and maces of differing shapes. Axes too had stone blades. Two types of axes were used by Egypt's troops; one form had a semicircular head, tied by cords, which were fed and tied through holes made in the blade. A second type had a long blade, with a flaring, curved edge. Although some copper daggers and axes are known from the Old Kingdom, they were not the norm.

Before the New Kingdom, soldiers didn't wear body armour or helmets, but did carry shields made from cowhides stretched over wooden frames. Middle Kingdom soldiers did, however, wear leather straps, crossed across the body for protection. The only other technological development, from a military perspective at least, were siege ladders, as shown in the late Old Kingdom tomb of Inti at Deshasheh, where Egyptians attack a fortress in the Levant.

Sieges in the Southern Levant

Having enjoyed his adventures, let's leave Weni now and take a look at the wider picture, picking up where we left off at the end of the previous chapter. Following the Egyptian withdrawal from the southern Levant at the end of the Early Dynastic Period, the local population were left to their own devices. Now cultivating crops with irrigation systems (as opposed to the dry-farming techniques used earlier), and with a developed bureaucracy and increasing social stratification, the region's towns transformed into fortified city-states, some on the sites of the earlier Egyptian colonies, including at Egypt's abandoned headquarters, Tell es-Sakan.

Since the Egyptians now traded directly with cities in the northern Levant, it had become normal for them to sail there, stopping at key points along the Levantine coastline and bringing them into contact with the local city-states and Asiatic 'sand-dwellers' that lived on the sandy shores (as mentioned by Weni). The land route across northern Sinai into the Levant – known as the Ways of Horus – did continue to be used, but it's impossible to know how often. Whatever the case may be, the route was monitored, enabling the Egyptians to control the movement of people. Heknikhnum, who lived during the 5th Dynasty, was an overseer of the Ways of Horus, and it was probably there that King Sneferu of the 4th Dynasty built the 'Wall of the North,' a fortress known only from textual sources.

Due to the reduced need for interaction, few Egyptian objects are found in the southern Levant during the Old Kingdom, and few objects of southern Levantine origin are known in Egypt. (A palace at Megiddo, built using Egyptian techniques, may suggest that Egyptian architects were active there, however.) The two regions mainly came into contact whenever Egypt's trading interests were threatened, leading to campaigns being launched under nobles like Weni; the Egyptians had no interest in controlling the Levant, they simply wanted to ensure the continued flow of luxury goods.

Whenever problems in the southern Levant arose, it led to an Egyptian assault on one (or more) of the region's fortified city-states. A depiction of a siege in the late Old Kingdom tomb of Inti at Deshasheh seems to show such an attack. Egyptians armed with axes chop at Asiatics, who raise their arms in terror. Asiatics fall from the city walls, multiple arrows piercing their bodies. Meanwhile, some Egyptians enter the city by climbing a siege ladder, while others use stakes to undermine the wall's foundations. Within the city, Egyptians hack at their enemies. Women and children search for a place to hide. The enemy chief, upon his throne, wonders what to do next. Outside, Asiatic prisoners, including children, are led away from the city, each tied together in a row, the adults' hands bound in excruciating positions. The Saqqara tomb of Kaemheset also shows the siege of a city, most probably in the Levant. Here, a wheeled siege ladder has been pushed against the city walls, and is being climbed by soldiers. Others undermine the foundations. Within the city, animals stand in rows, near men, women, and children.

The Sinai Peninsula and the Port of Ayn Soukhna

During the Old Kingdom, the Egyptians started to mine turquoise in southern Sinai. Their main source was at Wadi Maghara, known to the Egyptians as 'the Terrace of Turquoise,' where they also smelted copper on a small scale (and left carvings of the pharaoh smiting foreigners). Another major source was Serabit el-Khadim, though this was only extensively exploited in later periods. From the 4th Dynasty, and perhaps even earlier, the Egyptians used boats to transport their mined turquoise and copper ore from the Sinai port of Abu Zenima across the Gulf of Suez to Ayn Soukhna, from where it would be carried to the Nile Valley. Powered by sails and oars, and travelling between 3-4 knots in speed, these boats took around 14-18 hours to make the roughly 100 km journey, and when not in use, were dismantled and stored in rock cut galleries at Ayn Soukhna.

These Egyptian mining operations occasionally encountered dangerous nomads. So, to protect their ships at Abu Zenima from such troublemakers, the Egyptians built a fortress at nearby Ras Budran (though this was destroyed at the end of the 6th Dynasty). A man more aware than most of the Sinai's dangers was Pepinakht (called Heqaib), who lived in Aswan during the 6th Dynasty and held the title overseer of foreigners. He was also in charge of bringing the products of foreign lands to the king (and in later periods was treated like a saint – quite the promotion). The story goes that King Pepi II sent Pepinakht to Sinai to retrieve the body of Ankhti, another overseer of foreigners, who had been killed, along with his team, by Asiatics and sand-dwellers, while they were constructing boats to sail to the land of Punt – a major source of incense and luxury goods somewhere south of Egypt (see below). As well as having to retrieve Ankhti's body, Pepinakht was commanded to deal with the murderers, so he duly left for the Sinai with an army, and successfully killed or drove away his enemies.

Byblos and the Northern Levant

With the shift to the maritime trade route at the end of the Predynastic Period, the city of Byblos in the northern Levant became Egypt's main trading partner in the region; by boat, the journey from the Delta to Byblos took between seven to twenty days, and required nightly stops at natural harbours along the Levantine seacoast. Upon arrival at Byblos, the Egyptians would have entered a prosperous fortified city (it even had an early sewer network), its houses built around a spring, and there, would have traded their goods for timber, oil, resins, and wine to bring back home. They may also have visited the city's main temple; this was dedicated to Baalat-Gebal, 'The Lady of Byblos,' who was depicted in the same manner as the Egyptian goddesses Isis and Hathor – testament to Byblos' close ties with Egypt; in the late Old Kingdom, Egyptian stone vessels were given to this temple either as royal gifts or by the local elite.

Under King Sneferu, at the start of the 4th Dynasty, the Egyptians brought forty shiploads of cedar from Byblos, while Khufu, Sneferu's son, had funerary boats, constructed from Lebanese cedar, buried beside his pyramid at Giza. Royal funerary temples, such as those of King Sahure at Abu Sir and Unas at Saqqara, also included scenes of boats returning from the Levant – most probably from Byblos. In the Sahure scenes, the Egyptian crew is accompanied by Asiatics – seemingly dignitaries and their families – who shout 'praise to you, Sahure, god of the living, we see your beauty!'[1] Interestingly, some of the Egyptians on board are labelled as 'interpreters.' One tomb lintel in the Khufu pyramid cemetery is inscribed for 'the man of Byblos, Wentjet,' suggesting that people from Byblos settled in Egypt during the Old Kingdom.

A 6th Dynasty official named Iny, who held the intriguing title, seal-bearer of the god of the two big ships, left an account of his journeys to the northern Levant under different kings in his tomb autobiography. After being selected by King Pepi I to undertake these foreign missions, Iny relates that he travelled four times to the regions of Amaau, Khenty-she (probably Lebanon), and a place called Pawes[...], bringing silver and other goods back to the palace. Next, under King Merenre, he led three boats to Byblos, where he received lapis lazuli, lead/tin, silver, oil, and other commodities. Upon Iny's return, the king rewarded him with gold. Under King Pepi II,

Iny travelled once again to Khenty-she, arriving back in Egypt with his own boat and a number of cargo ships, loaded with silver, and Asiatic men and women (no doubt to be used as slaves). As reward, Pepi II allowed Iny to sit near him when eating at court.

Ebla (Tell Mardikh) is another city in the northern Levant that might have been in contact with Egypt during the Old Kingdom; this was an important trading centre for lapis lazuli and silver thanks to its position at the end of the caravan route from Badakhshan in modern Afghanistan, a major source of lapis lazuli. Controlling a large territory, and enjoying diplomatic relations with other city-states in the region, the rulers of Ebla controlled the onward flow of lapis lazuli; indeed, in what was most probably a royal treasury in one of the city's palaces, archaeologists discovered 22 kg of raw lapis lazuli, as well as Old Kingdom vessels of a type used to transport prestige items. Such vessels might have reached Ebla through middlemen at Byblos or through direct contact with Egypt. Beyond Ebla, a jar found at Giza, but made in northern Syria or southern Anatolia, also suggests that oils, resins, or perfumes were imported from that region, emphasizing Egypt long-distance contacts.

Early Relations with Crete

Although there's only limited evidence, it seems that Egypt had established contact with Crete by around 2600 BCE. Vessels, seemingly copying Egyptian originals, have been found at Mesara in southern Crete, and a piece of hippo tusk, potentially from Egypt, was discovered at Knossos. Egyptian stone vessels, made during the Predynastic and Early Dynastic periods, have also been found at Knossos; these could have reached the island during the Old Kingdom, but if sent earlier, would push the date of Egypt's first interactions with Crete back further. Crete's involvement in international trade reduced towards the end of the Old Kingdom, probably due to the wider climatic changes that were affecting the whole of the Near East.

Egyptians in Lower Nubia, and Nubians in Egypt

Having explored Egypt's relations with the east, let's now turn our attention south. Founded under King Khafre during the 4th Dynasty, seemingly on top of an A-Group site 500 years after it had been abandoned, the Old Kingdom town at Buhen was well-located beside the Nile's Second Cataract. No other settlements stood nearby – in fact, no one had lived in the region since the disappearance of the A-Group. Consequently, the town enjoyed great vistas over the surrounding landscape: an empty space that stretched all the way back to the First Cataract, broken only by overgrown tamarisk and acacia, a handy source of wood for the Egyptians. While Khafre's pyramid – the second largest in Egypt – was being erected 850 km north, the Egyptians at Buhen lived on the very edge of Egyptian control, far from the action. You get the feeling that many probably didn't want to be there: there's no evidence for Egyptian graves in the area, suggesting that people either moved away before death, or in death were brought back to Egypt.

But whatever their opinion of the place, the townspeople still had jobs to do. Within the great enclosure wall that surrounded the settlement and controlled access stood storage areas, residences, and administrative and cult buildings. The Egyptians at Buhen played a key role in the trade network with Upper Nubia, further south, and also processed gold, melting it down, and pouring it into ingot moulds, before sending it north. At the same time, the Egyptians sent out patrols to monitor any movement in the town's vicinity; the State clearly saw Lower Nubia as a strategic buffer zone between themselves and Upper Nubia. And if the need for a campaign south arose, Buhen was an excellent launch pad.

Yet Nubians did pass north of Buhen and make their way into Egypt. Elephantine, in the first half of the Old Kingdom, continued to develop as a border town, where Egyptians and Nubians lived and interacted, even though it was from there that the Egyptians had launched many of the campaigns that had decimated the A-Group. The Nubians already living at Elephantine were probably the descendants of A-Group settlers that had moved there before the loss of their culture, but after the unification of Egypt; these individuals may have acted as interpreters for Egyptian campaigns and expeditions during the Old Kingdom. As Lower Nubia was depopulated during the first half of the Old Kingdom, the Nubians arriving to trade at Elephantine and Buhen must have travelled from Upper Nubia, though little is known about them.

During this early phase of Egyptian history, either in the 2nd or 3rd Dynasty, a man died at Shellal, just south of Elephantine. He was buried there, holding two copper objects and wearing an elaborate gold necklace, with bracelets on one wrist, and each arm adorned with a v-shaped ivory armlet. We cannot be certain who this man was in life, but due to his elaborate grave goods – quite unlike those of the local Egyptians – he might have been a high status Upper Nubian trade envoy. On the other hand, he might have been an Upper Nubian ruler, who died during a trip to Egypt. A scene from the 5th Dynasty pyramid complex of King Sahure shows prisoners tied together, all except one man, who raises his arms in praise of the king; his arms are adorned with the same style of v-shaped armlet that the man buried at Shellal wore. Within the same complex, there's also a scene of foreign rulers being trampled by the king in the form of a griffin; here, the Nubian ruler again wears the same form of v-shaped armlet. Egyptologist David O'Connor has argued that because Lower Nubia was deserted at this time, the ruler depicted was probably from Upper Nubia. Similarly, a stele from Helwan, probably of 2nd or 3rd Dynasty date, shows a man named Sisi seated wearing armlets and with twisted locks of hair, both thought to be Nubian in style. Again, given that Lower Nubia was empty, he is perhaps another example of an Upper Nubian living in Egypt.

Other interactions between the Egyptians and Nubians were less friendly. King Sneferu, first ruler of the 4th Dynasty, brought 7,000 Nubians to Egypt in the 12th year of his reign, along with 200,000 cattle; we must presume that these individuals were brought from a campaign in Upper Nubia, and used as soldiers or slaves. Their descendants continued to work for the Egyptian State for generations. The Palermo Stone, for example, bearing annals of royal activity, mentions that in the 3rd year of King Userkaf's reign, 303 'acculturated' or 'pacified' ones – perhaps Nubians who had been living in Egypt for some time – and seventy female foreigners were brought to work at the royal pyramid. A heavily broken, but very similar, text from the reign of King Pepi I also seems to mention 'pacified' or 'acculturated' Nubians being sent to work on a royal project.

A decree at Dahshur, carved in stone during the reign of King Pepi I, says that 'acculturated' or 'pacified' Nubians were forbidden from taking people in active temple service away from the pyramid towns at Dahshur, or from requisitioning goods for state projects; this shows that outside of Dahshur, Nubians – perhaps the descendants of prisoners taken during Sneferu's raids – levied men for projects. Despite their family origins as prisoners, they now enforced the will of the Egyptian state. This isn't surprising, for the majority of Nubians in Egypt, famous for their skills as warriors, now fought for the Egyptians during campaigns as mercenaries. Nevertheless, not all Nubians became fighters: at Giza, inscriptions within 5th Dynasty tombs mention Nubian servants and a Nubian treasurer.

The Rise of the C-Group

In 2300 BCE, a new culture entered Lower Nubia, roughly at the same time that the Egyptians abandoned their settlement at Buhen; these are known as the C-Group (a culture identified as the B-Group turned out to be a misreading of the archaeological evidence by scholars). Whether the Egyptians left Buhen because of the arrival of the C-Group, or if the C-Group moved into the area because the Egyptians left, we cannot be sure. What is clear is that this new Nubian group repopulated the area between the First and Second Cataracts of the Nile, and remained there until around 1500 BCE. Although they had no written language, the C-Group used a great deal of cattle symbolism in their art, and are best known today because of their distinctive burials: their tombs had circular superstructures, made from stone (sometimes with an offering chapel at the side). Within, the deceased was buried in a flexed position, along with pottery and jewellery. During this same period, further south in Upper Nubia, the Kerma Culture was also developing (but we shall return to them in Chapter Five).

At about this time in the late Old Kingdom, references to specific Lower Nubian regions appear in Egyptian texts, as if the C-Group had founded a series of chiefdoms along the Nile. The main divisions in Lower Nubia were Wawat, Irtjet, and Setju, while somewhere further south was Yam (see below). Execration texts from this period – magical inscriptions intended to neutralize Egypt's enemies – mention even more Nubian locations, adding to the list: Kaau, Yankh, Masit(?), Medja (the land of the Medjay-Nubians), and Meterti.

Perhaps the earliest interactions between the Egyptians and the C-Group are recorded on rock inscriptions at Khor el-Aqiba in Lower Nubia; one of these refers to an army of 20,000 men hacking up Wawat, and another to 17,000 Nubians being taken prisoner. It seems that even from the start, relations between the Egyptians and the C-Group were far from peaceful. Indeed, perhaps to defuse tensions, King Unas, at the end of the 5th Dynasty, travelled to Elephantine to speak with the rulers of Nubia, while later, King Merenre of the 6th Dynasty apparently received the submission of the rulers of Medja, Irtjet, and Wawat.

Warfare in Nubia

After the C-Group's arrival in Lower Nubia, Elephantine, previously experiencing a period of decline, once again rose to importance. Trade increased with Upper Nubia and a large residence was constructed for the governor of the Aswan region. This might sound rather nice, but taking the job of governor of Aswan wasn't simply a cushy bureaucratic position, where you'd push a few papyri and get fat on beef: these men were expected to lead expeditions into Nubia for the purposes of both trade and war.

The Overseer of Foreigners (no doubt meaning Nubians here) Pepinakht called Heqaib was one such governor of Aswan (this same man also travelled to the Sinai to retrieve the body of Ankhti, discussed earlier). King Pepi II sent Pepinakht to attack the lands of Wawat and Irtjet, where he killed a large number of people, including the ruler's children and the commander of the Nubian troops. The Egyptians then brought back many of the Nubians to the royal residence as prisoners. After another campaign south, Pepinakht also brought two enemy chiefs, their children, commanders, oxen, and goats to the residence of King Pepi II.

A more sombre account is provided by Sabni, another governor of Aswan under King Pepi II (this king ruled a long time). A group of men arrived at Aswan to tell Sabni that his father, Mekhu, had died whilst travelling in a place called Wetjtj in Wawat. Sabni left immediately to retrieve the corpse, supported by an army of Egyptian and Nubian troops, as well as 100 donkeys laden with honey, linen, faience vessels, and oils – gifts for the Nubian rulers he'd meet along the way. At the end of his journey south, Sabni found his father's body upon a donkey in a place called Temetjer. He took the corpse, placed it in a coffin, and returned to Egypt, bringing along the luxury goods that his father had gathered in Nubia for the king in Memphis.

Another Sabni, perhaps a son of Pepinakht-Heqaib, also led an expedition into Nubia. Known as the 'throw-stick of Horus in the foreign lands,' he was sent to Wawat to construct boats for shipping obelisks from the stone quarries at Elephantine to Heliopolis. During the mission, he was accompanied by soldiers, and later proclaimed that neither a sandal nor a loaf of bread was stolen.

You Gotta Haggle! Trade and Barter in Ancient Egypt

Ancient Egyptian markets, like markets today, were a vibrant place to get to know the local culture. Markets were held at road intersections or on riverbanks, and people could travel great distances to take part; in the famous Middle Kingdom tale, 'The Eloquent Peasant,' the peasant travels with a donkey caravan from his home in the Wadi Natrun to a market at Herakleopolis, roughly 200 km away.

In Old Kingdom tomb scenes showing markets, the seller normally sits on a stool or kneels alongside his goods, shouting out the names of the items on offer. Buyers stand, sometimes with a shopping bag over one shoulder, explaining what they can offer in exchange for the goods presented by the seller. We must remember that there was no money in Ancient Egypt, save for some special cases late in Egyptian history. People exchanged goods and had to decide what assorted items, and in what quantities, might equal the value of the desired object. A scene in one Old Kingdom tomb, for example, shows a man exchanging sandals for a vessel of liquid. Another exchanges a fan for vegetables.

The most celebrated Old Kingdom market scene is found in the 5th Dynasty tomb of Niankhkhnum and Khnumhotep, who were royal manicurists. This vibrant scene shows barbers, manicurists, and pedicurists hard at work, even shaving faces and legs. Traders sell fish and sycamore fruits. Others take copper ingots in exchange for finished copper goods. One craftsman sits carving a seal. A woman sells cups, telling the buyer, 'see, something from which you can drink!' A cloth merchant offers two cubits of cloth for six *deben* of copper (*deben* being a unit of weight, one equalling roughly 27 g in the Old Kingdom, but changing to 91 g in the New Kingdom). All around, baskets are filled with fruit, dried and fresh fish, and vegetables. Perhaps for security reasons, men walk with baboons on leashes ('Seize him! Seize him!', one man says to a baboon), while another more unruly baboon steals an onion from a stall.

Searching for Yam

Locating the land of Yam has been a goal of Egyptologists ever since they first became aware of its existence. With its ruler controlling the regions of Wawat, Irtjet, and Setju, it was from Yam that the Egyptians received many of their sub-Saharan luxury goods, such as panther skins, ebony, and ivory. The most detailed account of Egypt's interaction with Yam is found in the tomb of Harkhuf, yet another governor of Aswan under King Pepi II. Harkhuf visited Yam a number of times during his career and provides details on its location and organization.

Harkhuf first travelled to Yam under King Merenre of the 6th Dynasty, departing with his father, the Lector Priest and Sole Companion Iry, to 'open the way' to this mysterious land – a phrase that implies that they were the first to initiate diplomatic relations. The mission lasted seven months and ended with Harkhuf bringing rare and beautiful gifts back to the king. On his second trip, Harkhuf travelled alone, along a different route from that used on his first mission. Following the 'Yebu Road,' he passed through Mekher, Terers, and Irtjet, regions controlled by the chiefs of Setju and Irtjet. Once again, he returned to Egypt with gifts for the king, having spent eight months away.

For his third trip, Harkhuf headed west from Abydos and took the 'Oasis Road' south to Yam. But upon arrival, he found that its ruler had departed to wage war in the land of the Tjemehu-Libyans. Rather than wait around for the absent ruler to return, Harkhuf set off to find him, sending a courtier and a man from Yam to the Egyptian court to inform the king of his unexpected movements. Afterwards, escorted by soldiers from Yam, Harkhuf returned to Egypt with 300 donkeys, carrying incense, ebony, panther skins, elephant tusks, throw-sticks, incense, and other goods. The soldiers of Yam safely led him through Irtjet, Setju, and Wawat, and along the dangerous mountain paths. Upon returning to Egypt, Harkhuf received presents from the king.

When returning from Yam in the second year of King Pepi II's rule, Harkhuf sent a letter to the king explaining that he was bringing a dancing pygmy back to the Egyptian court. The king, only a child at the time, was very excited to hear this, especially because he'd never seen a pygmy before. Pepi replied to Harkhuf, saying that the pygmy must be protected at all times: 'Cause trustworthy people to be around him on deck, lest he fall into the water!', the young king wrote. 'When he sleeps in the night, cause trustworthy people to sleep around him in his tent. Inspect ten times a night! My Majesty desires to see this pygmy more than the tribute of the mine land of Punt!'[2]

Other sources for Yam provide far less detail. The 6th Dynasty stele of Iwet from Naqada mentions an overseer of interpreters of Yam; this is significant because it's probable that one of the routes to Yam started near Naqada, leading first to Dakhla Oasis, and onwards south to Yam. In 2007, a stele mentioning Yam, erected during the reign of King Montuhotep II of the 11th Dynasty, was found at Gebel Uweinat, in the far south-west of Egypt. Given Gebel Uweinat's position on the Abu Ballas trail (see below), which starts at Dakhla Oasis, the stele probably stood on the desert road to this mysterious land. It bears the last known reference to Yam.

The Land of Punt

The land of Punt, which the Egyptians also referred to as 'God's Land,' is another mysterious location that cannot be pinpointed exactly. Among the suggested locations for Punt over the years, there's the Somali coast; somewhere between the Sudanese cities of Atbara and Khartoum; between Port Sudan and Massawa in Eritrea; and along the entire west coast of the Arabian peninsula. Recent analyses of mummified baboons thought to come from Punt show that eastern Ethiopia and Eritrea are the most likely locations. Meanwhile, excavations at the Red Sea port of Mersa Gawasis, from which many of the expeditions to Punt were launched, have revealed obsidian and ebony from Sudan and Eritrea, and ceramics from Yemen, produced in the Aden region, indicating contact with southern Arabia.

Wherever Punt was located, Egypt procured many of its southern luxury goods from there, especially incense. The first reference to Punt is found on the 5th Dynasty Palermo Stone, which simply says that products from Punt were imported in the 13th year of King Sahure; these products included 80,000 measures of *antyu*-myrrh, 6,000 measures of electrum, 2,000 measures of *sen-seshemet*, and 23,020 staves. The recent discovery of a decorated block from the pyramid causeway of Sahure, depicting the return of this expedition from Punt, now adds extra detail to the Palermo Stone's account. This shows at least five Egyptian ships with Egyptians and Puntites standing on board. Dogs (some leashed to the ship) also stand on deck, and baboons are tied to the lowered masts. The Puntite men wear short kilts and short wigs, secured to the head with cloths. The women from Punt have long hair, and like the men, have tied pieces of cloth around their wigs. Among the crew is their overseer, User; an overseer of quarry work called Kaaper; and an overseer of prospectors called Menia, showing that quarrying work was also part of the mission. A man described as an interpreter is also present. Among the items transported were frankincense trees, which were to be planted in the garden of the royal palace; the king is shown standing in front of a row of these trees, while his great royal wife and the queen mother witness the historic event. Courtiers also stand, awaiting the arrival of the ships. Afterwards, a great banquet was held, attended by officials and craftsmen, and accompanied by music.

Further evidence for Old Kingdom missions to Punt is rather limited. The account of Harkhuf, presented earlier, mentions that before Harkhuf brought a pygmy back to Egypt from Yam, the seal-bearer of the god Werdjededba had brought a pygmy from Punt under King Isesi of the 5th Dynasty; Werdjededba's fame continued into the Middle Kingdom, when a boat at Mersa Gawasis – a harbour on the Red Sea – was named after him. The only other Old Kingdom reference to Punt has also already been mentioned: the account of Pepinakht-Heqaib, who travelled to the Red Sea coast to retrieve the body of an official killed by Asiatics whilst building a boat meant for Punt.

Egypt's Wild West

The great expanse of the Western Desert was of little interest to the Egyptians; they didn't regard the various Libyan groups living in the desert region as a threat, and no fortifications existed to protect Egypt from potential incursions. Nevertheless, from Dynasty 0, a label of King Narmer show's an image of the king's name executing members of a Libyan group called the Tjehenu – a people who seem to have lived in the northern part of the Western Desert. In the 6th Dynasty, the Tjemehu, another Libyan group, are first mentioned in texts; these appear to have lived further south, near the Bahariya and Farafra oases, but perhaps even as far south as the Third Cataract. Although these Libyan groups occasionally caused trouble for Egyptian traders, most of the sporadic violent interactions in the Old Kingdom were motivated by the Egyptians.

According to the Palermo Stone, King Sneferu took 1,100 Tjehenu-Libyans as captives and 23,000 sheep and goats; this was probably an Egyptian raid, launched to gather people (to be used as soldiers or slaves) and livestock. In the 5th Dynasty pyramid complex of King Sahure at Abu Sir, scenes depict rows of animals walking in a line, with specific numbers recording those taken: 123,400 cattle; 223,200 asses; 232,413 goats; and 243,689 sheep. Three named Libyan prisoners are also shown: Wesa, Weni, and Khu-ites. Early Egyptologists believed this scene to depict a historical event – a time when Sahure attacked the Libyans and brought back prisoners and livestock, much as Sneferu had done. But later kings – including Niuserre and Pepi II of the Old Kingdom, and Taharka of the 25th Dynasty – also decorated their monuments with the same imagery, to the extent that the Libyan prisoners bear the same names. As a result, it's impossible to know if the Sahure expedition was the first, true campaign that captured these individuals, or if he too was copying an earlier original. Further Old Kingdom references to Libyan groups are brief, and have already been mentioned: Weni included Tjemehu-Libyans among the mercenaries for his Levantine campaign, and Harkhuf says that the ruler of Yam had gone to fight the Tjemehu-Libyans in the desert.

The Oases of the Western Desert

For much of Egyptian history, the Western Desert oases were ignored both by Egyptians and foreign groups alike. Siwa Oasis, perhaps the most famous of them all, was only used by the Egyptians from the 26th Dynasty; Bahariya Oasis only had a small population before the Middle Kingdom; and Farafra wasn't occupied until the Roman Period. Of the more southerly oases, Kharga was little used before the arrival of the Persians and Romans (although archaeological remains of a Second Intermediate Period administrative centre and bakery have recently been unearthed), serving solely as a stopping off point for those wanting to feed animals and restock their water supplies during their journey to Dakhla Oasis – the only oasis of interest to the Old Kingdom Egyptians.

From as early as the 4th Dynasty, Egyptians, or people who had been 'Egyptianized,' lived in various settlements across Dakhla Oasis. These were buried according to Egyptian custom, and potters made vessels in Egyptian styles from local clay. Across the oasis, farms, hamlets, and villages were supervised by overseers of fields, who acted as intermediaries between the local people and the administrative centre at the oasis' major settlement: the fortified town of Ain Asil. In addition to the Egyptians, the Sheikh Muftah people were also active in the region; these made their own distinctive pottery, and seemingly traded goods – such as pottery and lithic tools – with the Egyptians in the west of Dakhla.

From a palace at Ain Asil, the governors of Dakhla Oasis held authority over all the western oases, including Bahariya, from which people were enlisted to work on projects at Dakhla. Controlling their own mini-courts, managed by family members in important positions, the governors kept in contact with the central court at Memphis through messengers, and also stationed people elsewhere, including Bahariya Oasis and unidentified locations called Mesqet and Qedeset (which may have been other oases). Administrative documents were stored in an archive at the governor's palace; the scribes composing these documents recorded important information on papyri, and wrote information of only short-term importance, such as records of goods, on clay tablets.

As well as ruling their own mini-courts, the governors of Dakhla were buried in monumental tombs, about 1 km away from Ain Asil in Balat. Chapels to their *ka*-spirits – an aspect of the deceased that required magical or physical food offerings – were built in Ain Asil, however; not only was this handy for residents wishing to pay their respects, but they were also close to an area of pottery production, should anyone wish to buy and leave offerings for them.

The Western Desert Trails

Dakhla's importance stemmed from its location at the end of an important trade route, known today as the Abu Ballas Trail; this is named after the route's mid-point, 200 km south-west of Dakhla. Travellers had walked this trail since Predynastic times, and continued to use it until the Roman Period, although most of the evidence for its use is concentrated in the late Old Kingdom and First Intermediate Period. Dakhla's governor was responsible for accepting goods from traders passing along this route, and for sending these goods onwards to the Nile Valley. He also ensured that Egyptian goods were available to trade, and that supplies, especially water, were dotted along the route at staging posts, easing the movement of people through the inhospitable desert.

We can imagine then, in around 2400 BCE, a group of traders based at Ain Asil departing the relative comforts of their town to begin their two week, 400 km journey south-west, through the desert to the region of the Gilf Kebir Plateau. From there, the path might have led towards Gebel Uweinat, 200 km further south-west, at the edge of modern Egypt's territory, or perhaps even as far as Kufra Oasis or Chad's Ennendi Mountain. It's possible that the trail ended at Gebel Uweinat, however, where Libyan traders, acting as middlemen for luxury goods delivered from Yam, could have met the Egyptians.

Whatever the case, leaving Dakhla Oasis, our traders would have first passed watch posts, built during the 4th and 5th Dynasties on hilltops to control access to the oasis, observing the roads to the east and south. Leaving Dakhla behind, as the traders journeyed through the desert, they were well-provisioned: thirty staging posts linked Ain Asil and the Gilf Kebir, each marked by cairns of loose stones. These outposts, many at the foot of prominent hills, were also equipped with huge pottery jars, capable of holding thirty litres of water. Each would have been filled before the arrival of a caravan and sealed. Other jars were filled with grains, used to feed the travellers and their donkeys. Some of these outposts were manned, at least temporarily – perhaps only when a caravan was expected. Cups and bowls were kept there, and vats were used to prepare dough for bread. Some ancient guardians scratched notches into the stone, each perhaps representing days passed in boredom, protecting the supplies. Others carved senet boards – a popular board game in Ancient Egypt – into the rock, providing a source of entertainment. Some men whiled away the hours carving images into other nearby stone surfaces, including one scene that appears to show a man with two dogs chasing a gazelle.

It was not only Egyptians heading south-west from Dakhla that received good treatment, but also foreign traders entering the oasis, probably along the Abu Ballas trail. An administrative letter, found at Ain Asil, mentions the failure to arrive of a potter at a place called Rudjet – perhaps to be located on the outskirts of the oasis – who had been meant to 'prepare the way' for the chief of Demi-iu – 'the Village of the Island.' Another letter mentions the need to provide grain for this chief along the way. Although Demi-iu cannot be located, it is possibly Gebel Uweinat, with its chief only occupying the site during the desert's rainy season.

Further evidence for Egyptian activities in the Western Desert can be found at a place known today as Redjedef's Water Mountain or Khufu Hill, a 20 m high rock face about 60 km south-west of Dakhla Oasis. There, in the twenty-seventh year of the reign of King Khufu, an expeditionary force of 400 men rested on a terrace at its foot, surrounded by a stone wall, some of them ready to tuck into a meal of roast locusts. The leaders of this force were the Overseers of Recruits Iymery and Beby, and their aim was to procure *mefat* – probably a mineral pigment used for paint – from the 'desert district.' To mark the event, Iymery and Beby had scratched their names, titles, and mission onto the rock face, close to images of ostriches, giraffes, and antelopes carved by much earlier visitors. This wasn't Beby's first trip to the mountain, for he'd led 200 men there two years earlier, again in search of *mefat*. Another individual, perhaps a member of one of these expeditions, also carved a boat being pulled along, and left a reference to quarry workers.

Getting Around: Travel by Land

When not travelling along the Nile on boats, the Egyptians made use of tracks along its banks, often marked by cairns and cleared of gravel. One particular ancient route led from Dahshur to the Faiyum Oasis. Some Egyptian roads were even paved, including one that connected Widan el-Faras and Qasr es-Sagha in the Faiyum (dubbed the world's oldest paved road).

Of course, if you were a member of the elite, you could get around Egypt without the need for all that tiresome walking thanks to the invention of carrying chairs. These are first attested in the 1st Dynasty, and archaeologists found a physical example among the burial equipment of Queen Hetepheres, mother of King Khufu of the 4th Dynasty. Most people, however, travelled by foot (probably barefoot if they couldn't afford sandals), and used donkeys as pack animals (the Egyptians seem to have preferred not to ride donkeys). From the New Kingdom, wheeled carts were used too, although it's not clear to what extent.

The End of the Old Kingdom

Thanks to new discoveries, Egypt's Old Kingdom interactions with the wider world are slowly becoming easier to reconstruct. What had previously been regarded as a period of limited contact with the outside world is now proving itself to be quite the opposite: the account of Iny reveals extensive relations with the northern Levant; the Abu Ballas trail shows early connections with the south-west, perhaps even leading to Chad; Elephantine was a cultural melting pot; the recently published blocks from Sahure's pyramid complex have provided more detail about an early voyage to the mysterious land of Punt; and excavations at the fort of Ras Budran and the port of Ayn Soukhna have enhanced our knowledge of the Egyptians' early exploitation of the Sinai mines. Already, foreigners lived in Egypt in large numbers and Egyptians travelled abroad, for both war and trade. It was a period of political development, bureaucratic expansion, and monuments on an extraordinary scale. Egypt flourished. But all good things must come to an end, and the Old Kingdom was no different. We will explore the reasons for its collapse, and the aftermath, in the next chapter.

Chapter 3

A Country Divided
(2117–2066 BCE)

There's still no definite explanation as to why the Old Kingdom came to an end, leaving Egypt to enter a phase of political disunity known as the First Intermediate Period. Certainly, King Pepi II of the 6th Dynasty reigned for an extremely long time, leading to dynastic succession troubles, chaos at court, and numerous short-lived reigns, to the extent that the 7th and 8th Dynasties are hard to reconstruct (indeed, the 7th Dynasty probably never existed). There was also a growth in provincial power at the expense of the central court. Egypt, from the Mediterranean Sea down to Aswan, was divided into a series of provinces, often referred to as 'nomes,' each overseen by its own nomarch, appointed by, and responsible to, the king at Memphis. But in the late Old Kingdom, nomarchs started to hand down their powerful office to members of their immediate family, creating lines of hereditary succession across the country. They were also buried in their own nomes, rather than close to the royal pyramid, as was traditional. By the end of the Old Kingdom, Egypt's nomarchs had created their own mini-courts, and the central power suffered.

To add to the court's woes, there might also have been a foreign invasion. A Middle Kingdom text, known as 'The Prophecy of Neferti,' says 'foreign birds' were breeding in the Delta, having entered the region during the First Intermediate Period because of the people's laxness. Asiatics were wandering the land, the text adds, and they'd seized Egypt's fortresses. Although this text as a whole is filled with hyperbole, there's further evidence for a foreign presence: a text known as the 'Teaching for King Merikare' also mentions Asiatics in the Delta. As king, Merikare's father had attacked these Asiatics, until they loathed Egypt, the text says. These enemies moved from place to place in search of food, and were always fighting, attacking without announcing the day of combat (which was apparently very rude).

Such accounts could be entirely fictional, but with the collapse of central power and the start of the First Intermediate Period, the royal court did move from Memphis to Herakleopolis, south of the Faiyum Oasis. Was this move prompted by instability in the north? Furthermore, at the end of the 6th Dynasty, the town of Mendes in the north-east Delta was violently destroyed and its inhabitants killed. It's not possible to reconstruct who attacked the town, and it's highly likely that the damage was caused by Egyptians fighting one another, but an Asiatic invasion cannot be discounted. The governor's palace at Ain Asil and part of the town in Dakhla Oasis were also burned down at this time, but it's extremely unlikely that these were attacked by people from the Levant.

If Asiatics did contribute to the political problems of the First Intermediate Period, why did they enter Egypt in the first place? The answer could be rapid climatic change. From 2250–2050 BCE, the Near East suffered through a period of drought, brought on by an unusually dry climate. People were forced to move in search of food. Violence erupted. Cities and states collapsed. Among its casualties, many settlements in Syria, and others further south, were abandoned, and people from Anatolia spread west, causing the destruction of settlements in the Aegean islands. It may also have contributed to the collapse of the Akkadian Empire. Egypt appears to have been largely unaffected by these climatic changes, although some scholars argue that the country experienced a period of low Nile floods.

Whatever the cause of the Old Kingdom's demise, with the political fragmentation at the start of the First Intermediate Period, Egypt found itself divided between northern nomes loyal to the royal family based at Herakleopolis, and the nomes of the south, independent of the northern royals and each competing for territory and power. Further fractures existed within individual nomes: rulers of towns acted independently of the nomarch, and even pledged their allegiance to nomarchs from other areas.

To complicate matters further, our evidence for a reconstruction is heavily weighted to the south, creating a one-sided view of events. Little can be said about the northern rulers during the first half of the First Intermediate Period. Comprising both the 9th and 10th Dynasties – though no family break is apparent – this line was founded by a man named Kheti, whose influence stretched as far south as Abydos. Manetho, who in the third century BCE compiled a list of Egypt's kings, including major events from their lives, describes Kheti as 'behaving more cruelly than his predecessors,'[1] indicating that the king probably came to power by force. So, given the lack of sources for the north, we shall first head south, and focus our attention on a local warlord named Ankhtifi.

Ankhtifi: A Man Without Equal

When his artists arrived at Moalla, just south of Thebes, to decorate his tomb chapel, Ankhtifi surely already had a good, clear idea of what he wanted them to paint: based on his tomb inscriptions, he wasn't a man who lacked vision, and he certainly thought highly of himself. A nomarch and warlord, Ankhtifi wanted everyone entering his tomb chapel to immediately recognize his power. This is perhaps why he instructed his artists to include only one example of the northern king's name on his walls: in an extremely tiny cartouche (an elongated ring, containing a royal name) painted directly beneath Ankhtifi's feet. To further stress his importance, Ankhtifi even had his tomb chapel excavated within a pyramid-shaped hill. No one can accuse him of lacking self-confidence. His inscriptions are full of bombastic statements, presenting him as 'Ankhtifi the strong,' as a 'man without equal,' and as the 'beginning of people and the end of people.'[2]

Ankhtifi began his career as nomarch of Hierakonpolis – the third nome of Upper Egypt – whilst the 9th Dynasty were ruling in the north from Herakleopolis. But he also held the titles: general, commander of mercenaries, and commander of foreign lands. During these early years, he led a campaign south into the neighbouring nome of Edfu to overthrow 'rebels' and restore order. He justified his invasion by stressing that the nome was a mess, 'neglected by the one in charge.'[3] He also said that the god Horus had requested him to enter the nome. Basically, Ankhtifi argues, his actions weren't selfish or a simple power grab: the people of Edfu needed him and the god Horus wanted him to take action. To heal the region's wounds, he made men embrace those who had killed their fathers and brothers. But taking Edfu wasn't enough. Ankhtifi went on to lead his army beyond Edfu into the nome of Elephantine, uniting Egypt's three southernmost nomes under his rule.

Ankhtifi's later attempts to expand north of Hierakonpolis were less successful. The nomarchs of Thebes and Coptos had formed an alliance against him, and were uninterested in battling the boastful southern warlord. On one occasion, Ankhtifi says, his troops challenged the Thebans to a fight. His men searched for battle throughout the Theban nome, but nobody dared to fight them. Most seem to have just shut themselves behind their city walls until Ankhtifi went away. Ankhtifi accuses them of being afraid, but they were probably just trying to ignore him.

Predictably, it wasn't just in warfare that Ankhtifi believed himself to excel. In his tomb autobiography, he describes Egypt as living through a time of famine, when people were forced to eat their children. Naturally, such chaos was confined to the areas north and south of Ankhtifi's own well-managed territory: he had plenty of barley to feed his people, and traded his surplus for oils from other nomes. He even sent barley to Lower Egypt (but doesn't mention the ruling 9th Dynasty), and far south into the region of Wawat in northern Nubia. By presenting Egypt's situation as so terribly dire, he was amplifying the success of his own actions. Not only was Ankhtifi a perfect warrior, but an excellent manager, and a philanthropist too.

Despite his exaggerations, however, Ankhtifi's claims of famine are reflected in other contemporary accounts. The Steward Seneni of the Coptite nome mentions measuring out Upper Egyptian barley to give to his whole town 'in the painful years of distress.'[4] Meanwhile, in the Theban nome, a royal treasurer named Iti says that he fed the village of Gebelein, and gave barely to Armant and Moalla. Whatever the case may be – and these men could each simply be playing on the same theme popular in self-presentation at the time – there's currently no firm scientific evidence to prove that Egypt went through a period of famine during the First Intermediate Period.

So what made Ankhtifi tick? Was he truly a person fighting for the people of his nomes? Had he tired of royal control from the north, and wanted better lives for the people of the south? Or was he simply a warlord, boastful and bombastic, whose ultimate aim was to expand his territory until he could declare himself the new king of Egypt? If the latter, he never achieved his aim. But the rulers of Thebes that came after him did.

The Rise of Thebes

The Theban nomarch that had tried his best to ignore Ankhtifi's 'invasion' was probably Intef the Great, born of Iku, who describes himself as a priest and great overlord of Upper Egypt. He appears to have extended Theban control north into Dendera, marking the beginning of the region's ascendancy in the south, and is the first in a line of Theban rulers that would eventually become the 11th Dynasty – the kings of a newly united Egypt. Intef the Great was succeeded by Montuhotep I (called *tepi-a:* 'the ancestor'), who in turn passed his office to Intef I. To ensure the safety of the Theban nome from a hostile neighbour, and to stop his enemies from controlling the desert, Intef sent his troops to close off one of the desert routes leading west. This forced Tjauti, nomarch of Coptos – loyal to the Herakleopolitan king – to create a new desert road. War followed, but it worked out well for Intef: he seized the nomes of Coptos, Dendera, and Diospolis Parva, and may even have pushed into the Abydos nome. The Thebans were taking over.

The wars for territory continued under Intef I's son, Intef II, who ruled for around fifty years and called himself king of Upper and Lower Egypt, despite not controlling the north. Someone should have told him that such hyperbole was unnecessary, for Intef's 'kingdom' – stretching from Elephantine to Abydos, according to his chancellor, Tjeti – was surely extensive enough to be worth boasting about without such exaggeration. Ankhtifi's southern nomes had by now been swallowed into Intef's territory, and the nomes further north remained loyal to the Theban. But it was a different situation at Abydos: the Herakleopolitans wouldn't give up this sacred city without a fight. The Overseer of Scouts Djari says that he fought to the west of the Abydos nome; and a letter sent from Intef II to the Herakleopolitan King Kheti says that Kheti had raised a storm over Abydos. Despite these setbacks, Intef eventually managed to push further north beyond Abydos to establish his new border at the tenth nome of Upper Egypt – the region of modern Qau el-Kebir. The stele of Redikhnum from Dendera mentions Intef II moving men from Elephantine into the tenth nome, presumably to defend his new border.

Whilst fighting to seize more territory in the north, Intef II reorganized the nomes already under his control. He assigned Hetepy from el-Qab to manage Egypt's seven southernmost nomes, with particular attention given to Elephantine, Edfu, and Hierakonpolis. Egypt's nomes would no longer be assigned to individual (potentially troublesome) nomarchs, but were to be overseen en masse by royally appointed managers. The governors of individual towns within the nomes received greater powers, and men of importance once again began to be buried close to the king, rather than in their own nomes. Intef II had broken the power of the nomarchs and succeeded in pushing his territory to the edge of Asyut in Middle Egypt. On the basis of a single inscription at Aniba in Nubia, he may also have expanded his influence south beyond the First Cataract, where he could find highly-skilled fighters to join his cause.

The Nomarchs of Asyut

Intef II's advance north must have worried the nomarchs of Asyut, Egypt's thirteenth Upper Egyptian nome. This family were loyal to the Herakleopolitan kings and had actively tried to block the Theban king's progress. The first of these nomarchs, Kheti I, lived during Thebes' rise to power. On campaign, he organized his troops into divisions of 1,000 men, some placed into teams of bowmen, and others into teams armed with shields and spears. This same division of troops – between bowmen and spearmen – can be seen in the tomb models of Mesehti, a descendant of Kheti I, who also lived at Asyut. One set of models represents forty Nubian archers. Another represents Egyptian spearmen carrying shields. Nomarch Kheti also commanded a fleet of ships, capable of transporting his troops along the Nile to defend the interests of the Herakleopolitan kings.

Kheti's son and successor, It-ibi also fought against the southern king. His troops travelled by boat to different locations along the Nile, and he apparently succeeded in halting the southern advance north. After It-Ibi's death, his son Kheti II was installed as nomarch by King Merikare, one of the last Herakleopolitan kings (and the man whose father may have fought Asiatic invaders in the Delta, mentioned at the start of this chapter). He too commanded ships, perhaps during the final war of reunification between the Thebans and the Herakleopolitans, and mentions the temporary loss of Asyut to the southern invaders, followed by his successful attempt to remove them.

Nubians at Gebelein

During the First Intermediate Period, a population of Nubians lived at Gebelein, about 25 km south of Thebes. They probably reached this village via the desert and oasis routes from Nubia. As Nubians were famous among the Egyptians as archers, they probably served in the Theban army, helping to seize the north of the country.

These men were buried according to Egyptian tradition, but portrayed themselves as Nubian on their monuments. One man, Nenu, is depicted on his funerary stele wearing a red sash around his waist, typical of Nubian dress at this time, and holds a bow and quiver. His son wears a pin through his hair, a style not followed by the Egyptians. Nenu's wife, however, is shown in a traditionally Egyptian manner. The village's Nubian population is also mentioned by the local Egyptians on their monuments.

Further attestations of Nubians in Egypt during these troubled times are rare: a bowl of First Intermediate Period date depicting a Nubian archer was left in the forecourt of one of the tombs of Aswan's late Old Kingdom governors; and two stelae from Naga ed-Deir in Middle Egypt mention a man named Nefernehesy, who might have been of Nubian origin. Nubian archers are depicted in various tombs of the First Intermediate Period, and imported vessels show that the Egyptians continued to trade with the C-Group in the south.

Montuhotep II: Man of Many Names

Montuhotep II, son of Intef III (who reigned for less than a decade), led the Thebans in the final war against the Herakleopolitans. It's an important moment in Egyptian history, but the events surrounding this final push for unity are obscure, forcing us to rely on extremely limited evidence, including changes to royal names: you see, each pharaoh, upon his coronation, was given four additional names, among them one called a Horus Name. Normally, these names remained the same throughout a king's life, but he could alter them if he so desired, particularly if he wanted to highlight an important event or change in policy. After being crowned king, Montuhotep's Horus Name was Sankhibtawy, 'the one who causes the Two Lands to live,' but sometime after his fourteenth year he changed it to Netjeryhedjet, 'Divine one of the White Crown.' You'd think this would be enough name changes, but by at least his thirty-ninth year as king, he'd changed it once again, this time to Sematawy, 'Unifier of the Two Lands.' This has led scholars to argue that Montuhotep's unification of Egypt occurred sometime before this date. And with the reunification of Egypt under a single king, the Middle Kingdom began.

Following Egypt's unification, the king stripped all nomarchs of their office, but allowed their families to remain in key positions in their home regions. In Asyut, Kheti II's son Iti-ibi-iqer, unable to inherit the office of nomarch, became an overseer of priests and general. In his tomb, he depicts rows of marching soldiers, including one Nubian. Iti-ibi-iqer was succeeded as overseer of priests by his son Mesehti, owner of the model soldiers of Nubians and Egyptians, discussed earlier. Given that this family, once so hostile to the south, remained in power after unification, we must wonder if they switched allegiance to the Thebans during the final war, allowing their former enemies to pass north unopposed through Asyut to take Herakleopolis.

Montuhotep II's Foreign Wars

As we can't say for sure when exactly Montuhotep II unified Egypt, it's possible that he was already campaigning beyond Egypt's borders before he seized the north. One of his early targets, seemingly before unification, was Libya: at Gebelein, scenes show Montuhotep (still Netjeryhedjet at this point) clubbing a Libyan chief called Hedjwawesh. Another has him smiting an Egyptian, Nubian, and Asiatic, with a Libyan waiting in turn. And at Dendera, he is described as beating the Libyans, along with the Eastern Lands, Nubians, and Medjay (a Nubian group from the Eastern Desert). He is also shown smiting the symbol of Lower Egypt.

Montuhotep II also sent troops south into C-Group Nubia, initiating the Middle Kingdom domination of this territory. In an inscription from Deir el-Ballas, the king says that he annexed an oasis and the region of Wawat, and decapitated desert dwellers. It's unclear which oasis he meant, but if Montuhotep had taken Kurkur Oasis, west of Aswan, he would have secured an important desert route into Wawat. A carved scene of Montuhotep at Wadi Schatt er-Rigal might mark the starting point for this Nubian campaign. Montuhotep II also seems to have married a Nubian woman named Kemsit, who was buried in a shaft beneath his mortuary temple at Deir el-Bahri in Thebes. On the sarcophagus of Ashayt, another of his wives, one servant is identified as a Medjay.

Scenes from Montuhotep's mortuary temple at Thebes, showing an attack on an Asiatic fortress, probably represents events after unification. Egyptian soldiers march carrying axes, and use a siege ladder to enter the fortress. Enemies fall, pierced by arrows. A Nubian mercenary, armed with a bow, escorts a captured female prisoner, who carries a child. A similar scene is found in the tomb of the Overseer of Troops Intef, who served Montuhotep II: soldiers march towards an Asiatic fortress; they carry axes, bows and arrows, shields, and spears. Some archers have placed their quivers on the ground while they shoot their arrows. Others have climbed a siege ladder to the top of the fortress and are attacking their enemies. Asiatics fall to the ground.

An insight into military life under Montuhotep II is provided by a Nubian soldier named Tjehemau, who left a rock inscription about his career at Abisko, south of Aswan. Tjehemau enlisted into the Egyptian army at Buhen (bringing along his son), during a visit by Montuhotep II to Nubia. Just as in the Old Kingdom, Lower Nubia was a major recruiting ground for Nubian mercenaries: men who would give the Thebans the extra fighting power needed to dominate and consolidate their control of the north. Tjehemau says that he attacked and defeated Asiatics in an obscure place called Djaty – perhaps in the Delta – and travelled to the Lake of Sobek in the Faiyum. He also seems to have fought in the region of Irtjet in

Nubia, a place that may have bordered the emerging Kingdom of Kerma in Upper Nubia (discussed in Chapter Five). Afterwards, Tjehemau returned to Thebes, where the population gathered on the riverbanks to praise him.

The End of the 11th Dynasty

Although Montuhotep II initiated the Middle Kingdom, his family line – the 11th Dynasty – didn't last much beyond him. Two further Montuhoteps (III and IV) reigned in succession after his death, making little impact at home or abroad. In fact, the best-known event from this period occurred under Montuhotep IV, and the king isn't even the star.

In around 2000 BCE, Montuhotep IV sent a procession of Egyptian workmen, administrators, and soldiers into the Wadi Hammamat in the Eastern Desert – a region famous for the quality of its stone – to procure a block of stone suitable for the court artisans to carve into a royal sarcophagus. The leader of this 10,000 strong expedition was the Vizier Amenemhat, overseer of everything in the land, who would find himself bearing witness to some rather dramatic 'miracles': for one, during the march to the quarry, a pregnant gazelle approached the expedition members and led them to a particularly lovely piece of stone, where she gave birth – an event that the Egyptians took as a divine sign that this was the stone they'd been searching for. Such was the men's devotion that they slit the gazelle's throat and offered her as a burnt offering to the gods. As a second miracle, during a flash flood, the god Min unveiled a secret well, kept pure from the animals and the sight of all previous expeditions.

Dramatic indeed. But not as dramatic as what Amenemhat had planned next. Not content with being vizier – the second most important man in the land – he set his sights on the only promotion available: the kingship.

Chapter 4

An Expanding World
(2066–1781 BCE)

The events surrounding Amenemhat's rise to power are not clearly known. One moment there's a king called Montuhotep IV and a vizier named Amenemhat, the next, there's a King Amenemhat sitting on the throne as the first ruler of the 12th Dynasty. Although it can't be proven that both Amenemhats were the same man, it would seem a rather huge coincidence.

There are, however, a few pieces of evidence that can shed light on these murky events. A series of inscriptions at the calcite quarry at Hatnub, in Middle Egypt, mention infighting among Egyptians. Nehri, the local nomarch, proclaims that he rescued his city on a day of terror brought about by the King's House – seemingly the forces of the 11th Dynasty. Nehri's son Kay similarly describes a time of warfare, during which he recruited and trained men from his home town. His opponent is again said to be the King's House, aided by people from all directions – Nubians, easterners (perhaps mercenaries), and people from the Delta. If Kay is to be believed, despite everyone in his known world ganging up against him, he was still the ultimate victor. It's probable that this family of nomarchs had been caught up in a civil war, and had taken Amenemhat's side against the 11th Dynasty.

More evidence for internal strife comes from the tomb of Khnumhotep I, a nomarch buried at Beni Hassan, who served Amenemhat I. What's unusual here is that his tomb is decorated with scenes of Egyptians fighting Egyptians, armed with bows and arrows, axes, and shields, while the accompanying text describes the king as leading a military expedition of twenty ships against a rebel in the south, launched in order to expel this enemy from Egypt. One register, though perhaps unrelated to this campaign south, shows an Egyptian leading away Asiatic prisoners: men, women carrying babies on their backs, and livestock. Clearly, Khnumhotep was on Amenemhat's side in the civil war: the winning side. Finally – and perhaps the most gruesome testament to warfare in the early 12th Dynasty – archaeologists found the skeletal remains of soldiers from Amenemhat I's army in a cave at Thebes, many still with arrowheads embedded in their skeletons. Others were killed by falling projectiles, suggesting that they'd taken part in an attack on a fortified city, perhaps Thebes itself.

Although there's little detail about these battles, one thing is quite clear: by the end of it all, Amenemhat I sat on the throne. His dynasty ruled Egypt for the rest of the Middle Kingdom, overseeing a period of high prosperity, when Egypt's interactions with the wider world expanded and the presentation of kingship itself changed. Inheriting elements of the First Intermediate Period nomarch approach to rule, it was no longer enough for a king to be a distant god, his personality hidden from view; now, the king had to present himself as caring for his people, and in turn – because of his hard work – the people were meant to show him their loyalty. It was also in the Middle Kingdom that court scribes composed various classics of Egyptian literature. From wisdom texts and loyalist instructions, to fictional tales, such as the 'Tale of the Shipwrecked Sailor' and the 'Tale of Sinuhe (Sanehat)' – the court did not lack entertainment.

The kings also wanted to connect themselves with Egypt's already great past, and so started building pyramids again. Unlike their Old Kingdom predecessors, these pyramids had complex interior arrangements designed to confuse thieves, an indication that the pyramids of the Old Kingdom had been robbed, probably during the First Intermediate Period. More nefariously, the state began to impose on society as a whole, creating state settlements with rigid grid layouts and inflicting brutal punishments on anyone who avoided, or fled, state labour.

Trading with the East

While the Egyptians were becoming accustomed to getting along with each other again, their neighbours to the east were experiencing their own time of recovery. Following a period of rapid climatic change across the Near East, which had caused mass movement and the destruction of cities, by around 2050 BCE, life was returning to normal. People across the region were once again free to go about their daily lives without fear of violence (although they did live within fortified cities, suggesting the presence of at least some danger). At the same time, the Minoans on the island of Crete also entered a period of growth and prosperity. Things were looking up.

After the establishment of the 12th Dynasty, the Egyptians began to take a renewed interest in their neighbours. As in the Old Kingdom, they made no attempt to occupy the Levant, rather it was seen as a source of luxury goods – a place to be exploited as much as possible. When Egypt's ships left the Delta, they stopped at various locations along the Levantine coast as they travelled north, leaving traces of their presence at places such as Ashkelon and, further north, Dor. Their crews traded with local people, so that items of Egyptian origin passed from person to person until they ended up spread across the Levant and beyond – from scarabs and pottery at Megiddo, for example, to Egyptian statuettes at Qatna, in modern Syria; and a *djed*-pillar – an Egyptian symbol of stability – as far from Egypt as Alaca Höyük in Anatolia.

Some light is cast on the extent of Egypt's trading ventures thanks to the 'Annals of King Amenemhat II,' a detailed breakdown of the most important events from this king's reign, inscribed on a stone block, reused as a pedestal under King Ramesses II of the 19th Dynasty. Among its various entries, the inscription records a visit by tribute-bearing Nubian and Syrian dignitaries to the royal court; an Egyptian expedition to the 'turquoise terraces' – probably the Sinai mines; and the arrival of the Tempau-people (perhaps Bedouin), who came with 'bowed heads' carrying 238 ingots of lead. It also says that two boats were sent to Khenty-she (Lebanon), and returned to Egypt with 1,675.5 *deben* of silver, 4,882 *deben* of bronze and 15,961 *deben* of copper (one *deben* of weight being equal to 27 g in the Middle Kingdom). Also among the cargo was gold, lead, marble, daggers (some made from bronze, gold, and silver, others of bronze and ivory), plants and fruits, oils, resins, and cedar trees. People were aboard too: sixty-five male and female Asiatics. According to another section of the Annals, the princes of Asia sent 1,002 Asiatics to the Egyptian court, along with items of silver and lead, and domestic animals.

The extent of foreign trade under King Amenemhat II appears to have been unusual, for before his reign contact was more sporadic. It's perhaps not coincidental then that under Amenemhat II, the 'Tod Treasure' was assembled: four copper chests, discovered at Tod (just south of Thebes), containing precious items from across Egypt's known world, including rings, bracelets, a mirror, copper, pendants, carnelian beads, fragments of quartz, amethyst, and obsidian, as well as over 150 bowls. In total, this amounted to about 7 kg of gold and more than 9 kg of silver. Based on style, and from scientific analysis, the silver items came from the Aegean and Anatolia; the cylinder and stamp seals from Iran, Mesopotamia, and Syria; and the lapis lazuli from Afghanistan. And this is not the only example of items from across the world finding their way to Egypt: a single carnelian bead, made by the Indus culture, but unearthed at Abydos, is the oldest Indian object discovered in Ancient Egypt. It was probably traded in around 2000 BCE.

Not only did Egyptian traders enter the Levant during the Middle Kingdom, but Asiatic traders came to Egypt too. In the sixth year of the reign of King Senwosret II, an Asiatic caravan arrived in Egypt to trade in galena eye-paint, an event depicted in the tomb of Khnumhotep II at Beni Hassan. The caravan, led by a man named Abisharie, consisted of eight men, four women, three children, and two donkeys. Each person wore a multicoloured robe, and some of the men were armed with weapons, including a composite bow – not used by the Egyptians until the New Kingdom – spears, and throw-sticks. Another man carried a stringed instrument, perhaps played to entertain his companions during their long journey. In Egypt, the caravan was met by the Royal Document Scribe Neferhotep, who is shown in the scene holding a piece of papyrus; the tiny text on this papyrus says that there were thirty-seven Asiatics in total (despite the number of people painted), and these had been invited from a place called Shu by the local mayor's son. (Given its content, this document can perhaps be viewed as a form of ancient 'entry visa,' enabling the Asiatics to pass into Egyptian territory.)

Behind Neferhotep in the caravan scene stands the Overseer of Hunters Khety, who probably monitored and patrolled the desert routes, acting as border security. Such methods of controlling the movement of people were not unusual in the Middle Kingdom. The Egyptians had always monitored the 'Ways of Horus' – the coastal road connecting Egypt and the Levant – and in the Middle Kingdom constructed a series of fortresses there, called the 'Walls of the Ruler.' Although not known archaeologically, these are mentioned in literary tales: 'The Prophecy of Neferti', set during the 4th Dynasty, predicts the rise of King Amenemhat I, who would build the 'Walls of the Ruler' to protect Egypt from Asiatics; and 'The Tale of Sinuhe' has its eponymous hero hide in a bush to avoid a sentry at the 'Walls of the Ruler' while attempting to flee into the Levant. Later, when crossing back into Egypt, Sinuhe speaks with the head of a patrol. He then continues his journey, but his Asiatic companions return home, perhaps because they weren't allowed into Egypt.

The Tale of Sinuhe (Sanehat): An Adventure in the Levant

Sinuhe (more correctly Sanehat), an official of the royal harem, had accompanied Prince Senwosret, the future King Senwosret I, and his army on campaign in Libya. The mission was a success, but during their return to Egypt – prisoners and cattle dragged along with them – tragic news reached the prince: his father, King Amenemhat I was dead and there was trouble at the royal residence. As a harem official, Sinuhe overheard this message while it was being delivered to the royal children, and in a state of panic, fled (he was a harem official after all, and harems have a nasty habit of being involved in royal assassinations in Ancient Egypt, just ask King Ramesses III of the 20th Dynasty).

Sinuhe crossed Egypt and reached the fortresses known as the 'Walls of the Ruler,' where he hid in a bush until nightfall to avoid the guards. Later, enshrouded in darkness, he entered the Levant, but soon after, at a place called The Great Black Water, dehydration overwhelmed him. In this shattered state, expecting death, he suddenly heard the sound of lowing cattle and saw Asiatics approaching. Their chief recognized him as an Egyptian and offered him water and boiled milk. Sinuhe, now saved and recovered, joined the chief's tribe, and travelled with them to Byblos and Qedem.

A year and a half later, Amunenshi, the ruler of this Syrian territory, sent for Sinuhe – other Egyptians, already serving the ruler, had vouched for their fellow countryman's useful skills. In audience, Amunenshi asked Sinuhe how he ended up in Syria: had something happened at the Egyptian residence? Sinuhe told him about the king's death, and the mysterious circumstances surrounding it. Although he himself had not been mentioned or implicated, Sinuhe added, he fled, but didn't know why. Treating the Egyptian like one of his own children, Amunenshi then appointed Sinuhe as the ruler of a clan, and married him to his eldest daughter. He also gave Sinuhe control of a place called Iaa – a land with figs and grapes, abundant in wine, plentiful in honey, barely, wheat, and cattle. Many years passed, and Sinuhe's children became adults, each now with his own clan. Egyptian envoys, passing through Iaa, stopped to meet Sinuhe during their travels, enabling him to keep up-to-date with events back home.

Sinuhe also became commander of his ruler's army, attacking and killing many enemies. His fame as a warrior must have spread, for at one time, a hero of Syria arrived at Sinuhe's tent to challenge him. Sinuhe was forced to accept, and prepared his weapons for battle. The next morning, the local people gathered to watch the fight, wondering if anyone was capable of defeating the hero of Syria. The battle began, and the hero launched himself at the Egyptian. But Sinuhe dodged and loosed an arrow straight into the hero's neck. His enemy now weakened, Sinuhe took the hero's own dagger from the ground and made the final, deadly blow.

Upon entering old age, Sinuhe began to long for home: the Egyptian royal residence. King Senwosret I heard of his wish, and sent a message, inviting him to return to Egypt. Sinuhe agreed, but before starting his journey home, gave his property to his children and appointed his eldest son as leader of the clan. The Syrians escorted Sinuhe to the Egyptian border, located along the 'Ways of Horus,' where they parted. From there, he travelled to the royal city of Itj-Tawy, founded under Amenemhat I, which probably stood somewhere in the vicinity of Lisht. The next morning, Sinuhe met the king during a royal audience, and was given accommodation. Because he was unshaven and dressed as a Syrian, the Egyptians cut Sinuhe's hair, gave him the fine linen of an Egyptian to wear, and anointed him with high quality oil. The king also gave him a tomb, so that he could be laid to rest in suitably Egyptian surroundings now that his foreign adventures were over.

War in the East

Of course, Egypt's relations with the Levant weren't always peaceful: raids – following the Old Kingdom tradition of using muscle to ensure the steady flow of goods and slaves – were probably reasonably frequent. Unfortunately, most of the preserved accounts of Middle Kingdom warfare are quite brief. At the start of the 12th Dynasty, in the twenty-fourth year of King Amenemhat I's reign, a general named Nesumontu demolished fortresses in the Levant, and, in his account of these events, says how he prowled like a jackal on the desert's edge, walking up and down the Asiatics' streets. King Senwosret I describes himself as severing the necks of Asiatics, and his vizier, Montuhotep, says that he pacified the 'sand-dwellers.' Senwosret I's pyramid complex at Lisht included a battle scene, showing Asiatics fighting. Egyptian soldiers, armed with bows and arrows, and spears, can be seen besieging an Asiatic fortress in the tomb of the Nomarch Amenemhat, buried at Beni Hassan under Senwosret I.

In addition to recording the trading ventures mentioned above, the 'Annals of Amenemhat II' include more violent interactions too. One entry says that the Egyptian army travelled to Setjet (Asia) to destroy a place called Iaw, while on another occasion, they returned home after attacking the fortifications of Iawi. These were probably the same location, and can perhaps be equated with Ura, a port city in southern Anatolia, mentioned in later Babylonian sources and the Ugarit archives. The army also attacked the fortifications of Iasy, perhaps a city in Cyprus. From the mission to Iawi and Iasy, the Egyptians brought back 1,554 Asiatic captives (perhaps the total from both cities), copper, bronze weapons, silver, jewellery, amethyst, malachite, ivory furniture pieces, household goods, lead, and combs. For their service, they were rewarded with slaves, fields, gold of honour, clothing, and generally 'beautiful things.' They also got to eat the Asiatics' food supplies.

One of the more detailed accounts of warfare in the Levant during the Middle Kingdom is found on a statue of the Soldier Sobek-Khu, who served in the army of King Senwosret III. The troops were travelling home from a campaign when they were attacked by Asiatics at Sekmem (probably Shechem). Sobek-Khu, serving at the back of the army, says that he fought an Asiatic and took his weapons. For his bravery, he was rewarded with a throw-stick of electrum, a dagger of electrum, and a sheath.

Asiatics in Southern Sinai

Egypt's mining activities in southern Sinai resumed during the Middle Kingdom, with expeditions sent to exploit the mines at Serabit el-Khadim and Wadi Maghara under various rulers. During these expeditions, the Egyptians worked alongside people of Asiatic origin. Their presence is reflected in numerous inscriptions and drawings, many within the Temple of Hathor at Serabit el-Khadim. Various stelae mention a brother of the prince of Retenu (roughly Syria-Palestine) called Khebded as present, and he is depicted riding a donkey. Another scene on a stele, from the reign of King Amenemhat III, also shows an Asiatic riding a donkey, accompanied by two further Asiatics: Shekam and Apim. Archaeologists have found stone foot bellows at the site identical to examples found in the Levant, suggesting that these Asiatics worked as metalworkers and in other craft-related roles. Others may have travelled from the Levant to bring the Egyptians charcoal or wood as fuel. Interpreters, travelling as members of the expeditions, helped the Egyptians to communicate with their Levantine neighbours.

During the Second Intermediate Period – the phase after the Middle Kingdom – Asiatics left Proto-Sinaitic inscriptions in the mines at Serabit el-Khadim; around half of the symbols in this alphabetic system were inspired by Egyptian hieroglyphs, showing a merging of cultural ideas. Asiatics, probably serving as mercenaries, also left Proto-Sinaitic inscriptions at Wadi el-Hol, north of Thebes, in the early Middle Kingdom.

War and Peace at Byblos

For the first half of the Middle Kingdom, Egypt did not enjoy friendly relations with Byblos – the country's most important trading partner in earlier times. This is made clear in the tomb autobiography of Khnumhotep III at Dahshur, in which he describes his adventures during a trading voyage in the Levant. Khnumhotep III was the son of Khnumhotep II, the man famous for his tomb's depiction of the Asiatic caravan entering Egypt, mentioned above. Like his father, Khnumhotep III played an important role in Egypt's foreign relations, being referred to as a 'doorway of foreign lands' and as 'one who brought what is useful for its owner (the king).'[1]

According to Khnumhotep III, Egypt's main Levantine trading partner during his voyage was the city of Ullaza, about 50 km north of Byblos. It had probably been this way for much of the early Middle Kingdom. The inscription is not entirely clear, due to frequent breaks, but it appears that Khnumhotep had hoped to trade for cedar in Ullaza, and somehow ended up in Byblos. There, the king of Byblos, hostile to Egyptians, questioned Khnumhotep on his unexpected appearance. At the time, relations were tense between Byblos and Ullaza: war had erupted between the two cities, and the king of Byblos had already sent his son at the head of an army into his enemy's territory. He had also written to the Egyptian king to ask him to show restraint, perhaps in an effort to stop the Egyptians from intervening. This was disregarded, for in the sections that follow, the Egyptians are described as arriving on Asiatic soil and a battlefield is mentioned. The Egyptians appear to have mobilized in order to protect Ullaza – their trading partner – from Byblos, ensuring their own interests in the region.

The text breaks off here, but later in the 12th Dynasty, Egyptianized governors rule Byblos. It is probable that the events described in Khnumhotep III's autobiography were a key turning point in Egypt's relations with their former trading partner, when the Egyptians overthrew Byblos' unruly king and established in his place a line of rulers more favourable to Egypt's influence. So dramatic was this shift that Byblos now resumed its position as Egypt's main trading partner in the region, and the city's rulers became known as *haty-a*, the Egyptian word for 'mayor.' They even began to write in hieroglyphs, and developed their own short-lived 'pseudo-hieroglyphic script,' inspired by the Egyptian writing system. Byblos' Temple of the Obelisks, full of standing stones with pyramidal peaks, was also influenced by Egyptian architecture. There, copper or bronze figurines once stood, gilded, and wearing conical hats, seemingly inspired by statues of the Egyptian king wearing the White Crown of Upper Egypt.

Both King Amenemhat III and King Amenemhat IV sent gifts to their new allies, which ended up buried within the mayors' tombs at Byblos. Among these gifts was a grey stone vase, and a small chest of obsidian and gold. On one gold pendant, embellished with semiprecious stones, the Mayor Ip-shemu-abi wrote his name in a cartouche. His sickle-sword, also buried with him, bore hieroglyphs, and uraei – symbols of royal protection. Egypt's royal workshops produced scarabs bearing the names and titles of the mayors of Byblos, which were then sent to the city for them to use.

Cyprus in the Middle Kingdom

Trade between Cyprus and Egypt during the Middle Kingdom is mentioned on a recently discovered cuneiform tablet from Tell Siyannu, close to the Syrian coast, proving that relations between the two countries existed. Furthermore, if Iasy in the 'Annals of Amenemhat II' (mentioned above) can be equated with Cyprus, it would be an early reference to Egypt's relations with the island. The main problem with this attribution, however, is that there is no evidence for large settlements on Cyprus at this time, and archaeologists haven't found any Egyptian objects of Middle Kingdom date there. Nevertheless, wealthy cemeteries are known, particularly those at Lapithos-Vrysi tou Barba and at Bellpais-Vounous, and so undiscovered settlements, perhaps home to the people that interacted with the Egyptians, may lie hidden in their vicinity.

Asiatics in Egypt

By the Middle Kingdom, people from the Levant had been settling in Egypt for centuries, either as prisoners of war, traded as slaves – as highlighted in the 'Annals of Amenemhat II' – or as mercenaries. Such individuals now started to appear more frequently in art. One wooden statue of an Asiatic woman, dated to the early 12th Dynasty and found at Beni Hassan, depicts her wearing yellow boots and a brown garment decorated with zigzags. Her hair is tied upwards, with a band around it, and she carries a baby on her back. A similar statuette, again depicting a woman carrying a baby on her back, also probably dates to the Middle Kingdom. This woman wears a thick cloak, decorated with a chequer board pattern, with a fringe at the bottom and seam at the front; this garment is quite unlike anything typically worn by Egyptian women in art, and highlights the woman's foreign origins. Her hairstyle is similar to that of the Beni Hassan figurine, and both may have worn combs in their hair. Foreigners with such hairdos are depicted in the 12th Dynasty tomb of Ukhhotep at Meir, where they appear to be either acting as household or temple servants.

Foreign slaves often worked as household or temple servants. One stele, now in the Garstang Museum, Liverpool, shows a priest of Onuris named Si-Anhur ploughing. Behind him, a man labelled as 'the Asiatic, Sobekiry,' sows seeds with one hand, taken from a bag carried with his other hand. A female Asiatic servant called Seneb-Ameny-Nebtiti grinds grain. A further Asiatic servant is 'the brewer, the Asiatic Iry,' who strains a mash of liquid and dough. Meanwhile, Sobekiry, appearing for a second time, pours beer into jars. A stele of 13th Dynasty date, now in the Metropolitan Museum of Art, shows rows of offering bearers bringing items for the Vizier Reniseneb; among them is an Asiatic woman named Seneb-Reniseneb. Some Asiatics also held special-ized positions: the stele of a man named Karu, now in Rio de Janeiro, mentions an Asiatic named Tuti acting as chief of craftsmen, while another man men-tioned is the Chief of Craftsmen Aper, born of Ibi. On the stele of Minhotep in Florence, the name of the Asiatic Wahka is included beneath Minhotep's chair.

One section of Papyrus Brooklyn 35.1446 – a document re-used over the course of many years – was drawn up by a 13th Dynasty noblewoman named Senebtisi in order to prove that her late husband, seemingly the Vizier Resseneb, had given her ownership of his estate's slaves. It lists ninety-five slaves in total, of which at least forty-five were Asiatics of both sexes; on the whole, these per-formed skilled labour for the household, while the Egyptians worked in the fields. Among the male Asiatics was a house servant, a brewer, cooks, and tutors or guardians of children. Most of the women mentioned were cloth-makers, but a maidservant, magazine employees, and a labourer were also present. Many of the children were too young to work. Although it was normal for Asiatic slaves to be given Egyptian names – usually compounded with that of their owners or with statements that the lord or mistress 'be well' – here five of the adults still retain their Semitic names, as do all of the children. Some adults have both Semitic and Egyptian names. Because Asiatics born in Egypt usu-ally have Egyptian names, scholars have suggested that the majority of these people were brought to Egypt shortly before the document was drawn up, and, because Asiatic women outnumber men by three to one, they may have been taken during raids in the Levant, in which most of the men were killed.

Papyrus documents from Lahun – a town associated with the pyramid of King Senwosret II in the Faiyum Oasis – also attest to an Asiatic presence, many as specialized workers. Living among the villagers were Asiatic tem-ple singers, serfs, doorkeepers, and weavers in the households. At the local temple, there were more Asiatic and Medjay dancers than Egyptians. None, however, performed ritual roles in the temple cult. Without these papyrus documents, Egyptologists would never have known the extent of the foreign presence at Lahun because excavations had only revealed metal torques – a type of necklace popular in the Levant – and Asiatic weights. As metal torques have also been found at sites in other parts of Egypt, the country may have been home to a larger Asiatic population than previously thought.

Egypt's Relations with Crete

During the Middle Kingdom, there was a sudden explosion of interaction between the Minoans of Crete and the Ancient Egyptians. The Minoans imported Egyptian scarabs and stone vessels, or made their own local imitations; perhaps adopted a new form of Egyptian potter's wheel; and seem to have been inspired by the Egyptians to use hand drills to make stone vessels and seals. Within tombs on Crete's Mesara Plain, clay coffins, stone cosmetic palettes, and model bread loaves may all have been inspired by Egyptian art, while at the Phourni Cemetery, archaeologists found the earliest Cretan hieroglyphic script, perhaps inspired by Egyptian hieroglyphs. The Egyptian goddess Taweret was assimilated into Minoan religion, but rather than protecting mothers and children as she did in Egypt, on Crete, she became a goddess associated with water and sacred stones.

In return for Egyptian goods, the Minoans probably exported silver, timber, spices, herbs, and decorated fabrics. On the ceiling of the tomb of Hepdjefa at Asyut – from the reign of King Senwosret I – artists painted heart-shaped spirals, perhaps influenced by Minoan textiles; and archaeologists have found Minoan pottery at sites across Egypt, including Abydos, Lisht, and Qubbet el-Hawa. The greatest quantity of Minoan pottery sherds in Egypt, however, was excavated at Lahun and Haraga. Representing about thirty-one vessels, these probably entered Egypt as part of palatial exchange. The treasure of Princess Khnumet, a daughter of King Amenemhat II, also reveals Minoan influence, particularly her bird pendants and painted rock-crystal pendant.

Intriguingly, despite the extensive archaeological evidence for Egyptian contact with Crete, there is only a single reference to the Minoans – called Keftiu – in an Egyptian text from this period, found in 'The Admonitions of Ipuwer,' composed in the late Middle Kingdom.

Securing the Western Desert and Oases

Beyond a depiction of King Montuhotep II smiting the Libyan ruler Hedjwawesh at Gebelein, and a reference to the Libyans in the 'Tale of Sinuhe,' the Middle Kingdom evidence is rather quiet concerning the people of the Western Desert and the oases. Much of what is known relates to border security, for just as they had done in the south (see below), and along the 'Ways of Horus' in the east, during the Middle Kingdom, the Egyptians attempted to strengthen their control over their western territory. They constructed a fortress in the Wadi Natrun, on the western side of the Delta, seemingly to monitor and control the movement of people into this region, and appointed officials to travel the borderlands in search of potential threats to Egypt's security. The Policeman Beb, operating in the 12th Dynasty under Senwosret I, says that he policed all the deserts for the king, and on patrol, travelled to a land called Nehu (location unknown) before returning to Upper Egypt; from the late 11th Dynasty, a man named Kay – the overseer of the hunters of the desert districts – travelled to the oases in search of a fugitive hiding in the west, his mission to bring the criminal back to Egypt; and under King Senwosret I, the Steward and Leader of Recruits Dediku left Thebes to secure the land of the oasis dwellers. During his return journey, he erected a stele at Abydos (perhaps while enjoying a bit of religious tourism).

Egypt and Nubia

Unlike the Levant, which was seen as a place to exploit and send troops when necessary, from the early Middle Kingdom, the Egyptians regarded Nubia as a place to occupy and dominate – as a land along the Nile, it was an extension of Egyptian territory, and so could be formally integrated into the whole. The C-Group Nubians felt the brunt of this new approach to foreign policy from the start of the 12th Dynasty, when King Amenemhat I sent troops into Nubia three times – in his tenth, eighteenth, and twenty-ninth regnal years. His army included the Vizier Antefiker, who says that he slaughtered Nubians in Wawat (Lower Nubia), stripped the land of crops, and burned Nubian homes.

With Lower Nubia's population devastated by these violent attacks, King Senwosret I set about further exploiting the region's rich mineral wealth. He sent expeditions to Toshka in search of diorite, to Wadi el-Hudi for amethyst, and to Wadi Allaqi for gold and copper. The Nomarch Amenemhat (buried at Beni Hassan) joined Senwosret I on a military campaign to expand Egypt's influence further south. It was a success, and Amenemhat returned to the region afterwards to collect gold for his king. Senwosret also commanded an inscription be carved at Wadi el-Hudi, proclaiming that only Nubians who acted as servants for the king would see their descendants live. The message was clear: submit to Egypt or die.

Later in the Middle Kingdom, King Senwosret III launched four campaigns into Nubia (in his tenth, twelfth, sixteenth, and possibly nineteenth regnal years). During his sixteenth year as king, he erected a stele at Semna, marking his southern border at the point where the impassable waters of the Second Cataract become navigable again for those sailing south. Here, he describes plundering Nubia's women and dependents, attacking their wells and cattle, and setting fire to their grain. 'Aggression is valour, retreat is cowardice,'[2] the king says, after calling Nubians a people unworthy of respect. The king then sent a team of men to cut a channel around the dangerous waters of the First Cataract zone, enabling his ships to sail south, even at times of a low Nile. Luxury goods could now flow into Egypt from Nubia all year round.

Nubians in Egypt

As in earlier periods, during the Middle Kingdom, Nubians of different ethnicities continued to live in Egypt: there were the Pan-Grave people of the Eastern Desert (known to the Egyptians as Medjay – more about them below); the C-Group of Lower Nubia; and the Kermans of Upper Nubia. And, although most references to Nubians are found on the monuments of prominent Egyptians – such as the two Medjay servants, Fedeteyet and Mekhenet, shown on a sarcophagus from the mortuary temple of King Montuhotep II – some commissioned monuments of their own, such as 'the Nubian Ankhetneni,' a wealthy noblewoman, who erected her stele at Dahshur.

Nubians are also attested archaeologically in Middle Kingdom Egypt. From the 11th Dynasty through to the early Second Intermediate Period, the C-Group population of Hierakonpolis was buried in the city's local cemetery. There, archaeologists found sixty graves, the vast majority built according to C-Group custom and containing distinctive Nubian pottery, leather skirts, sashes, and jewellery, including rings. One necklace, left as an offering, was composed of around 1,600 tiny faience beads. Living as members of the local community, rather than as foreign slaves, these individuals may have initially entered Egypt to fight for Egyptian nomarchs during the First Intermediate Period.

The Pan-Grave Culture of the Medjay

Among the various Nubian cultures living in Egypt during the Middle Kingdom were the Pan-Grave people. This nomadic (or semi-nomadic)

group, known from the Middle Kingdom to the end of the Second
Intermediate Period, were buried in distinctive shallow, oval graves (hence
'Pan-Grave'), normally marked by an oval tumulus. Within, the dead were
placed on mats, lying on their right side in a contracted position, accompanied by pottery vessels and sometimes Egyptian weapons. Cow skulls,
painted red and black, are typically found in the graves too – one cow
skull, found at Mostagedda, bore an image of a man holding an axe and
throw-stick. Pan-Grave burials are most often unearthed in Lower Nubia
and Upper Egypt, but their pottery is attested as far north as Memphis.
Excavations at Hierakonpolis revealed Pan-Grave burials at two different
sectors of the site; these contained red-dyed leather garments, some with
tassels, and armlets formed of shell plaque beads. Textiles with raised knot
patterns were also found, as were beads, most often of ostrich eggshell or
blue faience.

The owners of these graves were probably the Medjay mentioned in
Egyptian texts – a people who had their origins in the Eastern Desert,
beside the Red Sea. They enjoyed good relations with the Egyptians, acting as temple security at Lahun and often serving as mercenaries in the
army. According to Papyrus Boulaq 18, an administrative text from the 13th
Dynasty, one group of Medjay visited the Egyptian court and were given
food. Over the course of the Second Intermediate Period, Pan-Grave burials became increasingly Egyptianized, and they disappear entirely from the
archaeological record in the New Kingdom. The word Medjay, however,
continued to be used, often in reference to people acting in police roles,
such as the guards of the Valley of the Kings.

The Nubian Forts

The Egyptians' greatest intervention in Nubia during the Middle Kingdom
was a series of mud-brick fortresses constructed between Aswan and the
southern edge of the Nile's Second Cataract zone, primarily under Kings
Senwosret I and III. Each fortress was unique in design, but had similar features, such as massive enclosure walls, fortified gates, ditches, and ramparts.
Between fifty and 300 soldiers lived at any one time in a single fortress, and
all were fed by the State. To keep track of who received what, the authorities
handed out tokens, their shapes representing different types of bread and
inscribed with quantities, which the soldiers swapped for the real thing. So
that the tokens couldn't be lost, they were pierced with holes, allowing them
to be worn.

Senwosret I constructed five fortresses between the First and Second Cataracts to protect Egypt's interests in the region: namely its access to natural resources. The furthest north were Ikkur and Kubban, flanking the Nile at the end of the road leading to the Wadi Allaqi gold mining region; these were most probably built to protect Egypt's gold and copper mining expeditions. The fortress at Aniba, further south, may have been connected with the diorite quarries to its south-west, or was perhaps constructed to keep an eye on C-Group settlements in the surrounding area. At the southernmost extent, close to the Second Cataract, were Buhen and Kor, where trade goods were stored. Buhen was the most elaborate of these fortresses, its enclosure wall protecting administrative, economic, and residential buildings.

Under Senwosret III, some of these earlier fortresses were altered – Buhen in particular received a new outer enclosure wall, 4 m thick – and new fortresses were constructed in the Second Cataract zone down to Semna, where the king established Egypt's new southern border. Of these, the Egyptians used the fortress at Mirgissa as a storage centre for campaigns, and Askut a little further south as a grain reserve. Uronarti was the campaign headquarters, and the fortresses of Semna and Kumma, flanking the Nile, guarded the entrance to Egyptian territory. The Egyptians didn't build these extra fortresses to protect themselves from the Lower Nubians; for one, it would have been easy for the Nubians to simply avoid them, and two, the Egyptians don't seem to have regarded the Nubians as a major threat anyway. (In fact, many C-Group Nubians lived in the vicinity of the forts, and the C-Group as a whole prospered during this time, even founding new settlements.) No, these southernmost fortresses were launching pads for campaigns beyond the Second Cataract zone, into territory controlled by the Kerma Civilization (discussed in greater detail in the following chapter). The Egyptians probably perceived this prosperous and expanding civilization, based at Kerma, just south of the Third Cataract, as a threat, both to Egypt's control of Nubian trade and its security, and sought to prove their domination of the region.

We can gain an insight into the work of the soldiers at the Nubian forts thanks to the survival of the 'Semna Dispatches,' a collection of papyri, found in a Middle Kingdom tomb at Thebes. These show that the Egyptians not only monitored the movement of Nubians and Medjay near the forts – sometimes tracking them for days – but that they captured and interrogated people too. Other dispatches talk of five Medjay travelling to Elephantine to ask for jobs as mercenaries, because 'the desert is dying of hunger,' and of

Nubian merchants arriving by boat and donkey to trade at one of the forts. In fact, Nubians (presumably not including C-Group Nubians living north of the Second Cataract) were not allowed to pass the fortress of Semna, either by water or land, unless they were traders, in which case they received permission to exchange their goods at Mirgissa. Only in special circumstances could this rule be broken.

The soldiers stationed at the forts didn't just rely on weapons and defensive architecture to achieve and sustain their domination of Lower Nubia. Magic – *heka* to the Egyptians – was just as powerful in their worldview. They were particularly fond of execration rituals – known in Egypt from the Old Kingdom through to the Roman Period – in which a person destroys a symbol representing his enemies in order to harm or neutralize them. Sometimes red pots were smashed, the colour red being associated with evil, or clay figurines of bound enemies were broken or burnt. The names of foreign princes and civilizations, and lists of locations in Nubia and the Levant could also be written on the objects destroyed. The most extreme example of execration so far known in Egypt was discovered by archaeologists in pits close to the fortress at Mirgissa. These contained nearly 200 broken inscribed red vessels and ostraca, 437 uninscribed broken red pots, 346 mud figurines (including severed feet, heads, torsos, and animals), three limestone prisoner figurines and the head of a fourth. Other objects appear to have been burnt. But, most grisly of all, there was also the decapitated body of a Nubian. The skull, placed upside down on a cup, was found nearby, melted red wax beside it, and a flint sacrificial knife.

Punt and Mersa Gawasis

If visiting Mersa Gawasis, a port with a shallow bay on the Red Sea coastline, in around 2000 BCE, you'd have been met with the sight of twenty-four small huts erected on a coral terrace, providing space for around forty to fifty soldiers as temporary accommodation. Although the site lacked permanent structures, rock cut galleries penetrated the mountain side, where the Egyptians stored disassembled boats, as well as ropes and other equipment. One gallery might have served as a workshop. All around, men would have been grinding emmer and barley, baking bread, and making beer. Others would have been eating seafood – fish and crabs – as well as domesticated and desert animals. The men made fires from whatever wood was at hand – even fragments of valuable foreign imported woods, such as ebony and cedar, too small to be used for other purposes – and found fresh water at nearby Bir Umm Al-Huwaytat. Small shrines and ritual platforms served the soldiers' religious needs. One stele was dedicated to Osiris of the Sea, a local maritime version of the god, and there was probably a shrine to Hathor. An open air altar bore 650 conch shells, seemingly dedicated to the god Min.

In ancient times, this port was known as Saww. It was from here that the Egyptians launched missions to Punt in the late Old Kingdom and First Intermediate Period, and then again in the 12th and early 13th Dynasties, as well as in the early New Kingdom. Every item used by the sailors, soldiers, and workmen had to be dragged across the Eastern Desert from the Nile Valley; even the boats were designed to be disassembled and reassembled, making it easier for the Egyptians to store them when not in use, or to move them across the desert. Boxes used for transporting goods – a useful resource – were re-used: these were sent to their destination, filled with items, sealed by an administrator, and only opened again after arrival at Mersa Gawasis. From there, the goods were transferred across the desert to the Nile Valley.

The Egyptians launched many missions to Punt during the Middle Kingdom. In the eighth year of Montuhotep III, a man named Henenu led one such mission, reinitiating contact with Punt after a hiatus during the First Intermediate Period. He travelled from Coptos to Mersa Gawasis via the Wadi Hammamat, supported by 3,000 men. Each man received twenty loaves a day and two jars of water, as well as a carrying pole and an animal skin – perhaps combined for carrying items – and sandals when needed. It's unclear whether soldiers normally received sandals when on the march, because those trudging through the rocky Eastern Desert plateau may have needed extra foot protection. Similarly, at the start of the 12th Dynasty, Antefiker, vizier under Senwosret I, led an expedition of 3,200 soldiers, 500 sailors, fifty escorts, five scribes, and one steward to Punt. If these numbers are to be believed, it was a large scale operation. Missions to Punt are also attested under Amenemhat II, Senwosret II, Senwosret III, Amenemhat III, and Amenemhat IV. Another location that the Egyptians sailed to during the Middle Kingdom was Bia-Punt, which may have been a gold mining region south-east of Kerma.

And it wasn't only goods that travelled from Punt in the Middle Kingdom. On the stele of Ded-Sobek, dated to the end of the 12th Dynasty, one woman, only partly preserved due to a break in the stele, is referred to as 'the female servant of Punt, Sat-Mesuty(?).' This is the only reference to a servant from Punt known on an Egyptian stele.

The End of the Middle Kingdom

By the end of the 12th Dynasty, the Egyptians had reasserted themselves on the world stage, putting the turmoil of the First Intermediate Period behind them: Nubia, down to the Second Cataract, had been pummelled and placed under Egyptian rule; and routes into Egypt from the west and east were closely monitored. Whether in the south, east or west, fortresses built in the borderlands physically represented the edge of Egyptian control, providing secure bases from which the Egyptians could track the movements of people and goods coming and going from their territory. Meanwhile, maritime trade missions brought prestige goods to the Egyptian court from across the known world; and any threats to their access to these luxuries met with swift action: violent raids, which not only brought war plunder to Egypt, but thousands of prisoners too – people that were forcibly settled across the country, and particularly in the eastern Delta. But Egypt's renewed phase of unity and dominance would not last: like each stable phase in the country's history, the Middle Kingdom came to an end, bringing about a time of foreign domination: the Second Intermediate Period.

Chapter 5

The Hyksos and the Kermans: Their Rise and Fall (1781–1549 BCE)

The events surrounding the demise of the Middle Kingdom are rather shadowy. When King Amenemhat IV died towards the end of the 12th Dynasty, a female pharaoh came to power, named Queen Sobekneferu. She reigned for four years, after which a new line of kings took the throne: the 13th Dynasty. Their appearance marks the start of the Second Intermediate Period, a 200 year phase of renewed disunity and warfare. Many of the 13th Dynasty kings ruled briefly and only a few monuments attributed to them are known; indeed, because their reigns were so rapid, some scholars have argued that power cycled between important families (and some kings even appear to have been of foreign origin, adding to the confusion). The 13th Dynasty, however, was not immediately a time of collapse – some Egyptologists even prefer to include it in the Middle Kingdom. The government remained strong, at least initially, and the people of Lower Nubia continued to live under Egyptian control. Scribes of the vizier even escorted Nubian rulers to the 13th Dynasty court.

Foreign trade continued in the Levant under the 13th Dynasty. Archaeologists have found seals, many dating to the reigns of King Neferhotep I and King Sobekhotep IV, at Tell el-Ajjul, Lachish, Jericho, Megiddo, and Byblos, indicating a renewed escalation in foreign relations during their reigns. Egyptian treasurers, stewards, soldiers, and priests were all active in the Levant, and ties with Byblos remained strong. Items buried with the rulers of Byblos even mention the names of 13th Dynasty kings: a relief of the Mayor Yantinu depicts him seated on a throne in front of the name of King Neferhotep I, and a cylinder seal of Mayor Yakin-Ilu includes one of the royal names of King Sewesekhetawy and makes reference to Hathor, Lady of Byblos. The Egyptians continued to receive wood from Byblos at least until the reign of King Sobekhotep IV, who imported cedar to make two doors for the Temple of Amun at Karnak in Thebes.

Slowly, however, Egypt weakened and royal influence waned. This provided an opportunity for various regions to declare independence. Notably, an Asiatic line of rulers – though heavily Egyptianized – took control of the north-eastern Delta, becoming the 14th Dynasty. At the same time, the weakened 13th Dynasty fully withdrew from Nubia, enabling the Kerma Civilization (centred on the city of Kerma, just beyond the Third Cataract) to expand into what had previously been Egypt's Lower Nubian territory. Faced with all these troubles, the 13th Dynasty eventually abandoned the north entirely, leaving their Egyptian successors to rule a portion of Egypt stretching from Cusae in Middle Egypt to Aswan at the First Cataract, with their major royal residence at Thebes. So, for much of the Second Intermediate Period, Egypt's fortunes were influenced by three major players: the Kerma Nubians in the south; the Egyptians at Thebes; and the rulers of Levantine descent in the Delta, better known as the Hyksos.

A general breakdown of the overlapping dynasties of the Second Intermediate Period (and their major residences) can be visualized as follows:

Nubian Kings	Asiatic Kings	Egyptian Kings
Kings of Kerma		13th Dynasty (Itj-Tawy)
	14th Dynasty (Tell el-Daba)	
	15th Dynasty/Hyksos (Tell el-Daba)	16th Dynasty (Thebes)
		17th Dynasty (Thebes)

Disruptions in Lower Nubia

Lower Nubia remained under Egyptian control until the reigns of King Neferhotep I and his successor King Sobekhotep IV of the 13th Dynasty, when the unified Egyptian State began to fragment. However, the Egyptians had been closing their Nubian forts since the late 12th Dynasty: Amenemhat III abandoned Semna South, and Amenemhat IV closed Serra West. During the 13th Dynasty, the closures continued, with the most expensive forts to operate abandoned first. Askut, as one of the largest, shut its massive fortified gateway at the start of the Second Intermediate Period. The most southerly forts closed last, indicating that the Egyptians wished to monitor their Nubian territory's southern border until the last possible moment.

The soldiers stationed at the Nubian forts had by now, after generations of service, grown used to their surroundings and probably didn't want to leave, despite the volatile political situation. Indeed, around the reign of Neferhotep I, just as society began to crumble, some of Lower Nubia's Egyptian soldiers attempted to create their own mini-state. These ephemeral individuals, attested at various locations, awarded themselves royal titles and names ('why not?' they probably thought), allowing us to identify 'kings' Kakare Iny, Ii-ib-khent-Re, and Segerseni. Under the last of these, Segerseni, warfare broke out in a region called Per-senbet, a so far unknown location. If scholars are correct in regarding these individuals as wannabe kings of Lower Nubia, their reigns didn't last long. The entire period can only have lasted between twenty and thirty years, and ended with the kings of Kerma – the powerful Nubian state to the south – absorbing the soldier-kings' territory into their own expanding kingdom, which now stretched from Kurgus in the south to Elephantine in the north – a distance of about 1,200 km along the Nile.

The Egyptian soldiers garrisoned in the Nubian forts now served Kerma, alongside newly arrived Nubian soldiers – cemeteries at Buhen and Mirgissa attest to the presence of these newly installed Kerma garrisons. Among the remaining Egyptians at Buhen were the descendants of an administrator named Sobekemhab I, who had served there under the 13th Dynasty. One member of this family, Sopedhor, 'built' (more like renovated) the Temple of Horus 'to the satisfaction of the ruler of Kush.'[1] Another family member, called Ka, says on a stele, 'I was a brave servant of the ruler of Kush. I washed my feet in the waters of Kush in the following of the ruler of Nedjeh. I returned safe and sound with my relatives.'[2] Such individuals were not only invaluable for the continued running of the fortresses under their new management, but were useful as traders and intermediaries between the Kermans to the south and the Egyptians to the north. That trade continued between the Kermans and the Egyptians – now confined to Upper Egypt – after the collapse of the unified state is attested by archaeological findings, including seals at Kerma, which identified trade goods. But the Kermans also traded with the Hyksos in the north – the Asiatic dynasty that took advantage of Egypt's political fragmentation to set up their own state in the north-east Delta (more about them soon). The Kermans transported these goods along desert routes via the oases, bypassing the Egyptians in the south.

The Kingdom of Kush at Kerma

The centre of this expanding Nubian empire was the city of Kerma, just south of the Third Cataract. It had existed since around 2100 BCE, and had become powerful due to its fertile fields and its domination of trade routes. Although the origins of the Kerma Culture are unknown, it may originally have been the Yam known from Old Kingdom and early Middle Kingdom sources. During the Middle Kingdom, the Egyptians began to refer to Upper Nubia as 'Kush.' This word is first found under King Senwosret I, on a stele set up to commemorate his wars in the region; here, Kush is one of nine places represented by bound prisoners. After also being mentioned by a couple of Senwosret I's courtiers, 'Kush' isn't found again until the reign of Senwosret III, when it is repeatedly cited as a place to be overthrown. Egypt's construction of the Second Cataract forts under Senwosret III was probably a reaction to the growing importance and power of this expanding 'Kingdom of Kush,' controlled by its rulers from the city of Kerma.

As a prosperous city, Kerma boasted a harbour, religious structures, palaces, storehouses, kilns, bakeries, and domestic and administrative buildings. Workshops produced high quality bronze items, such as daggers and razors, others made faience figurines, vessels, and tiles to decorate funerary chapels. The ceramics produced by the Kermans were of the highest quality. Dry ditches and a mud-brick wall surrounded Kerma as protection from danger; nonetheless, the city was burned down multiple times and rebuilt. A large circular building, surrounded by smaller huts, was probably a royal audience hall, and the city's most prominent buildings were the two *deffufa*, massive mud-brick constructions that dominated the skyline. The Western Deffufa was the city's main temple, around which the early city seems to have expanded during the Middle Kingdom. The Eastern Deffufa was a funerary chapel in the eastern necropolis; this was surrounded by the tombs of Kerma's kings, who were buried beneath enormous tumuli – the largest burial structures in Nubia. Within these mounds, the Kermans laid their kings to rest on wooden beds, surrounded by grave goods. They sacrificed human retainers – men, women, and children – at the time of the king's death too, burying them alive during the tumulus' construction. Tumulus KX, for example, contained over 400 sacrificed individuals.

From clothing remains found during excavations in Kerma's necropolis – which contained over 20,000 graves, as well as large funerary monuments – it's possible to reconstruct how the city's population dressed in life. Leather was the most popular material: people wore leather sandals and loin-cloths, and even wrapped themselves in either linen or leather. Women sometimes wore leather hairnets. In Kerma's graves, archaeologists also found bronze mirrors, distinctive pottery, and jewellery with semiprecious stones. Men in particular were sometimes buried with weapons, including bows; some bodies bore injuries inflicted during life, perhaps during combat. The graves of certain members of the elite featured a crescent of cow skulls to one side – one had around 4,000 skulls. The Kermans buried sheep and dogs within their tombs too.

Within Tumulus KIII – a massive construction, 90 m in diameter – excavators found Egyptian statuary, including a statue of a woman named Sennuwy and fragments of a statue of her husband, Hepdjefa, who was active in Asyut under Senwosret I. The Kermans probably brought these, and other Egyptian statues, to Kerma as plunder from raids in Egyptian territory during the Second Intermediate Period. This interpretation is backed up by the inscription of Sobeknakht of el-Kab, an Egyptian who describes an attack by a king of Kerma on Upper Egypt, aided by allies from Wawat, Punt, an oasis, and the Medjay. This inscription shows that the kings of Kerma ruled over their neighbouring Nubian territories too. Many campaigns into Egypt must have occurred, for archaeologists at Kerma discovered items taken from temples and tombs from as far afield as Asyut, Thebes, Hierakonpolis, and Elephantine. Still, although the Kermans clearly launched military campaigns into Egyptian territory, at other times, the two civilizations enjoyed more peaceful relations, reflected by the ongoing trade mentioned above. It's even possible that some Egyptian artisans lived at the city, for flourishes of Egyptian art – such as a winged sun-disc in royal Tumulus KIII – can be found. Such art, however, may simply have been inspired by Egyptian motifs, rather than created by Egyptian artisans.

Unfortunately, little is known about the kings of Kerma themselves. An Egyptian execration text mentions a Nubian ruler called Awawa, born of his mother Kouna, but his father's name is lost; and an Egyptian figurine refers to a king of Kerma named Utatrerses, born of his mother Teti and his father Awa'a – seemingly the Awawa of the other text. Both sources mention further Nubian districts and rulers, perhaps controlled by the Kerman kings. Other kings attested include Kaa and Teriahi, who seem to have ruled before Awawa and Utatrerses.

Lower Nubia Under Kerman Rule

As the city of Kerma prospered further south, Lower Nubia, now under Kerman control, became a place where Egyptians, C-group Nubians, Pan-Grave people, and Kerma Nubians all lived and mingled in the same space, many involved in the lucrative business of long distance trade. The C-Group built more houses and tombs than in previous times, and more

Egyptian imports arrived than before, but the threat of violence remained, as shown by the fortification of the C-Group settlements at Wadi es-Sebua and Areika.

In this cultural melting pot, traditions began to fuse. This can be seen quite clearly in a settlement just outside the walls of the fortress of Askut, where a household ancestor shrine was maintained throughout the Second Intermediate Period. Placed on a bench in a reception room, with an altar for libations, the focal point of this cult was a stele dedicated to a man named Merikare. Although people placed Egyptian votive figurines and food offerings in Egyptian pots before this shrine, they also left offerings in Nubian pots, and a Nubian fertility figure of either Kerman or C-Group origin. Egyptian and Nubian figurines are found across the settlement at Askut, and intriguingly, many of the other Nubian objects discovered were associated with women; this has led some scholars to argue that Egyptian men married C-Group women at Askut.

The Rulers of Foreign Lands

Returning to the Egyptian Delta now: when the 13th Dynasty weakened, a north-eastern province centred on the city of Tell el-Daba (also known as Avaris) broke free of Egypt's centralized State. The kings of this territory are today known as the 14th Dynasty, with many of Asiatic ancestry. These were the descendants of immigrants from the Syrian region, who had settled in Egypt during the late 12th Dynasty – soldiers, administrators, and servants; increasing their wealth and status over generations, they became a powerful local elite with high-level roles in the administration. One burial at Tell el-Daba, dated to the late 12th Dynasty, contained the broken statue of an Asiatic man, twice life-size with a mushroom-shaped hairstyle, painted red, and wearing a long multicoloured robe. He was an important individual, who might even have been an Asiatic prince. Also of late 12th Dynasty date, a seal, mounted on a gold ring and found in a tomb at Tell el-Daba, bears an inscription for the ruler of Retenu – roughly Syria-Palestine. These immigrants built their houses at Tell el-Daba in the style of contemporary homes in north-east Syria, and buried many of their men as warriors. They also constructed Asiatic temples during the 13th Dynasty, close to buildings of purely Egyptian type. Hybrid Egyptian-Asiatic temples were also built. So, by the time that the 13th Dynasty weakened, the 14th Dynasty kings were in a position to transform Tell el-Daba into the north-east Delta's major hub for Asiatics in Egypt.

After declaring independence, the 14th Dynasty kings continued to rule their province according to typical Egyptian administrative practices, with only some adaptations influenced by their original homeland. Although few monuments are associated with these rulers, archaeologists have found seals and scarabs bearing their names as far afield as the Levant, the 13th Dynasty's remaining Egyptian territory, and Nubia. This shows that trade continued in all directions and that they enjoyed good relations with the Egyptian royals (despite taking a chunk of their country). Unfortunately, little else is known about the 14th Dynasty rulers other than their names. Better attested than most, however, is King Sheshi, who appears to have married a Kerman queen called Tati. It was perhaps under their son, King Nehesy – meaning 'the Nubian' – that the 14th Dynasty state formally separated from 13th Dynasty Egypt.

Under the 14th Dynasty, a large residence was constructed at Tell el-Daba, and wealthy individuals were buried in its courtyard – a very un-Egyptian practice, given that the Egyptians preferred to be buried out in the desert, away from settlements. The Deputy Treasurer Aamu (meaning 'the Asiatic') was among those buried in its grounds. This man lived during the mid- to late 14th Dynasty and was interred alongside five sacrificed donkeys, a bronze dagger, and a battleaxe, among other items. Burials from other locations in Tell el-Daba also belonged to warriors, who entered the afterlife with non-Egyptian weapons. Donkey burials are also known in the Levant, for example at Tell el-Ajjul.

Despite their success, and having expanded their influence to encompass most of the Delta, making vassals of the Egyptians along the way, the 14th Dynasty appear to have met an unfortunate end: large communal graves at Tell el-Daba suggest that a plague rampaged through the city, killing off much of the population. This then gave rise to a new ruling elite, known to us as the 15th Dynasty. Like the 14th Dynasty before them, these were probably the descendants of Asiatics already living in Egypt, who now moved to Tell el-Daba to fill the power vacuum. Nonetheless, they still referred to themselves as *heka khasut*, 'the rulers of foreign lands' – a title found on 15th Dynasty scarabs, but also on the lintel of King Sikri-haddu, where it is used like a royal epithet; it is from this phrase – *heka khasut* – that later Greek writers derived the word 'Hyksos.' These 15th Dynasty Hyksos kings ruled the north roughly concurrently with the successive Egyptian 16th and 17th Dynasties, who by this time, from their residence at Thebes, controlled territory from the region of Cusae in the Nile Valley down to Aswan.

Like that of their predecessors in the 14th Dynasty, Hyksos culture continued to display a mixture of Levantine and Egyptian traditions. A palatial compound, built at Tell el-Daba, reflects the influence of both cultures, and two scarabs, each depicting a Hyksos ruler in the manner of an Egyptian king, show the figure holding a twig in one hand and a raised club in the other – motifs associated with the Levantine weather god. Hyksos kings also used Egyptian royal titles, such as 'Son of Re' and 'Good God,' while retaining their foreign names (e.g. Khayan), written in hieroglyphs. An inscription on the scribal palette of Atu describes King Apepi – sometimes called Apophis – as being able to read hieroglyphs. This king ruled at the zenith of Hyksos power, and seems to have had a particular interest in Egyptian traditions: it was under Apepi, for example, that scribes copied the Rhind Mathematical Papyrus, a work that required a great deal of skill.

One advantage that the Delta's Asiatic kings had over the Egyptians was access to higher quality weaponry. Egypt had long lagged behind the rest of the world in military technology, and even by the Second Intermediate Period, bronze weapons were rare in Egypt. In contrast, archaeologists have excavated bronze scimitars (called *khepesh* by the Egyptians), axe heads, spearheads, and daggers, all of Levantine type, at Tell el-Daba. The people of the city also used moulds to produce both Egyptian and foreign style axes. Still, although the Hyksos are often said to have brought such advanced military technology as the composite bow and the chariot to Egypt, there's little evidence to back up these claims. Both composite bows and chariots appear to have been adopted from the Near East by the Egyptians and Hyksos at roughly the same time. And the Hyksos no doubt had them first: the earliest horse bones found in Egypt were excavated at Tell el-Daba, and the first textual reference to horses comes from an inscription of the Theban King Kamose, which describes them being used by the Hyksos. Whatever the case may be, Egypt's terrain does not lend itself well to large-scale chariot warfare, and so for the most part, chariots would have been ineffective in the battles of this period. This isn't to say that the Hyksos weren't great warriors, however: four pits, excavated in a Hyksos palace, contained severed hands. These were probably cut from fallen enemies, for in the New Kingdom, the Egyptians took hands to keep track of the number of enemies killed.

Whilst ruling northern Egypt, the Hyksos maintained their relations with the Levant, engaging in trade and sending diplomatic gifts. Archaeologists have discovered Levantine pottery in Hyksos graves, and trade further afield is shown through the presence of Cypriot pottery at Tell el-Daba, dated to the 15th Dynasty. A fragment of a cuneiform tablet, also found at Tell el-Daba, might show connections with southern Mesopotamia.

The Abydos Dynasty

Recent excavations at Abydos have proven the existence of an additional ruling family, active in the Abydos region during the Second Intermediate Period, roughly contemporary with the 15th and 16th Dynasties. The burials of eight kings from this mysterious line have so far been uncovered, and are currently being studied. Senebkay, one of these kings, came to a violent end. Eighteen wounds are spread across his body, each penetrating to the bone, including in his feet, ankles, knees, hands, and lower back. Senebkay also received three major blows to his head, leaving an imprint of the battleaxes used. It's thought that he was attacked by multiple enemies, but the identity of his killers is unknown: the most probable perpetrators are the Hyksos, others Egyptians or Nubians. What is clear is that quite a long time passed between his death and the preparation of his body for burial, suggesting that he was far from home. Based on an analysis of his muscle attachments, Senebkay spent a great deal of time riding horses. Another body, found nearby, showed similar evidence. This is curious, for in art, Egyptians are not typically shown riding donkeys or horses, and horses are not thought to have been common in Egypt until the New Kingdom.

The Theban 16th and 17th Dynasties

At the end of the 13th Dynasty, the Egyptian royals either fled south to Thebes to continue their rule, or vanished from history, leaving space for a new Egyptian dynasty to emerge. Either way, the Theban 16th Dynasty was roughly contemporary with the early Hyksos/15th Dynasty phase. During this turbulent time, the Egyptians lived under constant threat of attack. At Gebelein, King Dedumose II of the 16th Dynasty erected a stele with an inscription proclaiming that he'd been chosen by the god Horus, and had increased the size of his army. King Montuhotepi commemorated his defence of Thebes on a stele at Karnak Temple, saying that he was beloved of his army, drove back 'all foreign lands,' and rescued Thebes. King Ikhernofret, an ephemeral ruler, was 'a strong king beloved of his army,' and one 'who caused his city to be protected when it was immersed, and cared for it with the foreigners; who pacified the rebellious lands for her through the manifest power of his father Amun; who overthrew the guilty ones for her who had rebelled against him; and dealt terror to those that attacked him.'³ Nowhere does Ikhernofret say who his enemies were – they may have been the Hyksos, but, as we've already seen in the above mentioned text of Sobeknakht, the Kerman kings also launched frequent campaigns into Egyptian territory. In his account of this Kerman campaign, Sobeknakht says that he prepared the town of el-Qab by repairing its ramparts. He also mustered his troops and travelled south to meet the Kerman army. In the ensuing battle, Sobeknakht says, the goddess Nekhbet burned all her enemies, leaving the Egyptians victorious.

Re-conquering Egypt, or at the very least, making themselves more able to defend their territory, was a major concern of the 16th Dynasty's successors: the 17th Dynasty Theban kings. To solidify the allegiance of important provincial families, they awarded some nobles the title king's son, enabling them to feel part of the royal family. The governors of major towns, such as Abydos, Thebes, and Tod, also acted as garrison commanders, and were similarly awarded the title of king's son – some even married Theban princesses. Meanwhile, the Thebans took the first steps towards creating a professional army, with a fully fledged military hierarchy. For the Egyptians, enough was enough. The scene was set for war.

The Egyptians Strike Back

The Theban King Seqenenre Tao II of the 17th Dynasty probably launched the first campaign against the Hyksos. The Soldier Ahmose Son of Ibana (buried during the 18th Dynasty at el-Qab) says that his father served in Seqenenre's naval fleet, and this king also constructed a new settlement at Deir el-Ballas, 40 km north of Thebes, which boasted huge defensive walls and a military observation post. It was manned in part by Kerman mercenaries, raising the possibility that Seqenenre first launched a campaign south, securing a portion of Lower Nubia and enlisting the prisoners into his army. More unusually, a literary tale, known today as 'The Quarrel of Apophis and Seqenenre,' describes the king as getting into an argument with his Hyksos counterpart: Apepi/Apophis complains that the noise of the Theban hippos is keeping him awake at night, so Seqenenre assembles his courtiers to discuss the matter. Sadly, the text breaks off at this point, but it probably went on to describe the outbreak of war.

The mummy of Seqenenre Tao II provides the most significant evidence for warfare during his reign. When unwrapped, the body displayed multiple fractures in the king's skull, caused by a series of violent blows. Experts then matched the shape of these wounds to the types of weapons that inflicted them: two match the shape of a Hyksos-style axe; one was caused by an

Egyptian axe; the handle of an axe or a mace caused a blunt blow to the nose; and the final injury, perhaps caused by a spear, was below the left ear at the base of the skull. Significantly, Seqenenre's body displays no other signs of wounds or bone breakage. The only blows were to his head.

It is commonly argued that Seqenenre was either killed fighting on the battlefield against multiple assailants, or that he was assassinated while sleeping in his palace. Elsewhere, however, I've argued that Seqenenre was ceremonially executed following the loss of a battle against the Hyksos. His body was then left where it fell, only to be recovered later by the Thebans. The remains of King Senebkay, recently discovered at Abydos (see box text) re-enforce this new theory: the extent and spread of the wounds across his body reflect the frantic chaos of fighting multiple assailants on the battle-field. Seqenenre's wounds, however, are the product of targeted precision, ending with a coup de grâce: the blows were entirely against his head, sug-gesting that he was not actively fighting at the time of his death, and that he was probably bound and unable to defend himself.

With Seqenenre dead, it now fell to Kamose, probably Seqenenre's brother, to deal with the Hyksos and Kerman threat. A letter, sent from Apepi to a newly crowned Kerman king, mentions that Kamose had attacked Nubia, suggesting that the king first sought to weaken his Nubian counter-part and gain access to the region's gold supplies and mercenaries before tackling his northern enemy. (Apepi also complains that the Kerman king had failed to inform him about his recent coronation – the meanie!) Kamose's mission seems to have been successful, for by his third year on the throne, a soldier had been assigned to rebuild Buhen fortress' walls (and archaeo-logical investigations have shown that work was indeed undertaken there at this time). A soldier named Ahmose also mentions a campaign in Nubia, perhaps under Kamose, and two rock inscriptions in Lower Nubia indicate that Egyptians loyal to Kamose were active in the region.

Lower Nubia secure, at least for the time being, it was time to turn north. King Kamose, unhappy with Egypt's political situation, called a meeting with his courtiers, and, like the hero in a sword-and-sandals epic, tried to inspire his followers with a powerful speech: 'To what effect do I perceive it, my might, while a ruler is in Avaris and another in Kush, I sitting joined with an Asiatic and a Nubian, each man having his (own) portion of this Egypt, sharing the land with me. ... I shall engage in battle with him and I shall slit his body, for my intention is to save Egypt, striking the Asiatics.'[4] But rather than feeling inspired by their king's rousing words, the court-iers were far from enthusiastic about his plan. Speaking as one – there's safety in numbers after all – they explained that Kamose already ruled as far as Elephantine in the south, and as far north as Cusae in Middle Egypt. Not only that, but the finest fields were already being ploughed for them, and their cattle were allowed to graze in the Delta (and weren't being taken away). If the Hyksos attack us, they shrugged, then we'll attack them.

Kamose, unimpressed by his courtiers' lacklustre response, decided to royally ignore them. Perhaps after securing the approval of the oracle of Amun, he sailed north with his troops and sent his Medjay mercenaries ahead to burn enemy villages. Another Medjay patrol was sent to confront an Egyptian ally of the Hyksos, named Teti son of Pepi, at the town of Neferusy (80 km north of the Hyksos border at Cusae). The Medjay ensured that Teti couldn't escape Neferusy, and the next morning, once Kamose had arrived, the Egyptians attacked the town. By midday, they had destroyed its walls and slaughtered its population. The army divided up the spoils, and then left to attack other hostile towns nearby.

Continuing north, Kamose's army stopped at Sako – perhaps el-Qes – where he heard that a Hyksos messenger was travelling along the oasis route, bypassing the Nile Valley, to deliver a message to Kerma. Reacting fast, Kamose sent an army west to Bahariya Oasis to intercept the messenger. Their mission was successful, and the message – a request for assistance – fell into Egyptian hands. To provoke the Hyksos, Kamose returned the message to Apepi with an extra note explaining what his troops had done to the district of Cynopolis – a location under Hyksos control.

When the Egyptians finally marched on Tell el-Daba, the Hyksos smartly hid behind their city walls, leaving Kamose with no battle to fight. Perhaps not wanting to feel like he'd wasted his journey, the king resorted to taunting the Hyksos from outside, yelling that he was drinking wine from Apepi's own vineyards, pressed by Asiatics that he'd captured. The Hyksos still refused to fight. So, rather than taunt his enemies a second time, Kamose sent his army to cut down the Hyksos' orchards, capture women, and seize their goods, including gold, lapis lazuli, silver, turquoise, copper axes, oils, incense, honey, and different types of wood. He may have burned or taken everything that wasn't nailed down, but Kamose still didn't manage to take Tell el-Daba. Nevertheless, his army returned home in triumph to find Thebes in celebration.

Egyptian Statues in the Levant: Diplomatic Gifts?

Many Egyptian items dating to the Middle Kingdom have been found during excavations in the Levant, although it isn't always clear at which point in history they left their home country. Previously, scholars thought that such items represented Egyptian diplomats operating abroad, but it now seems clear that most were moved during the Hyksos Period. Statues of Queen Sobekneferu of the late 12th Dynasty were found at Tell el-Daba, for example, as was a statue of King Hetepibre of the 13th Dynasty and a statue of the king's mother Senet of 12th Dynasty date. Based on their inscriptions, these monuments originally stood in the regions of Memphis and the Faiyum Oasis and were moved north to Tell el-Daba for some unexplained reason. The Hyksos also carved them with new inscriptions: among the 'antiques' re-inscribed with the name of Apepi were four sphinxes of Amenemhat III and a sphinx of Senwosret II. Consequently, scholars argue that many of the Middle Kingdom statues found in the Levant were sent there by the Hyksos, perhaps as diplomatic gifts.

Made during the reign of King Amenemhat II, a fragmentary statue group of the Vizier Senwosretankh and his family, and a statue of a daughter of Amenemhat II were excavated at Ugarit. Sphinxes of Amenemhat III were found there too, as well as at Aleppo and Hazor. Numerous Middle Kingdom objects have also been excavated at Qatna, many in the city's palace area; here, a sphinx of 12th Dynasty Princess Ita was discovered broken into 400 pieces. Other Egyptian items were interred with Qatna's kings: one royal tomb, discovered in 2009, contained hundreds of Egyptian and Egyptian-imitating stone vessels, including one bearing the name of a Middle Kingdom Egyptian princess called Itakayet. Such items were probably regarded as exotic goods, carved from rare materials. Finally, four broken statues of the Nomarch Djehutyhotep, who held the title 'the door of every foreign country,' were discovered at Megiddo. As Djehutyhotep is depicted bringing cattle from the Levant in his tomb, he may be a rare example of a courtier who actually did travel to Megiddo in life and left his monuments there, rather than being just another post-mortem victim of Hyksos pilfering.

The Expulsion of the Hyksos and the Occupation of Nubia

Dying in his fourth year as king, Kamose didn't have the opportunity to continue his war against the Hyksos. Instead, that duty passed to Ahmose – son of King Seqenenre Tao II and Queen Ahhotep I – who ascended the Theban throne as a child. A few years later, Apepi, Kamose's nemesis, also died, passing the Hyksos crown to Khamudi. Liberating Egypt would have to wait until the young Ahmose reached adulthood. In the meantime, Queen Ahhotep I managed Egypt's matter's of state as queen regent. An inscription at the Temple of Amun at Karnak describes her as the mistress of the Two Lands, caring for Egypt, and looking after the country's soldiers and guarding them. But goes on to say that she also had to gather up deserters and fugitives, pacify Upper Egypt, and expel rebels. Clearly, not all was well at Thebes – much still needed to be done to strengthen control of Upper Egypt, let alone the north. To add to her military credentials, Ahhotep was buried with a ceremonial dagger and a lapis lazuli axe.

The sources for Ahmose's final campaign against the Hyksos are unfortunately scarce and uniformly lacking in detail. From what we can reconstruct, Ahmose first took Heliopolis before bypassing Tell el-Daba and seizing Tell el-Habua (Tjaru) to its east, probably to cut off the Hyksos' escape route or to block any support from arriving from the Levant. Only then did he attempt to take the Hyksos capital. Describing this campaign, the Soldier Ahmose Son of Ibana says that he and the Egyptian troops besieged Tell el-Daba and fought multiple battles. Fragments from King Ahmose's mortuary temple at Abydos also show archers and chariots at war, perhaps at Tell el-Daba. Eventually, the city fell, and the Hyksos survivors fled to Sharuhen in the southern Levant. The Egyptians pursued, and besieged the town for three years. Afterwards, Ahmose may have campaigned even further north, asserting his presence throughout the Levant.

Ahmose had removed the Hyksos from Egypt, simultaneously reuniting the Two Lands, ending the Second Intermediate Period, and starting the New Kingdom, a 500-year period of prosperity. And, though he was related to the 17th Dynasty bloodline, these major achievements led Ahmose to be regarded as the founder of a new royal line: the 18th Dynasty. The king now turned his attention south to Nubia. According to Ahmose Son of Ibana (who'll pop up a lot from now on), the Egyptians travelled to an area called Khenthennefer, south of the Second Cataract, where they killed 'a Nubian bowman' – perhaps a Kerman leader. The king then faced two rebellions: a Nubian named Aata led the first in an otherwise unknown location called Tent-taa, and an Egyptian called Tetian led the second; this man had raised an army, perhaps hoping to take advantage of the turmoil in Egypt while King Ahmose was restoring order. Both rebellions were swiftly quashed.

Ahmose now established Buhen as his administrative centre in Nubia, reclaiming control of the region, and placed the fort under the command of a man named Turi, who would go on to become the first king's son of Kush – the overseer of Egypt's Nubian territory (effectively the vizier of

Nubia). Ahmose also built a temple to Amun on the island of Sai, between the Second and Third Cataracts, where a Kerman population lived. This initiated a new phase of Egyptian temple construction in Nubia. Over the course of the New Kingdom, these new temples would assert Egypt's rule over Nubia, encourage Egyptianization, and manage the region's valuable resources, acting as hubs for redistribution in line with Egypt's own administrative system. For the next 500 years, Nubia would be an extension of Egypt, rather than a foreign land, a place to be taxed and exploited. Ahmose's army then pushed further south along the Nile towards the Third Cataract, bringing them closer and closer to their enemies at Kerma. The Egyptians had defeated the Hyksos. Now only the Kermans remained. Egypt's New Kingdom 'empire' was beginning to take shape.

Chapter 6

Meeting the Mitanni and Assimilating Kush (1549–1388 BCE)

W as it a knock to their self-esteem? A wake up call to the reality of the modern world? Simple revenge? Whatever the cause, once the Egyptians, now under the 18th Dynasty, had chased the Hyksos across the Sinai and into the Levant, the seeds of expansionism were sewn. The 'empire,' if we can truly call it that (it should perhaps be better categorised as a 'sphere of influence,' at least in Asia), had not yet begun, but the groundwork had been laid. King Ahmose, or his advisors, probably thought that if the Hyksos could enter Egypt and rule, then why couldn't they do the same in the Levant? No one at court would stand for a divided Egypt again, but dividing up other kingdoms was perfectly fine.

The scars must have run deep from the Hyksos interlude. Warfare had always been an important aspect of royal self presentation – we've already seen that the image of the smiting ruler dates back to Predynastic times – but this aspect of kingship would now be intensified: warfare and royal martial ability would become central to kingship. Through warfare, the pharaohs could display their strength, leadership, the approval of the gods, their protection of the people, and themselves as upholders of *maat* (order, justice, balance) – in short, all the aspects of a true and legitimate Egyptian king. Images of the destruction of foreign enemies would now be writ large across temple walls. Military exploits would be inscribed on stelae placed in temple courtyards, to be read aloud to gathered crowds on special occasions.

Egypt's technology of war had changed little between the final years of the Predynastic Period through to the end of the Second Intermediate Period. Now, as a result of the war with the Hyksos, not only had the Egyptians been exposed to more advanced weaponry (the pointy end), but resumed trading relations with the Near East had given them access to all the materials necessary to build their own. But access to materials alone wouldn't be enough, the Egyptians also had to encourage immigrants with the right technological know-how to settle in Egypt. Chariot building, for example, wasn't a simple task: just because you can buy all the materials you need to build a car, it doesn't mean that you can do it yourself, not without the right training.

For the Egyptians to construct their own chariots, they needed to bring in experts from abroad, whose expertise would be transferred over time.

But Egypt's re-entry into the world of international politics required something even more challenging than developing technology and managing an army: diplomacy. In this time of Bronze Age superpowers, Egypt's kings and their messengers were forced to deal directly with their foreign counterparts, talking with them as friends whilst simultaneously presenting the same people in temples and tombs as terrified weaklings. The New Kingdom was an age of brother-kings: ultimate rulers – gods in their home countries – forced by necessity to acknowledge that those evil personifications of everything horrible, those miserable rulers of foreign lands, had to be treated as equals.

The Wider World

While the Egyptians were dealing with the Hyksos, the wider world changed. Various international events conspired to bring into existence two powerful empires: the Mitanni and the Hittites, the fates of both intertwined. So, with the stage set, let's first pull back the curtains and introduce the Hittites. A civilization based in Anatolia (in modern central Turkey), the Hittites had strong expansionist aspirations. Perhaps with this goal in mind, they'd moved their capital city from central Anatolia to the north-east of their territory, to Hattusa, modern Boghazkoy. From there, they'd expanded eastwards, raiding cities in Yamkhad, an independent kingdom that roughly covers the same area as modern Syria. Yamkhad was one of a number of kingdoms established in the region by people of Hurrian origin – an ethnic group present in various kingdoms across northern Mesopotamia who spoke their own language.

At roughly the same time that King Ahmose I was ruling Egypt, Hattusilis I, king of the Hittites, launched an attack against the city of Alalakh in Yamkhad, causing devastation. He followed this with an assault on Urshu – a city on the Euphrates – and then four years later attacked Yamkhad's capital, Aleppo. Probably to much rejoicing in Yamkhad, Hattusilis died soon after, but his son, Mursilis I, continued the offensive. He returned to Aleppo and destroyed it, then set off down the Euphrates to loot Babylon, successfully ending the Amorite Dynasty in the process (most famous for King Hammurabi); this enabled the Kassites, a people from north-west Iran, to take power as the new Kassite Babylonian dynasty.

Who knows what Mursilis might have done next if his life hadn't been cut short, but cut short it was. Soon after arriving back in his home territory,

Mursilis was assassinated, leading to unrest across the Hittite Empire. The Hittite grip over Yamkhad now loosened. With the Hittites fighting amongst themselves, and Yamkhad in turmoil, a Hurrian group decided to take advantage of the situation: they founded a new kingdom, best known today as the land of Mitanni, though the Egyptians would know the territory as Naharin, and the Hittites would call it Hanigalbat. Their capital was established at Washukanni, a city that hasn't yet been firmly archaeologically identified. Quickly becoming the new major power in the northern Levant, and with the region's northern city-states under their control, the Mitanni would eventually push the limits of their territory against the Hittites to the north-west, the Kassite Babylonians to the south-east, and eventually, once the Egyptians had expanded their own influence far enough, against their territory too.

The New Kingdom Army

With the establishment of a standing army following the expulsion of the Hyksos, the Egyptian military entered a new phase of its existence (although men could still be levied against their will if necessary). As well as the troops – roughly divided into light infantry (armed with projectiles) and heavy infantry (handheld weaponry) – and charioteers (see the additional box text below), there were also numerous military scribes, administrators, and high-level generals. An army division consisted of *ca.* 5,000 men; within this, the troops were divided into squads of ten men, with five squads forming a platoon of fifty. Five platoons created a company of 250, and a host consisted of two companies, making 500 men. Each division was led by a great overseer of the division, who marched under the banner of a different state god, such as Amun or Ptah. With the increased presence of horses in Egypt, horse riding scouts also became part of the army.

The Birth of an Empire: Crushing Kerma

Ahmose I dead, mummified, and buried, King Amenhotep I ascended the throne as the second ruler of the 18th Dynasty. Despite the problems his father had faced with the Hyksos to the north-east, Amenhotep decided to focus his military attention southward. His goal was to strengthen Egyptian control of Nubia. Both Kamose and Ahmose had already made progress in Nubia: by Amenhotep's accession, the limit of Egyptian control was firmly at the Second Cataract – roughly at the spot where the Middle Kingdom kings had established their border. Ahmose Son of Ibana, a soldier that had earlier served in the wars of Ahmose, says that during his campaign south, Amenhotep I killed a Nubian bowman – presumably an enemy ruler – and that the Nubian army were brought away in fetters, without any missing. Amenhotep I is said to have seen Ahmose's bravery while the soldier was fighting at the front of the army. Later, Ahmose brought two hands – cut from fallen enemies – to prove his valour. Amenhotep rewarded him with a promotion to warrior of the ruler, and he was allowed to keep two Nubian women that he'd captured. Another soldier, Ahmose Pennekhbet, says that under Amenhotep I, he also received rewards, including gold, bracelets, necklaces, an armlet, golden flies, gold lions, and two golden axes. He fought for Amenhotep I in Kush – in the region of Kerma – and also faced a little known Libyan group called the Imukehek. Unfortunately, little else can be said about the campaigns of Amenhotep I. After a reign of twenty-one years, the throne passed to a man unrelated to the Ahmosid bloodline, but who nonetheless was regarded as a continuation of the 18th Dynasty line. This man was King Tuthmosis I.

Like Amenhotep I, Tuthmosis I initially focused his attention on Nubia. Ahmose Son of Ibana reports that the king travelled south to a place called Khenthennefer, where he crushed a rebellion and repelled intruders from the desert. We're also told that the king's first arrow pierced the chest of a Nubian, and that the Egyptians slaughtered many Nubians and took away some as prisoners. At Tombos – at the Third Cataract of the Nile – the Egyptians carved a stele into the rock, recording in poetic and violent phraseology the success of this campaign. Kerma, the capital of the Kingdom of Kush, was only a short distance south, and it's most probable that under Tuthmosis I this city was sacked and destroyed. Afterwards, the Egyptian army continued to the Nile's Fourth Cataract, where Tuthmosis marked his southern border. As a macabre footnote, Ahmose Son of Ibana says that during the army's return journey to Egypt, the Nubian 'bowman' – surely the king of Kerma – was hung, head down, from the front of Tuthmosis' boat.

With Kerma civilization crushed, Egypt was free to reorganize the region and incorporate it into its whole. Vassal rulers were appointed at Sai, Kerma, and Bugdumbush – three locations spread across the newly taken territory, and the king's son of Kush – a man with responsibility for the entire region – oversaw Egypt's interests there. Nubia was firmly under Egyptian control, and with it came access to the region's extensive natural resources, primarily gold, which would help fuel Egypt's growing imperial machine. Taxation of the region followed.

Tuthmosis Travels North

His southern territory now secure, Tuthmosis turned his attention north. Again, our major sources for his activities are the accounts of the soldiers Ahmose Pennekhbet and Ahmose Son of Ibana. Taken together, these relate that Tuthmosis and his army travelled north through the region of Retenu (roughly Syria-Palestine) and into the Mitanni controlled territory of Naharin, where vassals loyal to the Mitanni were gathering troops. A battle ensued, in which the Egyptians killed many enemies and took prisoners. Named on an artefact in Berlin, a charioteer called Karay served under Tuthmosis I and possibly accompanied this campaign, raising the likelihood that other charioteers came along too, even though the chariotry was not a well-established part of the Egyptian army at this time. After defeating the Mitanni vassals, Tuthmosis crossed the River Euphrates and erected a stele on its far side. This commemorated his achievement and marked the northern boundary of what the Egyptians now regarded as their territory. Finally, not too tired after all his campaigning, Tuthmosis turned around and went to hunt elephants in the region of Niy, about 50 km east of Ugarit. (Syrian elephants were hunted into extinction by around 100 BCE.)

This campaign marks a major turning point in Egypt's relationship with the Levant. Now, instead of sending trading missions and the occasional raiding force, a large Egyptian military contingent had marched through the Levant, seizing territory and demanding tribute from the city-states they'd encountered. The Egyptians also confronted, and presumably angered, the vassals of a major foreign kingdom – a true regional power, rather than a tiny city-state. With this campaign, Tuthmosis I set the blueprint for the New Kingdom attitude towards Egypt's eastern neighbours, creating expectations that would inspire and torment his royal successors: the River Euphrates was a goal to be reached, the extent of territorial control that a great king could achieve.

Charioteers: The Knights of Ancient Egypt

Although the Egyptians produced their own chariots from the early 18th Dynasty, it was not until the reign of King Amenhotep III that the chariotry became a separate division of the army, with its own ranking system.

Egyptian-made chariots were lightweight, open-backed, and tended to have either four or six spokes on their wheels. They were pulled by two horses yoked to the chassis by a long pole. Two men stood on board, one steering, and the other shooting arrows. To protect the horses, there was also a runner, who ran beside the chariot carrying a javelin. To keep themselves safe, charioteers wore scale armour, formed of bronze or leather scales attached to a linen or leather tunic. Bronze helmets, adorned with two tassels at the peak, protected their heads. In Egyptian sources, body armour is first mentioned in the Annals of King Tuthmosis III, and first depicted in the tomb of the courtier Kenamun. Bronze scales have also been found at the palace of King Amenhotep III at Malkata on the west bank of the Nile at Luxor.

Contrary to the imagery found in Egyptian scenes of royal warfare, chariots did not charge directly at the enemy – these were lightweight mobile platforms, not ancient tanks. Instead, they drove perpendicular to the enemy line, firing arrows from a safe distance. Nevertheless, charioteers were heavily armed: one text relates that standard chariot equipment included one or two bows, two to four quivers – with one on either side of the chariot chassis, providing access to around eighty arrows – a spear, with perhaps also a javelin, an axe, and shield. Such assortments can often be seen in battle depictions.

Being a charioteer conveyed a sense of social and political importance. To be a member of the chariot corps meant that you were an aristocratic warrior – a type of person known in the Near East as a *maryannu* or 'Young Hero.' As well as the status conveyed, the chariot itself was treated with love and care: one poem about the royal chariot assigns gods to each part of its body. Even more fun, Papyrus Anastasi I provides an account of a charioteer visiting a repair shop in Jaffa, much like a car owner today goes to get his car tuned up at the garage. It says, 'They take care of your chariot so that it is no longer loose. Your pole is freshly trimmed and its attachments are fitted on. They put bindings on your collar piece … and they fix up your yoke. They apply your ensign, engraved with a chisel, and they put a handle on your whip and attach a lash to it. You sally forth quickly to fight at the pass and accomplish glorious deeds.'[1]

War, Trade, and Diplomacy under Hatshepsut

Reigning only briefly, Tuthmosis II only had time to send a single campaign into Nubia before his death, leaving the Levant untouched (unless fragmentary scenes from his mortuary temple, showing Asiatics firing arrows, represent a true event). This Nubian campaign occurred during his first year on the throne, and is recorded near Aswan. Having been informed of a rebellion in Nubia, Tuthmosis made an oath that none of the Nubian males among the rebels would live. He duly sent out a large army to deal with the uprising, led by his own *bau* – a mystical manifestation of his anger at the loss of order. So, despite Tuthmosis not accompanying his army into Nubia himself, his scribes still presented the campaign as a personal royal victory. All the Nubian males were killed, just as the king had pledged, except for the son of a great one of Kush (along with his dependents), who was brought back to Egypt and dragged before the king.

Tuthmosis II and his Great Royal Wife Hatshepsut had no male offspring, so the royal successor, also called Tuthmosis, was born of a minor wife. With Tuthmosis III only a child at the time of his father's death, Hatshepsut ruled as queen regent. But slowly, over a number of years, she assumed the titles and regalia of a pharaoh herself. Tuthmosis didn't suffer during this time, instead he worked as a priest at the Temple of Amun at Karnak and later perhaps even led the army during a campaign in Gaza. Under Hatshepsut, rebellions continued to erupt in Nubia, and various courtiers describe battles fought to restore control. One such man was an official named Tiy, who says that under Hatshepsut, Nubians were overthrown, and the chiefs brought back to Egypt as prisoners. An official named Djehuty refers to booty being taken on the battlefield in Kush.

But it wasn't these successful military ventures that Hatshepsut chose to promote on the walls of her great mortuary temple at Deir el-Bahri, on the west bank of Thebes. Rather, an entire section of the temple's decoration was dedicated to, and dominated by, an act of trade and diplomacy: her mission to Punt. This event, in which Egypt reopened trade with the land of Punt for the first time since the end of the Middle Kingdom, occurred in the ninth year of Hatshepsut's reign. Five ships, loaded with gifts, journeyed south along the Red Sea, led by a chancellor named Nehesy and escorted by soldiers carrying shields and spears. Upon arrival, small ships helped the Egyptians offload their gifts and trade goods from the fleet to the shore. These were piled high for the Great One of Punt Parahu, who greeted the Egyptians with upraised arms – the customary Egyptian way of praising a person. He was quite surprised by their sudden appearance: 'How have you reached here, to this foreign land unknown to people?' He said. 'Have you descended through the ways of the sky? Have you travelled upon water and land? God's Land is happy because you have stepped on it as Re.'2

Soon after, the Egyptians erected a tent – a place for them to meet with Parahu and his wife. Puntite goods, including gold rings and ebony, were heaped outside, while the Puntites and Egyptians shared a meal together. On the menu, so the Egyptians tell us, was bread, beer, wine, meat, fruits, and all the good things of Egypt. Later, both Egyptians and Puntites carried incense trees in baskets (one Puntite apparently complained about his load being too heavy) to the waiting ships, as well as other goods, including ebony, panther skins, and animals, such as monkeys. Puntite families, including children, also went along. Later, back in Egypt, the goods were unloaded and the great ones of Punt prostrated themselves before Hatshepsut (who was awarded her own panther). The mission had successfully brought back thirty-one myrrh trees, a portion of which Hatshepsut offered to the god Amun.

Hatshepsut's Punt scenes are complemented by images in the tomb of the High Priest of Amun Hapuseneb at Thebes, which show a man (presumably Hapuseneb himself) leaning on his staff, while watching others chop down Puntite trees with axes. Hapuseneb had an interest in the supply of the incense that came from these trees, as it was used on a daily basis in the rituals performed before Amun and the other gods of Karnak Temple.

Life on Campaign

Due to the increased prominence of the military in New Kingdom Egypt, we start to find more scenes of army life appearing in tombs. One scene, for example, in the tomb of Userhat at Thebes, shows barbers cutting the hair of military recruits and rations being distributed. The tomb of Tjanuni, also at Thebes, shows cattle being brought to camp as food, as well as soldiers on the march.

One satirical papyrus – Papyrus Anastasi I – presents the life of a soldier in miserable terms (although we must bear in mind that it was composed to convince scribes that they'd chosen the best profession). This describes infantrymen as confined to their barracks and often beaten 'like a piece of papyrus.' Then, when on the march, they are forced to carry bread and water on their shoulders 'like a donkey's burden.' The soldier, the text goes on to say, has to drink disgusting water during the journey and feels weak by the time he reaches his enemy on the battlefield. And if he returns home, he's carried back as if paralyzed, with his clothes stolen and his servant having run away.

The arrangement of an Egyptian military camp can be seen in depictions of the Battle of Qadesh under King Ramesses II of the 19th Dynasty, and in the tomb of Horemheb at Saqqara. At the centre of the camp, these show the royal tent, one half low and rectangular, the other taller with a pyramidal peak – this pointed peak was created by a column within, holding aloft the fabric. To make it easier to transport the king's furniture, each item was foldable – such items can be seen in depictions, and a foldable bed was found in the tomb of King Tutankhamun of the 18th Dynasty. Guards' tents or those of generals were located nearby. As no tents for soldiers are shown in depictions, it's probable that they slept on the ground in the open air. Horses and chariots were lined up in rows, and the charioteers placed their helmets on the floor in front of them. Charioteers could also sleep in their chariots. Shields driven into the earth marked the camp's perimeter.

The Battle of Megiddo and Its Aftermath

After Hatshepsut's death, Tuthmosis III was left to rule alone. It seems that the young king must have regarded his grandfather, Tuthmosis I, as a great inspiration, for one of his first actions was to launch a campaign into the Levant, and he spent the rest of his reign attempting to secure the territory that Tuthmosis had once traversed. He even aimed to reach the River Euphrates. Tuthmosis III's first major campaign was among his most dramatic. The ruler of Qadesh (located in modern Syria), no doubt backed by the Mitanni, had expanded his influence and formed a coalition of city-states against the Egyptians. This force had gathered at the city of Megiddo – perhaps the southernmost stronghold of this new coalition – with the intention of pushing further south. Perhaps fearing invasion, Tuthmosis and his army departed Egypt, marched overland to Gaza, and onwards to the town of Yehem, reaching it in the twenty-third year of his reign (despite having just become sole king, Tuthmosis incorporated Hatshepsut's years of rule into his own).

An otherwise inconsequential town, at Yehem Tuthmosis and his advisors met to discuss strategy and the route to Megiddo. Three options presented themselves: a route that would bring the army out at the northern side of Megiddo, one that brought them out at its southern side, or a march through the narrow Aruna Pass, with its exit close to the city. Tuthmosis favoured the Aruna Pass option, but his troops were worried: due to the narrowness of the Pass, whilst on the march, the army would be in single file, horse behind horse. If they encountered an enemy force, only those at the front would be able to fight. Due to a break in the text relating these events, it's unclear what happened next; however, it appears that a messenger arrived with extra information, clinching the deal: the king was right all along (of course), and the best option was to march through the Aruna Pass.

Tuthmosis was not a despot, however (at least, he didn't like to present himself as such), and so gave those troops afraid of marching through the Pass the option to take a different road. None, of course, accepted his offer. But perhaps they should have: later, while marching through the Pass, the army's fears were realized – at least, as far as we can gather from this broken portion of the text. Enemy troops were waiting at its exit, and a small skirmish occurred. Afterwards, the Egyptians set up camp outside the Pass, and the king issued a command, telling his troops to sharpen their weapons in preparation for battle in the morning.

At dawn the next day, messengers entered the royal tent to inform Tuthmosis that the area was secure. The king duly prepared himself for battle. Speaking about the battle in poetic terms, the Annals of Tuthmosis III – inscribed on the walls within Karnak Temple – describe Tuthmosis as riding on his chariot of fine electrum, equipped with his weapons of war. The wings of the army went to their positions, and the king was among them, 'the strength of [Seth pervading] his limbs.'[3] The text doesn't dwell on the details of the battle, but rather on the Egyptians' success: 'Then his majesty prevailed over them at the front of his army,' the Annals relate. 'Then they (the enemy) saw his majesty prevailing over them when they were fleeing headlong [to] Megiddo with terrified faces.'[4] If the account can be trusted, the enemy coalition saw the Egyptian army approaching and fled. Although clearly exaggerated (the Gebel Barkal Stele, which also mentions these events, says that the battle lasted an hour), this might not be so farfetched. The Annals say that only 340 prisoners were taken during the battle – a relatively small number – and, more intriguingly, that the Egyptians only took eighty-three hands; as each hand represents a dead enemy, there can only have been a small-scale confrontation.

Showing a shocking lack of discipline, with the battle won, the Egyptian army looted the coalition camp instead of chasing their enemies down, giving the Asiatics enough time to flee and hide within the walls of Megiddo. This resulted in a siege that lasted seven months. 'Look, [all foreign lands] are placed (together) [in this town according to the command] of Re on this day,' said Tuthmosis. 'Because all the great ones of all rebellious northern foreign lands are mixing within it, the capture of Megiddo is the capture of a thousand towns.'[5] The Annals provide little more detail about what happened next, but the story picks up in Tuthmosis III's Gebel Barkal Stele. This says that the siege was a success, with the unfortunate inhabitants pleading with the king for the 'breath of life.' When the doors to the city finally opened, the enemy chiefs and their children brought gifts to Tuthmosis III, handily including their weapons. And after pledging oaths of allegiance to pharaoh, they were allowed to return to their homes.

Importing Glass

Glass was one of Egypt's major foreign imports during the New Kingdom. It is rarely found in the country before the 18th Dynasty, at which point, in around 1500 BCE, the Egyptians started importing it as a prestige item (in fact, it became so desirable that those who couldn't afford it painted wooden vessels to appear as if they were made from glass). Even the two Egyptian words for glass are of Hurrian and Akkadian origin, while 'lapis lazuli of Babylon,' mentioned in the Annals of Tuthmosis III, might be a further reference to the material.

Glass makers may have entered Egypt under Tuthmosis III as a result of his campaigns in the Levant. At this time, the Egyptians, lacking the ability to create the material from scratch, probably imported glass and melted it down to be re-shaped. By the Amarna Period, however, the Egyptians were producing their own raw glass, though it continued to be imported too (as mentioned in the Amarna Letters).

After Megiddo

Tuthmosis campaigned in the Levant on an almost yearly basis after the Battle of Megiddo, pushing Egyptian influence further and further north across the Levant. His eyes were focused on reaching the River Euphrates, where his grandfather had once erected his triumphal stele. The southern Levant was by now firmly under Egyptian control, with the kings of its city-states vassals, forced to pay tribute to pharaoh. Tuthmosis particularly ensured the loyalty of the region's harbour cities, as this enabled him to transport troops and supplies by boat, something he did during his sixth and seventh campaigns.

Despite the fame of the Battle of Megiddo, to Tuthmosis' soldiers, the most important campaign of their lives – the one most frequently mentioned in their tomb autobiographies – was the eighth campaign, launched in the thirty-third year of Tuthmosis' rule. During this campaign, Tuthmosis and his army finally reached the River Euphrates, fulfilling the king's dreams, and burned the region's cities. In order to cross the Euphrates, Tuthmosis had commanded boats be made at Byblos; in pieces, these were transported overland by oxen and carts to its banks, where they were reconstructed. Once on the opposite side of the river, mimicking his grandfather, Tuthmosis erected a stele, marking and reclaiming Egypt's furthest boundary north. The army took local people as prisoners, seized cattle, provisions, and grain, and cut down enemy plantations and fruit trees. After returning across the Euphrates, Tuthmosis, again in imitation of his grandfather, went hunting elephants in the region of Niy. Although it's recorded that he killed 120, he didn't have an easy time: the Soldier Amenemhab says that during the hunt, one of these elephants attacked the king. Luckily for Tuthmosis (though not the elephant), Amenemhab reacted swiftly, cutting off the elephant's trunk and saving his king. For his bravery, Amenemhab was rewarded by the pharaoh.

Managing the Levantine 'Empire'

During the New Kingdom, the Levant was dotted with a large number of city-states, each ruled by their own kings, some more powerful than others. Of these, the most powerful managed a great deal of territory, and could even hold influence over other, smaller cities. There was frequent competition for land, and they often came into conflict with one another. Political allegiances between states were in a constant state of flux, with diplomatic marriages capable of rewriting entire relationships.

After Egypt's campaigns in the Levant, each of these kings fell in status: they were forced to take an oath of allegiance to pharaoh and admit their subservience. To the Egyptians, these vassal kings were nothing more than local mayors – men who paid taxes to the Egyptian crown and provided the Egyptian army with supplies, troops, and accommodation whenever a campaign was underway. As long as they kept paying, and didn't obstruct the flow of luxury goods, the Egyptians gave them little attention, often leaving them to fight and squabble without interference.

Only certain cities, including Tyre, Byblos, and Beth Shean (though perhaps only from the 19th Dynasty onwards), housed Egyptian garrisons. Gaza, meanwhile, had a garrison and a commissioner's residence – home to a man known as the overseer of northern lands – who had responsibility for overseeing parts of the Levantine territory and made periodic tours of the region. Egyptian royal messengers, travelling between the Levant's city-states, also enjoyed a high status, and in particular had the power to collect taxes and administer justice.

Nubia in the 18th Dynasty

By the reign of Tuthmosis III, Nubia, as far as the Fourth Cataract, was firmly under Egyptian control, and there's little evidence for campaigning in the region during his time on the throne. The only detailed example is found in the account of the Royal Herald Djehutymose, who before his promotion to herald had been a messenger and overseer of the royal granary. In this latter capacity, he says that he helped to assemble and recruit troops for a Nubian expedition and organized the food supplies. Despite his purely administrative role, he took captives on the battlefield, suggesting that he also fought personally.

Since the early 18th Dynasty, Nubia as a whole, from the First to the Fourth Cataract, had been managed by the king's son of Kush. And like Egypt itself, Nubia was now divided in two, with Wawat referring to Lower Nubia, and Kush being Upper Nubia. Each division had a deputy governor, who lived locally in one of his region's major centres: the governor of Wawat lived at Aniba, roughly halfway between the First and Second Cataracts, and the governor of Kush was based at Soleb, before moving to Amara (both towns only a short distance away from the Third Cataract). Upper and Lower Nubia were further divided into a number of smaller provinces, each overseen by a Nubian vassal ruler.

Between Tuthmosis' years thirty-seven and forty-one, 200 prisoners were brought to Egypt from the region of Kush, including four of the ruler of Irem's children – Irem being a Nubian province, and its ruler a Nubian vassal of Egypt. These children were probably brought to the court to be 'Egyptianized,' exposing them to Egyptian culture and thus (theoretically) making them loyal to the Egyptian crown. At the same time, their presence at the Egyptian court would have ensured that the ruler of Irem followed pharaoh's commands. A similar policy was enacted in the Levant, from where the children of vassal kings were taken to the Egyptian palace and educated. One scene in the tomb of Menkheperreseneb shows the ruler of Tunip bringing a small boy, presumably his son, to the Egyptian court, probably for this reason.

Unlike in the Levant, where for the most part Egypt only expected loyalty and tribute from its vassal rulers, in Nubia there was a push to transform the region into an extension of Egypt; one way of achieving this 'Egyptianization' was through the construction of 'temple towns.' These settlements were managed by a commander or mayor, who had the role of generating income from the temple lands. Egypt's temples were involved in collecting and storing grain, as well as other goods, which could be redistributed locally or across the country (some went as wages to State employees); in this way, Nubia became incorporated into Egypt's wider economy. The temples also acted as a stamp of Egyptian identity and authority in Nubia, and so played a role in further Egyptianizing the local population, exposing them to Egyptian beliefs and deities.

One of the most important Egyptian temples founded in Nubia under Tuthmosis III was at Gebel Barkal, a small mountain near the Fourth Cataract of the Nile. Here, on a site probably already sacred to the Nubians, the Egyptians noticed that a rocky pinnacle resembled a uraeus (a rearing cobra that symbolized royal power) wearing the White Crown of Upper Egypt, leading them to identify the mountain as the Nubian home of the god Amun. Consequently, Tuthmosis founded a temple and fortress at the foot of the mountain, and a city, known as Napata, developed nearby. Additional temples were built under Tuthmosis' successors, creating a complex that would later have particular religious significance to the 25th Dynasty kings.

The Composite Bow and *Khepesh*

In addition to the chariot, one of the main technological developments adopted by the New Kingdom Egyptians was the composite bow – a technology that had been known in the Near East for some time. Composite bows, as the name suggests, were formed of multiple parts. To make one, a wooden bow was taken, and strips of horn and sinew were glued to it, making it more elastic and giving it a greater range – somewhere between 160 to 175 m. As composite bows were more powerful than standard bows, it was possible for archers to fire arrows with larger bronze heads. In turn, this meant that the Egyptians had to adopt better protection, and so started using bronze shields. The Egyptian word for quiver, '*ispet*,' was also imported from the Near East, it being based on the Akkadian word '*ispatu*.'

Another weapon, widely used in the Near East from around 2500 BCE, and introduced into Egypt during the New Kingdom, was the *khepesh*, a curved blade used for hacking. It is often shown held by the king in smiting scenes, or being handed to the king by a god as a symbol of certain victory in a coming campaign.

The World Comes to Egypt

Tuthmosis III's reign was not all about warfare and 'Egyptianization.' Egypt's exploits in the wider world had changed its relationship with its neighbours, and even more-so than previously, the country became a multicultural centre, attracting foreign merchants, messengers, and diplomats. Numerous people from the Levant lived and worked in Egypt, acting as shipyard workers, craftsmen, scribes, and vintners, among many other positions. At the royal dockyard of Peru-nefer in particular, a number of foreign people held jobs, and worshipped the gods Baal and Astarte; it's possible that these came to offer the Egyptians their specialist knowledge of shipping. One shipyard worker even travelled from as far away as the region of Arzawa in western Turkey. Foreigners also achieved high-level positions at court. There was a Hurrian overseer of works named Benya, and a chancellor named Nehesy, who may have been from Nubia. A man named Pas-Baal, captured during Tuthmosis III's wars in the Levant, went on to become chief draughtsman in the Temple of Amun. Egyptian soldiers married Asiatic women.

Across Egypt, there was a greater interest in all things 'foreign' than before: Egyptian workshops produced Syrian-style vessels, and Aegean textiles inspired the decoration of tomb ceilings. Foreign flora and fauna were also of interest: the Annals of Tuthmosis III record 'two birds that are not known and four birds of this (foreign) country that give birth every day'[6] among the gifts from a foreign country – the latter is possibly the first reference to chickens in Egypt. From his year twenty-five campaign in Lebanon, Tuthmosis III also collected plants and flowers; these were donated to the Temple of Amun at Karnak and recorded in detailed reliefs on the temple walls.

Egypt's enhanced foreign relations also boosted the economy. Independent countries and city-states brought expensive 'gifts' to the pharaoh's court, many of which were donated by the king to Egypt's temples. In the Annals of Tuthmosis III, such gifts arrive from Hatti (the land of the Hittites), Babylonia, Assyria, Cyprus, Alalakh, and mainland Greece, and included copper, lead, wood, silver, lapis lazuli, and even exotic animals. The foreign delegations bringing these gifts probably stayed at the Egyptian court for some months, enabling deals to be struck and bonds to be forged with courtiers.

Rather than giving gifts, conquered territories sent contributions to the Egyptian court as regular, obligatory tax; in the Annals, this was sent from locations in the southern Levant (showing a stronger hold over this region than the north), and included wine, honey, and cereals. Wawat and Kush in Nubia sent tax in the form of gold, cattle, slaves, ivory, and crops. Egypt's constant campaigning also brought the spoils of war: from prisoners and chariots, to women, children, and livestock.

Egypt's nobles must have found this all rather exciting, for it became fashionable for them to depict the arrival of foreign delegations in their tombs. Not only did such paintings show that you were a member of the 'in crowd,' invited to such lavish events, but it also added a touch of the exotic to your tomb. Among the foreigners depicted bearing gifts were people from the Levant, who were often painted bringing weapons, chariots, horses, metal vases, minerals, and other precious goods. In the tomb of Ineni, they're even shown bringing a bear.

Relations with the Aegean also became stronger in the 18th Dynasty. Artists decorated chambers in a palace of Tuthmosis III at Tell el-Daba entirely in the Minoan style, showing bull leapers, bull-grappling, hunts, and griffins, along with maze-patterns. These were made using non-Egyptian painting techniques, indicating that the artists were either Minoans or had been trained by Minoans. It's unclear why these paintings were made, and they didn't remain on the palace walls for long. Perhaps Tuthmosis simply wanted Minoan-themed chambers (the way rich Europeans often had themed rooms in their stately homes), or it may have been in honour of a Minoan delegation visiting the Egyptian court. Another suggestion is that a Minoan princess may have entered the pharaoh's harem, and that these chambers were associated with her. What is certain is that Minoan delegations did visit Egypt under Hatshepsut and Tuthmosis III, for they are shown among the foreigners bringing gifts to the Egyptian court. One Aegean delegation, depicted in the tomb of Senenmut, brought gifts of metal vases and a sword. Another, in the tomb of the Vizier Rekhmire, is shown carrying metal vases and jewellery.

Not to be outdone by Hatshepsut, trade with Punt continued under Tuthmosis III. But unlike his step-mother's famous mission, in which the Egyptians travelled to Punt, under Tuthmosis the people of Punt came to Egypt. Tuthmosis' Karnak Annals record 'marvels' arriving from Punt in years thirty-three and thirty-eight, and Theban Tomb 143 (owner unknown) includes depictions of Puntites arriving on the shores of the Red Sea aboard round watercraft with triangular sails (appearing a lot like modern dinghies). Scenes in the tombs of the Second Priest of Amun Puyemre and the Vizier Rekhmire show Puntites among foreigners bringing gifts to the royal court. As usual, these Puntite gifts are classified as 'marvels.' In Rekhmire's tomb, artists also painted Nubians bearing gold, ebony, ostrich feathers, and animals (including a giraffe), among other items. Nubian women and children, captured as prisoners of war, are depicted in the tomb of Ineni too, and are described as being sent to work for Egypt's temples. Goods and prisoners from Wawat were also once depicted in lost scenes in the tomb of Useramun.

Many foreign women entered the royal harem in the 18th Dynasty, accompanied by large numbers of attendants. The earliest known of these women are Manuwai, Manhata, and Maruta, each of Levantine origin, but unrelated to one another. They were buried with elaborate Egyptian grave goods in a joint tomb at Thebes, and are often described as wives of Tuthmosis III by scholars because they were interred shortly after Hatshepsut's death. In Tuthmosis' twenty-third year of rule (i.e. just after he became sole king), women and children associated with the leaders of the enemy coalition at the Battle of Megiddo were taken to Egypt; many were sent to work in the Temple of Amun's storehouse, and it's possible that some of the women ended up in the king's harem. Similarly, in Tuthmosis III's fortieth regnal year, among the tribute of Retenu was a chief's daughter, who came to Egypt with gold and lapis lazuli, along with attendants, servants, and slaves.

During the New Kingdom, foreign slaves, captured during campaigns, were brought to Egypt in larger numbers than before, and were often sent to work at the temples (for example in the fields of the Temple of Amun). The Annals of Tuthmosis III record around 7,300 slaves entering Egypt, with 2,500 captured during the Megiddo campaign alone. Slaves brought from Nubia and the Levant as prisoners of war are depicted in the tomb of the Vizier Rekhmire, including men, women, and children; these were sent to work for the Temple of Amun, where they were registered, and given clothes and ointment. Rekhmire's tomb also depicts Syrian and Nubian slaves making bricks at the Temple of Amun. Artists painted a Nubian girl dancing at a banquet in the tomb of the Butler Wah, while on the walls of the tomb of Tjay, a Nubian man and woman harvest a field. Nomadic people from the Levant, identified as Apiru, are shown making wine in the tombs of Puyemre and Intef. Sometimes, foreign prisoners given to individuals as slaves were freed by their owners. Under Tuthmosis III, for example, the Royal Barber Si-Bastet captured a slave during a military campaign and later allowed him to marry his blind niece. It was also possible for people to adopt their slaves, leading to them being freed.

Rewarding Soldiers

In addition to being rewarded for their service with 'gold of bravery,' slaves, and land, Egyptian soldiers could be awarded gold flies. It isn't clear why the Egyptians chose the fly-shape as a symbol of military valour; scholars have suggested that it was because the troops pestered their opponents like flies pester people, or because flies gather around the corpses of fallen enemies. Only five non-royal individuals – all from the 18th Dynasty and high-ranking soldiers – are currently known to have been rewarded with gold flies.

One 17th Dynasty queen, Ahhotep I, was also buried with gold flies.

Archaeologists have found large flies, each made from different materials, including gold, ivory, and bronze, in graves in Nubia, specifically at Kerma and Buhen. Made between 1700–1500 BCE, they predate those produced in Egypt. Although the Egyptian flies are different in size and appearance from these Nubian examples (which continued to be worn by Nubians through-out the New Kingdom), the Nubian flies may have inspired the Egyptian designs. Four of the 18th Dynasty soldiers that received golden flies were also rewarded with golden lions – symbols that appear to be associated with royalty and bravery.

Amenhotep II: Despot or Peacemaker?

Amenhotep II, the son and successor of Tuthmosis III, inherited his father's love of war. On many of his monuments, he flaunts his skill as a warrior and his athletic ability; in his own words, he was the greatest archer – capable of firing arrows through copper targets one palm thick (the arrows passing through and falling to the ground) – and boasted of his ability to row a boat with a single large oar, all by himself. He was the best horse rider too. (We can perhaps imagine him atop his chariot doing doughnuts in the palace courtyard, flexing his biceps and shouting 'look at me. I'm the best!') As we will see, Amenhotep also liked to emphasize his brutality, more-so than other pharaohs. It's possible that these bombastic accounts are all a reflec-tion of his personality, and that he wanted to be recognized for his aggres-sive treatment of his opponents.

Amenhotep's first campaign occurred in his third year as king, and was waged against the region of Takhsy, east of Byblos in the Levant. Although little information is provided beyond rhetorical praise, one gruesome detail does stand out: 'His majesty returned (to Egypt) with the joy of his father [Amun], (after) he had killed the seven chiefs with his own club, who had been in the district of Takhsy; and who were placed upside down at the bow of the falcon ship of his majesty…'[7] The Egyptians then hung six of these men in front of the rampart of Thebes, along with their hands (which had presumably been chopped off), and sent the remaining chief to Napata in Nubia, where he was likewise hung from the city's ramparts. They must have been rather rotten by the time they reached Thebes and Napata from the Levant.

For many, such behaviour conducted by the Ancient Egyptians might be shocking – to think that the walls of Thebes were hung with dead enemies, like heads on spikes at London Bridge, is not what many tourists imagine when wandering around modern Luxor. Whether this was a common practice or not is hard to say. Tuthmosis I makes references to bringing an enemy chief back to Karnak Temple, hung upside down at the front of the royal boat, and there is a depiction of a bound Syrian hanging in a cage in the war scenes from Tutankhamun's mortuary temple.

Amenhotep's next campaign occurred in his seventh year as king, and was directed against the northern Levant, where the Egyptians were having trouble maintaining control. One of the campaign's major events was the capture of a town called Shamash-Edom, which was plundered by the king. Afterwards, Amenhotep marched to the River Orontes, and there encountered enemies from the town of Qatna, who were chasing the Egyptians from behind. These were swiftly defeated, and the enemy commander placed at the side of the royal chariot (inside? Dragged along? It isn't clear). The king and his army then travelled north into the region of Niy – better known for the hunting escapades of Tuthmosis I and III. Here, a messenger informed Amenhotep of a rebellion in the town of Ikatj, in which a loyal chief had been overthrown. Amenhotep and his troops duly rode to Ikatj and executed everyone disloyal to the king. Then, in the area of Nukhasse – a large territory, roughly 100 km long, between Aleppo in the north and Qatna in the south – Amenhotep deported 15,070 people, forcing them to work for Egypt as slaves, and no doubt terrifying the remaining population into subservience. With typical bombast, Amenhotep says that he then travelled to a place called Hashabu alone, and returned after only a short time, bringing, 'sixteen Syrian warriors beside his chariot, twenty hands on the foreheads of his horses, and sixty bulls as a cattle-drive before him.'[8] One account of this campaign – known as the Karnak Stele – adds that Amenhotep captured the town's chief, along with his child. Afterwards, an enemy messenger was also captured, and placed on the king's chariot (presumably along with all the other captives already there).

Two years later, in his ninth year on the throne, Amenhotep returned to the Levant. This time, he remained in the region's south, directing his attention against the normally loyal area surrounding Megiddo, indicating an outbreak of unrest. After plundering a number of villages, Amenhotep's army travelled to the villages of Ituryn and Mektilyn, where a particularly gruesome event occurred. To present it in full: 'His majesty ... brought away thirty-four of their chiefs, fifty-seven Syrian warriors, 231 living Asiatics, 372 hands, fifty-four horses, fifty-four chariots, as well as all the weapons of war, all the "strong of arm" of Retenu, their children, their women, and all their belongings. After his majesty had seen the very numerous booty, they were made into prisoners. Two ditches were made all around them and filled with fire; his majesty was on guard over it until daybreak, his battle-axe in his right hand, alone, without anyone with him. Now, the army was far from him, apart from the servants of pharaoh.'[9] If this account can be believed, Amenhotep watched the people of the villages burn to death. It's perhaps one of the most violent descriptions found in an Egyptian royal text, and reveals the true brutality of warfare in the New Kingdom. After leaving Ituryn and Mektilyn, the Egyptians attacked further cities, taking prisoners as they went.

Peace Under Amenhotep II

After Amenhotep's year nine campaign, there was a sudden change in Egypt's relationship with the wider world: the Hittites (now on the rise again), the Mitanni, and the Babylonians all sent gifts to the pharaoh, delivered by their representatives to the court at Memphis. It's unclear why relations suddenly improved between Egypt and each of these great powers, but whatever the case may be, by the end of Amenhotep II's period campaigning in the Levant, Egypt had strengthened its territorial control, and now firmly held the region up to the River Orontes and Ugarit on the coast. More importantly, a time of peace could now be enjoyed.

Perhaps the Egyptians and Mitanni realized that they were evenly matched, and with their vassal states between them in the Levant serving as a buffer zone, neither could really pose a true threat to the other; if a treaty was formally created between the two superpowers, it probably stipulated that the territory north of Ugarit was off limits to the Egyptians. Due to aggression from the Hittites, the Mitanni were facing war on two fronts, and for this reason, may have wanted peace with the Egyptians – the lesser of two evils from their perspective.

It's possible that the Egyptians drew up a treaty with the Hittites at this time too, as one is mentioned in sources from a century later. Treaties were a normal aspect of Hittite international relations; during Amenhotep II's reign, for example, the Hittite king made a treaty with the state of Kizzuwatna, in south-eastern Turkey, ensuring that neither would be hostile to the other. From the Hittite point of view, having Kizzuwatna as a friend was beneficial, for the region provided a buffer zone between their heartland and Mitanni territory. At the same time, the Babylonians might also have made a treaty with Egypt, as indicated by a later Babylonian text, concerning the renewal of this earlier treaty.

We cannot know if making peace with the Hittites, Mitanni, and the Babylonians was an aim of Amenhotep's or something that he accepted begrudgingly as a political necessity. By making treaties, he would now have to accept these former enemies as 'brothers,' an admission of equality that would seem out of character for Amenhotep. Nonetheless, if it is accepted that these treaties date to Amenhotep's reign, they are the first that the Egyptians ever entered into with foreign states.

Perhaps Amenhotep II wasn't as self-obsessed and violent as he makes out, but then again, it's always how you spin it. In a letter written by Amenhotep to his King's Son of Kush Usersatet, in the twenty-third year of his reign, he refers to himself as giving orders to the Hittites, and possessing women from Babylon, Alalakh, and Arrapkha – these latter two places being in Mitanni territory. He also mentions having a servant from Byblos. With the end of warfare, and no significant threats to face, Amenhotep could now characterize himself as commander of a peaceful world, where even the greatest of kings couldn't oppose him.

A Time of Peace: The Reign of Tuthmosis IV

Under King Tuthmosis IV, a son of Amenhotep II, the 18th Dynasty's empire building phase ended. On the whole, Egypt's control of its Levantine territory was now stable and Nubia could offer little resistance against Egyptian occupation. Nevertheless, there were small scale campaigns in both regions. An offering list from Karnak Temple mentions booty taken from 'Naharin' on the king's first campaign – perhaps a small skirmish in the Mitanni borderlands – and Tuthmosis depopulated the area of Gezer in the southern Levant. Relations with the Mitanni nevertheless continued to flourish, with Tuthmosis marrying a Mitanni princess – a daughter of King Artatama I. Tuthmosis' campaigns also brought more foreign prisoners into Egypt, with his officials sending Nubians from Kush to work in the 'House of Bread' at the king's mortuary temple, and Asiatics to the 'House of Wine.' To promote his achievements, Tuthmosis had his artisans decorate the sides of one of his chariots with scenes of him defeating enemies from the north and south.

Tuthmosis IV's campaign in Nubia is the best known of his military exploits. The stele recording this event describes the king as at Karnak Temple, having just made offerings to the god Amun, when a messenger arrives to inform him of a Nubian rebellion; apparently, Nubians from Wawat had joined with other foreigners to cause trouble, probably disrupting Egypt's gold mining operations in the region. So, the next morning, the king returned to Karnak Temple to make additional offerings to Amun, and to consult with the god about the best way to deal with the uprising. It's also possible that Tuthmosis requested Amun's permission to launch a campaign, for divine sanction was seemingly needed before any action could be taken (later scenes on temple walls show pharaohs being handed a *khepesh*-sword by the gods as a symbol of assured triumph). Amun must have been happy to oblige, for soon afterwards Tuthmosis commanded his army to assemble. They then travelled south, stopping at cult centres along the way to make offerings to the gods. Upon arriving in Nubia, Tuthmosis is said to have discovered a new road in the Eastern Desert and found the rebels hiding in a secret valley. Alone, he killed them all, without bothering to wait for his army.

Despite Tuthmosis' attempts to promote his (minor) military successes, times had changed. The king may have wanted (and certainly tried) to portray himself as a powerful warrior, but the great battles had dried up. War was not what it used to be. It would be left to Tuthmosis' son and successor, Amenhotep III, to adapt to these new, more peaceful times. With wealth flowing in from across the empire, this king would turn his attention to grand displays of power, not through war, but a building programme of epic proportions. Amenhotep would also father one of Ancient Egypt's most controversial figures: the 'heretic' King Akhenaten, who ushered in a time of political and religious upheaval called the Amarna Period.

Chapter 7

Heresy and Diplomacy
(1388–1298 BCE)

By the time of King Tuthmosis IV's death, little had changed to upset the newfound peace across the Near East. Amenhotep III, successor to Tuthmosis, had no need to prove himself at war, and even if he'd wanted to, there wasn't much opportunity to do so anyway; instead, Amenhotep dedicated himself to producing art and architecture on a grand scale – the next time you see a large statue of the goddess Sekhmet in a museum, there's a good chance that you can thank Amenhotep for commissioning it. There's also a good chance that that beautiful statue of King Ramesses II you've always admired was also commissioned by Amenhotep, and later usurped by the better-known pharaoh. In fact, there are more surviving statues of Amenhotep III than of any other Egyptian king.

Many of Egypt's great temples also benefitted from Amenhotep's patronage, in particular Luxor Temple, and his mortuary temple on the west bank of Luxor – the largest mortuary temple constructed in Egypt – today most famous for the Colossi of Memnon, the two royal statues that still guard its entrance. Rather than spending his time directing troops on campaign like his predecessors, Amenhotep enjoyed the more pleasant side of life – perhaps too much, given that he had himself (quite unusually) portrayed portly and wearing a fringed tunic on a serpentine statue now in the Metropolitan Museum of Art, New York.

Amenhotep also found unusual ways to spread word of his achievements. Large commemorative scarabs bearing summaries of events from his coronation through to his tenth year have been found across the Mediterranean world; it's probable that these were handed out to loyal courtiers and visiting dignitaries, and afterwards were traded, passed from person to person, and eventually ended up all over the place. 'Brand Amenhotep' certainly had good PR. Of the various subjects recorded on these scarabs, there were the king's lion and bull hunts; the arrival of a Mitanni princess – Gilukhepa, sister of Mitanni King Tushratta – for marriage (one of two Mitanni princesses he would marry); the digging of a lake for his great royal wife, Queen Tiye, to sail upon; and a celebration of the parents of Queen Tiye. At the same time, the king also experimented with royal presentation in Nubia, where at Soleb and Sedeinga, he built temples dedicated to the royal cult, divinizing himself in his own lifetime (something else that Ramesses II would later copy). Through art and architecture, Amenhotep III proclaimed himself a god on earth: if he couldn't win glory on the battlefield, he'd at least tick every other box on the royal list of clichés.

But this isn't to say that warfare didn't occur under Amenhotep III, it's just that he had little interest in the opportunities available; there were at least two campaigns in Nubia during his reign, but Nubia – by now heavily Egyptianized – held little attraction. Faced only with minor rebellions, the challenge just wasn't there for the aggressive pharaoh seeking glory. The first of Amenhotep's Nubian campaigns occurred in his fifth year as king, but there's little information about it. As was often the case, a messenger came to inform the king that an enemy in Kush was planning a rebellion. The king duly sent out his army, who slaughtered their enemies and severed many hands. If the text is to be believed, 30,000 prisoners were taken, and Amenhotep set free as many as he liked, so that there'd still be some people left living there. The Nubian rebel leader was called Ikheny, described by Amenhotep as a 'boaster.' According to the king, Ikheny 'didn't know the lion that was in front of him: Nebmaatre (Amenhotep III) is the savage lion whose claws grasped impotent Kush. All its chiefs were trampled throughout their valleys, (being) overthrown in their (own) blood, one on top of another.'[1] Amenhotep III's second campaign was led by his King's Son of Kush Merymose, whose account is inscribed on a stele at Semna. This rebellion is blamed on the people of Ibhet, who were planning an attack on Egyptians in Nubia. Merymose assembled an army and attacked the Nubians during the harvest season, taking 740 prisoners and killing 312.

Relations with the Levant, on the other hand, continued to prosper. As already mentioned, Amenhotep married a sister of Mitanni King Tushratta, and later married a second Mitanni princess, named Tadukhepa. For this second marriage, letters preserve discussions about the dowry and its contents, and mention Tadukhepa's planned arrival in Egypt. Such family ties brought Amenhotep and Tushratta closer together, to the extent that after Amenhotep's death, Tushratta wrote to the widowed Queen Tiye, saying that he had mourned the death of his 'brother.' Letters record snippets of the peace treaty established between the Mitanni and the Egyptians too. Amenhotep's northern vizier was also of Levantine origin. His name was Aper-el, and he'd been a child of the royal nursery – brought up and educated at Egypt's court. His son became an overseer of horses, and recruited men for military service and labour projects.

Interactions with people from the Aegean are also found under Amenhotep III. Fourteen locations in the region are mentioned on a statue base from the king's mortuary temple at Thebes, and a kneeling Minoan is shown in the tomb of Anen, brother of Queen Tiye. More unusually, a medical text from Amenhotep's reign mentions a spell for curing an Asiatic disease, and proceeds to present the spell as pronounced in the Minoan language.

The Amarna Letters

Perhaps the best-known sources for international diplomacy during the reign of Amenhotep III, and into the reigns of his successors, are the Amarna Letters (so-called because they were found at the site of Tell el-Amarna). Providing an insight into the diplomatic correspondence between Egypt and its neighbours, about 380 of these small clay tablets are known, covering a period of about twenty years, give or take a few. Each is inscribed with cuneiform script, and in the Akkadian language: the *lingua franca* of the day. On the whole, the letters are responses to the pharaoh, often quoting from the original letters sent, providing us with some much-needed context. The letters fall into two categories: a minority represent letters sent between the pharaohs and the great kings of the Near East, such as those of Babylon, Assyria, Hatti (the land of the Hittites), Mitanni, and Cyprus, while the rest represent correspondence between Egypt and her vassal kings in the Levant. (Indeed, one fifth of the letters come from Ribaddi of Byblos, an Egyptian vassal, who seems to have been a rather obsessive letter writer.)

For the great kings of the Near East, irrespective of how they presented themselves back home, in the world of diplomatic correspondence they were equals, and referred to each other as 'brothers.' Over time, these powerful states became interconnected and interdependent, reliant on one another for luxurious trade goods to flaunt their status at home. Diplomatic marriage and luxury goods were the main topics of conversation, not political discussion. Some letters also include messages of congratulations between the great kings, particularly when one ascended the throne, as well as – more entertainingly – complaints, particularly regarding the non-arrival or the poor quality of gifts sent. As you might expect, the great kings took offense easily, so all efforts were taken to ensure that proper procedures were carried out and etiquette followed.

The king smiting foreign-
ers was a symbol of Egypt's
domination of its enemies.
This motif is found from the
start of Egyptian civilization. From Karnak Temple.
New Kingdom. Photo: ©
Garry Shaw.

The Egyptian kings recorded their exploits at war in great inscriptions,
carved into the walls of their temples. The Annals of Tuthmosis III at Karnak
Temple. New Kingdom. Photo: © Garry Shaw.

The Egyptians often depicted Nubians in a stylized manner as prisoners. From Abu Simbel. New Kingdom. Photo: © Julie Patenaude.

The head of an Asiatic enemy, seen through the spoked wheel of the royal chariot. As with Nubian and Libyan enemies, Asiatics were depicted in a stylized manner. From the Temple of Seti I at Abydos (in a section decorated under Ramesses II). New Kingdom. Photo: © Garry Shaw.

Egyptian temples were decorated with images of defeated foreign cities, represented as fortified ovals containing their names, surmounted by bound enemies. From Karnak Temple. New Kingdom. Photo: © Garry Shaw.

The nomarchs of Dakhla Oasis managed trade from the town of Ain Asil. They were buried in these massive tombs at nearby Balat. Old Kingdom. Photo: © Garry Shaw.

The Nomarch Ankhtifi's foot can be seen above the tiny cartouche of the king. From the tomb of Ankhtifi, Moalla. First Intermediate Period. Photo: © Garry Shaw.

Archers marching to war with their hunting dogs. From the tomb of Ankhtifi at Moalla. First Intermediate Period. Photo: © Garry Shaw.

In the New Kingdom, the smiting motif was expanded to include scenes of the king charging into war atop his chariot, firing arrows at his enemies. Ramesses II at the Ramesseum. New Kingdom. Photo: © Henning Franzmeier.

In New Kingdom battle scenes, Egypt's enemies were typically shown in chaotic disarray, either dying, fallen or fleeing. From the Battle of Qadesh, depicted at the Ramesseum. Photo: © Garry Shaw.

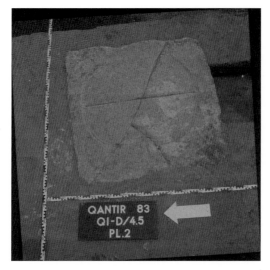

A mould for a Hittite shield, as found in situ at ancient Pi-Ramesses (modern Qantir). New Kingdom. Photo: © Projekt Ramses-Stadt, Norbert Boer.

A dagger found during excavations at Pi-Ramesses (modern Qantir). New Kingdom. Photo: © Projekt Ramses-Stadt, Axel Krause.

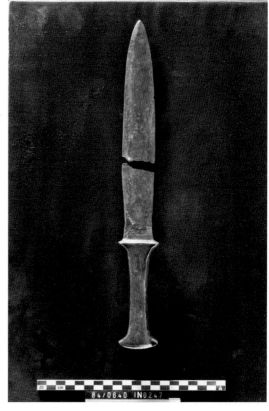

The Great Temple at Abu Simbel served as a symbol of Egypt's domination of Nubia in the New Kingdom. Photo: © Garry Shaw.

Ramesses III defeats the Sea Peoples, as shown in this complex battle scene at Medinet Habu. New Kingdom. Photo: © Garry Shaw.

Ramesses III stands upon fallen enemies to shoot arrows at the Sea Peoples. From Medinet Habu. New Kingdom. Photo: © Garry Shaw.

To keep track of the number of enemies killed in battle, the Egyptians severed and counted the hands or phalli of those killed. Here, a scribe depicted at Medinet Habu counts the hands of the dead. New Kingdom. Photo: © Garry Shaw.

But this could not always be achieved. King Kadashman-Enlil of Babylon, for example, sent a complaint to Amenhotep III after hearing that the chariots he'd presented to Egypt as a royal gift had been displayed among those sent by Egypt's vassal kings, and not reviewed separately. He regarded the situation as an insult. King Tushratta of the Mitanni was similarly offended, but by gifts sent to him by the Egyptians. Standing before his assembled court and dignitaries, Egyptian messengers among them, Tushratta ceremonially unveiled the gifts sent to him from Amenhotep III, only to discover that not everything was made of gold! (Perhaps he should have taken a peek at them before assembling the crowd?) On a later occasion, under King Akhenaten, Amenhotep III's successor, Tushratta complained that Egypt's gift of a solid gold statue turned out to be merely gold-plated wood (shocking!). Probably after double-checking the materials of all the other gifts he'd received, he wrote to Akhenaten asking him to speak with his mother Tiye about the matter. And, to emphasize his displeasure further, he also sent a letter directly to her.

As with any club, you couldn't just turn up and expect to be admitted: there were rules for joining the league of extraordinary kings, and sometimes the efforts of one kingdom to join annoyed certain existing member states. This was the case with Assyria, resurgent at the time and wanting to be recognized as a great state. The letter sent by King Ashuruballit I of Assyria to Akhenaten wasn't particularly offensive in itself: as you might expect, it includes some polite talk, the offer of gifts, and Ashuruballit's acceptance that his predecessors had not yet had a close relationship with Egypt. Nevertheless, a rising Assyria posed a threat to the Hittites, who weren't pleased with the country's attempts to woo the Egyptians. The Babylonians likewise had their own complaints, particularly as they regarded Assyria as part of their own territory. Their king, Burnaburiash II, wrote to Akhenaten, saying that he hadn't sent the Assyrians (his 'own subjects') to the Egyptians and wanted to know what they were doing. He then told Akhenaten not to do business with them, and to send them away 'empty-handed.' Despite these complaints, the Egyptians continued to have diplomatic ties with Assyria, even after Ashuruballit I sent a message moaning about the lack of gold among the latest diplomatic presents from Egypt. (His reason? He was building a new palace and needed the gold for adornment of course.)

Syrian Traders in the Tomb of Kenamun

On the walls of his Theban tomb, Kenamun, the mayor of Thebes under Amenhotep III, included a unique scene of Syrian traders arriving in Egypt to exchange goods. This scene is special due to the detail of the foreign boats and the clothing worn by the Syrians, as well as it being the only depiction of foreign traders disembarking from their vessels to bring goods to an Egyptian market. Although the location of the event is not stated, given Kenamun's position it probably occurred at Thebes.

This detailed scene shows two large sailing vessels, connected by ropes to seven smaller boats, which have reached the shore. The ships' crews wear highly detailed clothing, and are quite clearly Syrian due to their distinctive beards and hairdos (although some have shaved their beards). Men unload cargo, carrying it on their shoulders or in their hands, and some have carried a selection of items before Kenamun, who may have been making purchases on behalf of the local authorities, including the granary of Amun. Large vessels of wine or oil have been brought, as well as two large bulls, and vessels containing precious metals; the latter are quite elaborate in some cases: one is decorated with the figure of a bull, and another has a bull's head-shaped stopper. Two women and a young boy are perhaps being traded as slaves.

The Syrians bring other items before private traders, both men and women, who have set up their small booths on the riverfront. One of the shopkeepers owns a set of scales. Others display various items hanging around their stalls, including textiles, sandals, and foodstuffs. One Syrian merchant offers a large jar of either oil or wine to a shopkeeper.

The Reign of Akhenaten

Amenhotep III died after thirty-eight luxurious years on the throne, leaving a plump mummy and his son Amenhotep IV to take power. Thus began one of Egypt's most unusual phases, referred to by scholars as the Amarna Period. Soon after ascending the throne, Amenhotep IV changed his name to Akhenaten and refocused Egypt's state religion on the Aten, the sun disc, eventually proscribing the official worship of all other gods. With radical changes made to religion, art, and architecture, it wasn't long before the king announced a change of royal residence too. This new city, dedicated to the Aten, would be called Akhetaten ('The-Horizon-of-the-Aten'), better known today as Tell el-Amarna.

Although in older Egyptological literature Akhenaten is often presented by scholars as a pacifist, more focused on his religious movement than warfare, this interpretation is not accepted today. It's true that there's little evidence for large-scale campaigning, but this shouldn't be interpreted as the king having no interest in defending Egypt's interests abroad. Of the campaigns known from the time of Akhenaten, one was certainly waged in Nubia. This occurred during the king's twelfth year on the throne, when a rebellion was instigated by the people of Ikayta, a gold mining region in the desert just south-east of the First Cataract. Like his father, Akhenaten felt no need to personally accompany his Nubian campaign, and so instructed the King's Son of Kush Djehutymose to put an end to the uprising. Although the details of the campaign aren't clear, it seems that the Nubians retreated north of the mining region's wells, but were later discovered and dealt with harshly; Djehutymose took 145 captives, including twelve children, and there were 225 enemy casualties. The Egyptians then impaled the captured Nubians as punishment.

Meanwhile, there were developments in Hatti – the land of the Hittites. In year twelve, while Akhenaten's troops were fighting the rebellious Nubians, the Hittite Empire under King Suppiluliuma I was entering a phase of expansion that would have major repercussions throughout the Near East. Known as the 'Great Syrian Campaign,' this wave of expansionism effectively ended the Mitanni Empire. The Hittite military advance began as a way of halting an anti-Hittite uprising in Isuwa, in south-east Anatolia. But rather than turning back afterwards, happy to have dealt with the troublemakers, the Hittites continued onwards to the Mitanni capital of Washukanni, forcing King Tushratta – a friend and relative by marriage to both Amenhotep III and Akhenaten – to flee. Tushratta was eventually murdered by one of his sons – an unfortunate end to one of Egypt's closest allies. With Mitanni territory now under Hittite control, Suppiluliuma placed Tushratta's brother, Shattiwaza (who had married into the Hittite royal family) on the Mitanni throne to rule in his name. The Hittites next turned their attention to the Mitanni vassal states in Syria, absorbing them into their expanding empire. Among them, unexpectedly, was the city of Qadesh, at the time, an Egyptian vassal.

In these tumultuous times, Qadesh had the unfortunate luck of being caught between a number of competing powers: the Hittites to the north; Egypt's vassals to the south; and the state of Amurru to the west. It also stood at an important entry point into Egypt's Levantine territory from the northeast, giving the Egyptians a tactical reason to want to retain possession of it. By the reign of Akhenaten, the possibility of losing Qadesh hadn't worried the pharaohs for generations; it had remained firmly under Egyptian control since its capture by Tuthmosis III's army. It would have remained securely in Akhenaten's hands too if it weren't for the overeager actions of one individual: the city's king, Shutatarra. Seeing the Hittite army (who apparently had zero interest in taking Qadesh) nearing his territory, Shutatarra decided that the best defence was a good offence, and launched an attack, provoking the Hittites. Suppiluliuma's army swiftly defeated Qadesh's forces, took the city for themselves, and deported Shutatarra to Hatti. Afterwards, the Hittites put Shutatarra's son, a man named Aitakama, in charge of Qadesh as their latest vassal king. Things were starting to get messy.

What followed was a fair amount of double play behind the scenes. After taking power in Qadesh, Aitakama wrote to Akhenaten expressing loyalty to him and absolutely, definitely not to the Hittites. At the same time, Akhenaten was receiving letters from his other vassals, who claimed that Aitakama had been trying to tempt them to switch allegiance to the Hittites; Akizzi of Qatna, for example, wrote to Akhenaten saying that Aitakama had reached out to him, asking him to come to the king of Hatti, but he'd replied, saying that he was a servant of the king of Egypt. By writing to Akhenaten, the vassals were clearly (and cleverly) covering their own backs, just in case they were somehow implicated in Aitakama's treason. Meanwhile, Suppiluliuma was acting as if everything was business as usual, sending friendly letters to Egypt and pretending that nothing had changed.

At some point in the last years of his reign, Akhenaten must have felt that enough was enough, and started planning a campaign to retake Qadesh. His vassals – perhaps again fearful of being implicated in Aitakama's disloyalty – now fell over themselves in a desperate bid to prove their support for the king: Abimilki of Tyre wrote to Akhenaten, pointing out that the ruler of Beirut had offered the pharaoh one ship, the ruler of Sidon had offered two ships, but he would offer all his ships! What happened next is unclear, as we have no further details about the campaign. If it did in fact go ahead, Akhenaten can't have been successful, for Aitakama continued to rule as king of Qadesh into the reign of Tutankhamun and the city didn't yet return to Egyptian control.

Getting to Know Amurru

The Amarna Letters are a wonderful source for learning about the relations between the various vassal states of Egypt and the rulers of these lands. One of the more interesting examples is that of Abdiashirta of Amurru, a region on the edge of southern Syria. Though an Egyptian vassal, this local ruler had an expansionist policy, which particularly bothered another of Egypt's vassals, Ribaddi of Byblos, who frequently wrote to pharaoh to complain. When plundering local cities, Abdiashirta enlisted local 'Apiru' as mercenaries – these were people of various backgrounds, who lived in bands as refugees outside the cities. Most local rulers regarded them as violent outlaws. Abdiashirta's expansionism came to an abrupt halt when he occupied an Egyptian fortress in Sumur, arguing that he had, in fact, saved it. The Egyptians, unconvinced, captured Abdiashirta and dragged him to Egypt, where he was executed. One of his sons, Aziru, then took his place and immediately continued his father's expansionist policy, attacking neighbouring cities (including Sumur), showing a spectacular lack of learning from the past. As Aziru should probably have predicted, he was then summoned to the Egyptian court to explain himself. Surprisingly, he managed to convince the pharaoh that he was not rebellious at all, and that he was actually extremely loyal. The Egyptians allowed him to return to Amurru, where he immediately defected to the Hittite cause.

The Diplomatic Service

Archaeologists found many of the Amarna Letters in the 'Records Office' at Amarna, where such diplomatic correspondence was stored. Among the letters were also thirty-two 'scholarly tablets,' bearing mythological texts, vocabularies, and even literary narratives in cuneiform script. It appears that scribes versed in Akkadian were based in this office, who might themselves have been foreigners or Egyptians trained to understand cuneiform. If the latter, through training by reading and copying Mesopotamian literature and other such texts, foreign learning and cultural understanding would have passed into the Egyptian court as a form of cultural transmission.

There's no evidence for Egyptian dignitaries being permanently based in foreign countries (except for areas under Egyptian control). And foreign ambassadors didn't have an 'embassy' in Egypt; vassals, however, could own property: a chief of Sidon had a house at the city of Pi-Ramesses in the Ramesside Period, for example. Instead of being resident in foreign cities, envoys were sent from Egypt whenever a message needed to be delivered. Such long-distance journeys posed many dangers: King Burnaburiash of Babylon wrote to Akhenaten, saying that his merchants were travelling through Egypt's Levantine territory, on their way to Egypt, when they were beaten and robbed in the town of Hanatun by men sent by the ruler of Akko. As this region was under Egyptian control, he asked that the pharaoh bind the thieves and return the stolen goods.

Even after arriving at their destination, messengers could be treated miserably by their foreign hosts. In one of the Amarna Letters, an envoy is referred to as an 'ass-herder' and a liar. Even worse, Akhenaten forced Assyrian diplomats to stand in the blazing sun, probably whilst attending a royal ceremony or religious event, prompting King Ashuruballit I to write to Akhenaten in frustration. An envoy's return journey could also be problematic. Foreign messengers at pharaoh's court had to wait for the king to find the time to respond to the message delivered. This could take years. Afterwards, even with the reply in hand, they had to wait until the king gave them permission to return home and supplied them with provisions and protection for the journey. Spying at court was probably an element of life as an envoy too, but there is no evidence for it. Nevertheless, intelligence gathering was a topic of conversation between Egypt and her vassal states in the Amarna Letters. Akhenaten asked Zimreddi of Sidon to report to him on everything the vassal heard about Amurru, for example. The king was keeping an eye on his vassals, and expected them to snitch on one another.

Foreigners at Amarna

A great reception was held at Amarna in Akhenaten's twelfth year as king (with the campaigning in Nubia, and the expansion of the Hittite Empire, it must have been a busy year!). This reception is depicted in the tombs of the courtiers Meryre II and Huya at Amarna, which show large scenes of foreigners bringing tribute. Among the dignitaries present, people from the Aegean bring metal vessels; Puntites carry incense; there's Libyans with ostrich feathers and eggs; Asiatics offering horses and chariots; and Nubians bringing gold.

This great event isn't the only evidence for the presence of foreigners at Amarna. A fragmentary papyrus in the British Museum, found at Amarna, depicts two Libyan archers and a kneeling Egyptian. From the posture of the Libyans and the Egyptian, it appears as if the Egyptian is about to be killed. Another scene from the same papyrus shows Egyptians and Mycenaeans running. Although the Mycenaeans aren't identified in writing, their boar's tusk helmets are quite distinctive and unlike those worn by the Egyptians. At the top of this scene, an Egyptian thrusts a dagger into an enemy, probably a Libyan. These scenes are of interest, not only because they suggest that the Egyptians faced an incursion from Libyan groups under Akhenaten (an otherwise unattested event), but because they also suggest that Mycenaeans were fighting alongside the Egyptians, and may even have been living at Amarna. Intriguingly, the house in which this papyrus was discovered contained a complete Mycenaean vessel, further suggestive of a foreign presence. A large number of Mycenaean pottery sherds have also been found during excavations at the city; these probably contained oils brought from the Greek mainland.

The Uluburun Shipwreck: International Sea Trade

During the Amarna Period, a vessel was wrecked off the coast of southern Turkey, in an area today known as Uluburun. When excavated, this ship was found to contain goods from across the then known world: objects from northern Europe and Africa, Mesopotamia to the east, and as far west as Sicily formed its cargo. In total, items from about nine or ten different cultures were revealed, among them a gold ring bearing the name of Queen Nefertiti, wife of Akhenaten. The main commodity onboard was copper, made in an 'ox-hide' shape, followed by tin. There was also gold, silver, electrum, and even jars filled with seeds. Among the finished goods were glass beads, and gold and silver jewellery. Over 100 jars of terebinth resin for ritual use were also being transported, as well as glass ingots for glass production and un-carved hippo ivory.

The traders had stored various ceramic items in *pithoi* (large storage jars), including Cypriote oil lamps. Indeed, most of the ceramics in the *pithoi* seem to be of Cypriote origin, and were a secondary cargo, probably picked up along the journey (the oil lamps hadn't been used). It seems that the crew thought they could sell these items on, perhaps for their quality, but probably also in some cases as status symbols – in Egypt, foreign pottery was sometimes kept for show, and local imitations were even made. These normally display no signs of use, indicating that they were purely for decoration.

Given its contents, the Uluburun wreck has been identified as a merchant ship, travelling anticlockwise around the Mediterranean coastline – it was normal at this time for ships to remain in view of land as much as possible, rather than sailing in the open sea. Following a well-travelled shipping route, the vessel probably stopped at numerous ports along the way; from the north coast of Egypt, up the Levant, it would have stopped at cities such as Ashkelon, Byblos, and Ugarit, before travelling westward along the southern coast of Turkey towards Greece. Then, from Crete, it would have headed southward, crossing the open sea on its way to North Africa, where the aim was probably to reach Mersa Matruh in western Egypt. From there, the circle began again.

So who were these sailors, and where did their ship originate? The ship was probably constructed in the Levant, and based on the objects of daily use found onboard, as well as a votive figurine, its crew were a mixture of people of Levantine and Mycenaean origin. Some of the items found probably belonged to these sailors, including fishing equipment, used oil lamps (which had been charred), a writing panel, weights, and perhaps even some bronze bowls.

Foreign Relations Under Tutankhamun

With the death of Akhenaten, and the shadowy reigns of his immediate successors, we reach Tutankhamun, who came to the throne at a young age and died after only ten years. But although the boy king's reign was short, there was still time for warfare. He was perhaps particularly keen to re-establish Egypt's importance in the east, for in his Restoration Stele – erected at Karnak Temple to record the return to tradition following the Amarna revolution – it's said that before his reign, military ventures into the Levant had failed.

From Hittite sources, it appears that Tutankhamun launched a campaign against Qadesh in his final years on the throne. Egyptian temple blocks decorated under the boy king may depict events from this campaign. Among the dramatic scenes are images of the Egyptians riding their chariots towards an unnamed Syrian fortress; an enemy collapsing over the legs of an Egyptian horse; and Asiatics falling from the battlements of the fortress, while Egyptians, armed with shields and spears, climb ladders to gain entry. The Egyptians took prisoners and marched with severed hands on their spears; and, when sailing along the Nile, triumphant after the battle, they hung a cage from the royal barge, an imprisoned Syrian, dressed in a long robe, held inside. Tribute scenes at Karnak Temple, carved under Tutankhamun, also show Asiatic prisoners (as well as tribute arriving from Punt). All of this infuriated the Hittites, who retaliated by launching an attack on the Egyptian territory of Amka.

General Horemheb led the Egyptian army during this eastern campaign. Consequently, scenes of warfare from his royal mortuary temple – he later became king – perhaps show events from the boy king's reign: here, the battlements of a Syrian city are identified as Qadesh, a royal chariot battle rages, charioteers shoot arrows, and Asiatics lie dead. Horemheb also owned a tomb at Saqqara, constructed and decorated before he became king. The inscriptions stress his reputation among the Hittites and his presence on the battlefield; and in a depiction, bound prisoners are brought before Tutankhamun. Interestingly, another scene in Horemheb's tomb shows a delegation of foreigners from the east arriving at the Egyptian court and speaking to the king through an interpreter.

There was also warfare in Nubia under Tutankhamun. The royal chariot, marching troops, and singing Asiatic and Nubian mercenaries are all depicted on temple blocks; and the Nubians are described as having collapsed, their chiefs slaughtered, because they had violated Egypt's borders. This same campaign might be depicted at Gebel Silsilah, where Horemheb as king is shown returning from a campaign in Kush; again, because Horemheb served as general under Tutankhamun, this event may have occurred during the boy king's reign.

From the Theban tomb of Tutankhamun's King's Son of Kush Huy, we also gain an insight into Egypt's control of Nubia and the responsibilities of this important office in the final days of the 18th Dynasty. Huy mentions his appointment to king's son of Kush under Tutankhamun, and the treasury chief awarding him the seal of office. Afterwards, he held authority from Hierakonpolis to the region of Napata, effectively from southern Egypt down to the Fourth Cataract of the Nile – a significant amount of territory. As part of his work, Huy collected tribute in Nubia, to be presented at a royal audience before Tutankhamun. Huy's men loaded the tribute onto ships, which sailed north to the royal court. There, the various Nubian rulers of Wawat and Kush also presented offerings, prostrating themselves before the king. One Nubian princess arrived by chariot, pulled by two cows. Among the prostrating Nubian rulers was a man named Hekanefer, shown in full Nubian dress with feathers in his hair. Hekanefer, the ruler of Aniba, had earlier been a child of the royal nursery – meaning that he'd been raised and educated at Egypt's royal court with the princes. Interestingly, given his depiction in the Tomb of Huy, in Hekanefer's own tomb at Toshka in Nubia, he wears only Egyptian clothing, and was buried with a traditional Egyptian burial assemblage.

The Death of a Hittite Prince

With Tutankhamun's death at a young age, there was no successor to the Egyptian throne: the 18th Dynasty was in danger of collapse. This is when a rather shadowy series of events occurred, primarily known from the account of the Hittite King Mursilis II, written years after the events described. According to Mursilis, King Suppiluliuma I, his father, was in Carchemish after a successful campaign against the Egyptian territory of Amka – revenge for Tutankhamun's attempt to retake Qadesh. This, Mursilis adds, made the people of Egypt afraid because their king, identified as 'Nibhururiya' – most probably a rendering of Nebkheperure, one of Tutankhamun's royal names – had just died. Then, unexpectedly, a letter from the widowed Egyptian queen arrived, addressed to Suppiluliuma. 'My husband is dead! I have no son', she wrote. 'Yet I am told that you have many sons. If you would give me one of your sons, he would become my husband. Never shall I pick out a servant of mine and make him my husband!'[2]

This surprised Suppiluliuma, so he called a meeting of his council to discuss the matter. Sceptical of the queen's true intent, he sent his chamberlain to Egypt to investigate whether the Egyptians were trying to deceive him (and probably to see whether they had a secret prince stashed away somewhere). The Hittite's lack of trust angered the widowed queen, who sent him a second letter, reiterating her desperate situation. Despite his initial hesitation, Suppiluliuma became convinced of the queen's honesty, and sent his son to Egypt for marriage. The specifics of what happened next are obscure, only the outcome is clear: the Hittite prince died en route to Egypt. After hearing the news, Suppiluliuma became enraged; he accused the Egyptians of murder and sent his army into combat against them.

Tutankhamun dead and the Amarna movement buried, the elderly Vizier Aye, who was perhaps also father of Queen Nefertiti (wife of Akhenaten), ruled as king for a short time. To legitimize his claim to the throne, he might have married Tutankhamun's widow, Ankhesenamun (although evidence for this rests on a single ring bearing their names side by side). Meanwhile, following the death of his son, the Hittite king attacked Egyptian territory in the Levant, breaking an existing treaty between Egypt and Hatti. During this campaign, disaster struck: the troops contracted a plague, which they brought back to Hatti. It ravaged the Hittites for the next twenty years, and was regarded as divine punishment for them breaking the treaty with the Egyptians. Back in Egypt, because Aye had no heir, General Horemheb ascended the throne. His reign was reasonably uneventful: campaigning continued in the Levant and a new treaty with the Hittites possibly came into force, temporarily solving the Qadesh issue. Horemheb's greatest impact on history was his appointment of the Vizier Pa-Ramessu as his successor. It was a decision that would change Egypt's history forever.

Chapter 8

The Hittites and the Ramessides
(1298–1187 BCE)

With the Mitanni now swallowed by the Hittite Empire, and Egypt's dynastic succession severed, the wider world was changing. To make matters worse, a plague swept through the Near East, claiming both King Suppiluliuma I and his eldest son Arnuwanda a year later. This left another royal son, Mursilis II, to briefly reign over the Hittite Empire, after which, in around 1295 BCE, his own son, Muwatallis, came to power. It wasn't the best time to become king of the Hittites. Instability rocked the fringes of the empire, to the north and west, but also in the south, in the borderlands with the Egyptians. Muwatallis had to choose his battles carefully, for to strengthen one region would deplete his troops in another – and this could be disastrous. To enhance his control of the north, Muwatallis put his brother, Hattusilis, in charge of this rebellious territory, where the Kaska people lived. There, Hattusilis fought several campaigns.

Around this time, Muwatallis moved the Hittite capital from Hattusa (modern Boghazkoy in Turkey) in the north to Tarhuntassa – an as yet unidentified city much further south in central Anatolia. Muwatallis' reason seems to have been security: he wanted to keep his capital safe, far from the warfare threatening his empire's stability at its fringes. But its only result was to encourage further rebellion in the north. Hattusilis records that the king – his brother, let's not forget – sent only 120 teams of horses to fight with him against the rebels (who, he says, had 800 teams of horses). Nevertheless, against all odds, he managed to defeat the rebels and reclaimed the land they'd stolen. Muwatallis proclaimed his brother king of the north.

Meanwhile... Back in Egypt

While the Hittites had been expanding their influence, defeating the Mitanni, building their empire, succumbing to plague, and fighting rebellions, a man named Pa-Ramessu, born in the north-east Delta – close to where the Hyksos had once established their capital – had been working his way up through Egypt's military hierarchy. From the position of stable-master, he'd advanced to become commander at the fortress of Sile – a border fortification on the eastern edge of the Delta – and served as a royal messenger in foreign countries. Perhaps due to a combination of skill, pure luck, and nepotism, he was eventually appointed vizier by King Horemheb, who had been a military man himself before ascending the throne. Like his immediate royal predecessors, Horemheb had no surviving children, and having witnessed the problems that an unclear dynastic succession could bring, wanted to leave Egypt in stable hands upon his death. His solution was Pa-Ramessu, who, although quite elderly by this time, had both a son and a grandson to succeed him. And so, when Horemheb died, taking the 18th Dynasty with him to the grave, his appointed successor Pa-Ramessu was crowned as King Ramesses I. The 19th Dynasty, and the Ramesside Period, was born.

Crowned in his advanced age, Ramesses I was unable to rule alone, and so enlisted the help of his eldest son Seti, who took over his father's earlier position as vizier and even led a campaign into the Levant. Ramesses also resumed expeditions to the turquoise mines in Sinai – the first since the reign of Amenhotep III. Stability was returning to Egypt, and less than two years after his coronation, Ramesses was buried in a small tomb in the Valley of the Kings – in his youth, a place that he could never have imagined seeing, let alone being buried. Seti, in turn, perhaps similarly amazed by his family's sudden rise to greatness, took his place on the throne.

The Wars of Seti I

As king, Seti continued the restoration of Egypt following the turmoil of the Amarna Period, sending artisans to re-carve defaced inscriptions across the country, and undertook large-scale building projects, such as his temple at Abydos. He also sought to re-establish Egypt's authority over the Levant. He fought his first campaign as king against the Shasu-Bedouin, who, we are told, were being rebellious: on this occasion, their infighting was causing trouble for people travelling between Egypt and the Levant. Although you might expect such developments to be a bad thing, Seti was rather pleased; as one inscription at Karnak Temple explicitly states, he looked forward to seeing the blood of his enemies and to cutting off their heads. The game afoot, Seti departed from the fortress at Sile – where his father had once been stationed – and travelled by land towards Gaza. Two battles ensued, one fought on the coastal road leading into the Levant, and the other near Gaza. The Shasu attempted to flee from the Egyptians, while others broke their weapons and surrendered.

Later that same year, Seti returned to the Levant with his army, this time heading further north into Lebanon. There, he sent out three divisions to attack different towns: one to Beth Shean, another to Hamath (whose chief was the main instigator of the problems in the region), and a third to Yenoam. Afterwards, the army brought prisoners and booty back to Egypt and presented them before the Theban triad: the gods Amun, Mut, and Khonsu. Seti launched further campaigns over the following years, including one that led to a confrontation with the Hittites somewhere in Syria; this enabled the pharaoh to reaffirm Egypt's control over the routes leading into the northern Levant: a show of strength for this new military dynasty.

For much of our journey through history so far, the various Libyan groups west of Egypt have caused little trouble for the Egyptians; there were occasional raids, and some low level hostilities, but no serious invasions or campaigns. In the reign of Seti I, this all changed. In Seti's fourth or fifth year as king, the Egyptians launched a campaign against the Libyans, marking the first serious hostilities on Egypt's western border since the Middle Kingdom. Significantly, although there's little detail about this campaign, Seti's eldest son, the young Prince Ramesses – the future King Ramesses II – joined the mission; he was probably only fourteen or fifteen years old at the time. Even as a teenager, he was learning the art of war.

After defeating the Libyans, Seti once again turned his attention towards the Levant, and in particular to the issue of Qadesh. By this time, Qadesh, and the surrounding region of Amurru, had been lost to Egypt for about a century. Regaining the city would help Seti to reinstate the 'empire' created by Tuthmosis I and Tuthmosis III, and give the Egyptians a tactical advantage in the region. And so, wanting to 'vanquish the land of Qadesh and the land of Amurru,' Seti led a campaign against Qadesh, successfully taking the city and erecting a victory stele within its walls. But the city, and the surrounding region of Amurru, quickly fell back into Hittite hands. It's not entirely clear what happened, but it seems that Seti might have reached an agreement with his enemies, allowing the Egyptians to retain control over the seaports of the northern Levant, in return for giving up control of Qadesh and Amurru.

In his eighth year as king, Seti fought a war in Nubia, an event recorded on stelae at Sai and Amara West. A messenger informed the king that enemies in the southern region of Irem were plotting rebellion. At first Seti gathered information, and only after learning of the rebels' plans, did he send out his infantry and chariotry. Over the course of seven days, the Egyptian troops recaptured five wells – probably dotted along an important desert route that was being disrupted – and took 434 prisoners. The young Prince Ramesses later led a second Nubian campaign during the reign of his father, accompanied by two of his own sons (each in their own chariot); for the Ramessides – as the 19th and 20th Dynasty kings would be known – war was a family business.

The Reign of Ramesses II

Seti died after seventeen years as king, and passed Egypt's throne to his son Ramesses, aged only around twenty-five at the time. Ramesses would reign for the next sixty-seven years, with much of the first third of his reign dedicated to military endeavours. Idolizing Amenhotep III, Ramesses built on a massive scale across Egypt and Nubia – temples, colossal statues, the royal city of Pi-Ramesses – but also usurped monuments made under his predecessors, carving his name over theirs and even remodelling the faces of some royal statues to reflect the artistic style of his reign. Like Amenhotep III, he was also deified in his own lifetime, and had himself depicted offering to himself in some temple scenes. A self-styled god, who irreversibly changed Egypt's landscape, it should come as no surprise that Ramesses' family life was equally as epic: over his long life, he fathered around a hundred children, including the famous Prince Khaemwaset, who later became a hero in Egyptian literature. And, due to her beautifully painted and preserved tomb at Thebes and presence on religious monuments, Queen Nefertari, Ramesses' first great royal wife, is also one of Ancient Egypt's most famous names. With so much going on during his reign, there's a good reason Ramesses II was later dubbed Ramesses the Great.

Sherden Warriors

As well as Egyptians, Nubians, and Libyans (said to have been captured by Ramesses II and trained as soldiers), Ramesses' army included Sherden warriors – mercenaries, perhaps of Sardinian origin, first mentioned in the Amarna Letters, and one of the various groups classed by the Egyptians as 'Peoples of the Sea,' normally shortened as 'Sea Peoples.' In the final years of Seti I, or the early reign of Ramesses II, the Sherden sailed on warships to attack the Delta, an event described in passing on two of Ramesses' stelae – one from Pi-Ramesses, the other from Aswan. Said to be from the 'Great Green Sea' or the 'midst of the sea,' the Sherden were an unstoppable force that no one could defeat, but Ramesses still managed to capture them and save the Delta, enabling the region to 'sleep' once again. Sherden warriors are then described among Ramesses' troops at the Battle of Qadesh, having been captured and brought by his 'strong arm'; these mercenaries – probably prisoners taken during their attack on the Delta – can be seen in the Qadesh battle reliefs wearing horned helmets. Some acted as royal bodyguards.

The Battle of Qadesh

After his coronation, Ramesses quickly asserted his military power over the Levant. He focused his first campaign on reaffirming control over the coastal region, but it's probable that his main aim all along was to re-take the region of Amurru and the city of Qadesh. It was a foolish goal that would provoke and enrage the Hittites, but one that would associate his new dynasty – recently commoners, let's not forget – with the great kings of the 18th Dynasty and their glorious victories. To take Qadesh would be a much-needed symbol of legitimacy. Ramesses' chance came in his fifth year as king. He would record the events of this famous campaign – generally known as 'The Battle of Qadesh' – on a large-scale on various monuments in Egypt and Nubia: at Abu Simbel, the Ramesseum (Ramesses' mortuary temple at Thebes), Karnak Temple, Luxor Temple, and Abydos. No one would ever forget what happened. Ramesses would not let them.

Following Egyptologist Kenneth Kitchen's reconstruction of events, Ramesses' army was initially formed of four divisions: Amun, Pre, Ptah, and Seth, which started the journey to Qadesh together, marching across northern Sinai and into the Levant. After passing Gaza, in the vicinity of Megiddo, it was decided that an extra division should be created, formed of the best troops from all divisions. This new division, called Nearin, would be sent westward to the coast, and then north to Amurru, before travelling east to join the other divisions at Qadesh. The remaining divisions would travel with the king along the inland route northwards to Qadesh; as these four divisions marched north, they separated from one another: the king and his Amun Division were some distance at the front, followed by the Pre Division, the Ptah Division, and finally the Seth Division.

South of Shabtuna, about 10 km from Qadesh, Ramesses came across two Shasu-Bedouin. Pledging to abandon their allegiance to the Hittites and to serve pharaoh, they convinced the king that the Hittite army was still 190 km away in Aleppo – about nine days march – and were remaining there out of fear of the Egyptians. Now expecting an easy time, the Amun Division set up camp near Qadesh and released the Shasu, who (of course) immediately ran off to tell the Hittites – actually camped on the opposite side of the city – that the Egyptians had fallen for their ruse: their true aim was to report on the Amun Division's location.

This was probably when the Hittites – their army consisting of a coalition of various vassal states – launched their first attack. Bypassing the Egyptian camp, they marched south and sent their chariots against the Pre Division, by now at Shabtuna and unprepared for battle, scattering them and cutting off the Amun Division's support from behind. Next, chasing the Pre Division's fleeing survivors, the Hittites moved northwards, towards the Egyptian camp and the oblivious Amun Division within. Meanwhile, the Amun Division had captured two Hittite scouts, who after some violent encouragement divulged the true location of the Hittites. Unaware no longer, Ramesses ordered an emergency war council be held and sent his vizier along with messengers to hurry up the Ptah Division (clearly they were under no illusion that the distant Seth Division could make it in time). But it was too late. As the king and his advisors spoke, the Hittites broke into the western end of the Egyptian camp. The Pre Division already in disarray, and the Amun Division caught off-guard, the Egyptian camp fell into chaos. Ramesses says that he was totally alone, abandoned by his troops (except for his shield-bearer and butlers, naturally), and in this moment of despair, prayed to Amun. His mind now became joyful, his heart strong, and like a super-hero discovering his powers, he was suddenly unbeatable: on his chariot, he charged at wave after wave of enemies, slaughtering every Asiatic that dared attack him. To Ramesses, Amun had saved him: it was a sign that he was indeed a true, legitimate pharaoh.

In reality, although Ramesses may well have prayed to Amun, it's probable that at this point the Nearin Division arrived. Unaware of the existence of this extra division, the Hittites scattered in surprise, only to regroup near the fords of a river. The Egyptians took chase, forcing the Hittites across the water, and causing many to drown in the process (or to need resuscitation, as was the case with the ruler of Aleppo). The battle was over. The Egyptians returned to their camp. There, Ramesses scolded his troops for abandoning him, saying: 'I defeated a million foreign lands, alone, with Victory-in-Thebes and Mut-is-Content, my great chariot horses. It was they whom I found to support me, when I alone fought many foreign lands! I shall make them eat food, in my presence, every day I am in the palace. It was they whom I found in the middle of the battle, with the Charioteer Menna, my shield-bearer, and with my household butlers who were at my side...'[1]

The next day, Ramesses set out early with the Pre, Amun, Ptah, and the Nearin Divisions (the Seth Division still remained too far behind to join them). Their target was the Hittite camp, but their march was wasted: the Hittites fought off the Egyptians, forcing them to retreat to their own camp. At this point, Ramesses says that he received a message from the Hittite king, begging for peace ('Look, your manifest power is great, and your strength is heavy on the land of Hatti,'[2] he reportedly said). In reality, negotiations probably began: the goal being to reinstate the peace treaty that had existed under Seti I. But Ramesses rejected the offer, and commanded his troops to return home. The Hittites, including Hattusilis (Hittite King Muwatallis' brother), took chase, and briefly invaded the Egyptian territory of Upe before turning back north. The campaign was over. The Egyptians had gained no territory. The king had barely escaped with his life.

Why Advertise the Battle of Qadesh?

By anyone's estimation (except for Ramesses'), the Battle of Qadesh wasn't a fantastic victory for the Egyptians. At best, it was a draw. This is why it is unusual that after returning home, Ramesses decided to publicize the event on his most important monuments, including at Abu Simbel and his mortuary temple, today known as the Ramesseum (construction of which was overseen by a former charioteer and army commander named Amenemone). The accounts, full of royal boasting, focus on the large size of the Hittite coalition army and how Ramesses was abandoned by his troops (as well as his complaints about them). When disaster loomed, Ramesses says, it was the god Amun that saved him and gave him strength to win the day.

The question is why advertise the battle this way? Why not just forget about it? Born a commoner, Ramesses was only the third king of his new dynasty, and perhaps felt the need to legitimize his presence on the throne. To prove their kingliness (and providing an insight into their thinking), both Ramesses II and his father, Seti I, commissioned extensive king lists within their temples at Abydos, proclaiming themselves as the latest in a long line of pharaohs that stretched back to the beginning of time.

During the early 19th Dynasty it had become trendy for people to portray gods as personal saviours on their monuments: they erected stelae in thanks for deities saving or protecting them in times of need or danger, or to thank a god for healing. At Qadesh, if all had seemed lost, Ramesses might truly have regarded Amun as interceding on his behalf, protecting him and his troops in their moment of need. So, by advertising the events at Qadesh, the king was probably just following the popular trend of thanking divine saviours, but on a suitably royal scale. In turn, by publicizing Amun's protection of him, Ramesses was also emphasizing the god's endorsement of his new dynasty; it proved that these commoner kings were not so common any more.

Hail to the King(s) (of the Hittites)

Muwatallis, Ramesses' nemesis at Qadesh, died in around year eight or nine of the pharaoh's reign, just a few years after the famous battle. The Hittite throne then passed to Urhi-Teshub, a prince born of Muwatallis and a concubine, who from the time of his coronation took the name Mursilis III. As a child, Mursilis had been taught by his uncle Hattusilis – the same man that had taken on the northern Kaska rebels to protect the Hittite Empire under Muwatallis, and had later chased Ramesses south from Qadesh. Both tutor and pupil would now direct the future of the empire. Whilst dealing with continued instability in his borderlands – including constant campaigning by Ramesses in the Levant – early in his reign, Mursilis enacted a number of unusual policies, reversing decisions taken by his father. For one, he moved the Hittite capital back to Hattusa from Tarhuntassa, and re-installed certain banished and deposed vassals. It's possible that Hattusilis was behind the scenes influencing Mursilis in his decisions, continuing to 'teach' his old student. Perhaps he disagreed with some of Muwatallis' acts, and now saw an opportunity to reverse them.

But if Hattusilis had been behind some of Mursilis' early decisions, he might have pushed his luck in the end. By Hattusilis' own account, Mursilis eventually stripped him of his territorial influence, restricting his power almost only to the city of Hakpissa in the north. The more experienced warrior and leader did not take this insult lightly. In Ramesses' sixteenth year on the throne, aided by loyal nobles, Hattusilis assembled an army and captured and deposed Mursilis. He must still have had a soft spot for his nephew and former student, for instead of murdering Mursilis (a pretty common practice among rival Hittite royals), the newly crowned King Hattusilis III exiled him to Syria, awarding him control over a number of cities. But in doing so, Hattusilis underestimated the former king. Mursilis immediately plotted his return to power, reaching out to the kings of Babylon and Assyria in an effort to garner military support. Someone must have tipped off Hattusilis about his nephew's activities, for he then sent Mursilis to a more distant land – either to Cyprus or somewhere along the Turkish coastline. But again, Mursilis refused to give up: this time, he fled to Egypt. And when Hattusilis wrote to Ramesses asking for his nephew's extradition, the pharaoh refused.

Egypt's relations with the Hittites had hit an all time low; a state of war still existed between them, and the Egyptians now harboured a former Hittite king in exile. But in choosing how to respond, Hattusilis had to take wider concerns into consideration. The Assyrians had expanded their territory, swallowing the eastern Hittite territory of Hanigalbat (itself earlier the Mitanni homeland), pushing their border to Carchemish (today on the border between Syria and Turkey); Egypt continued to campaign in the empire's south, causing trouble in the Levant; and the Kingdom of Ahhiyawa (part of the Mycenaean world) was destabilizing the west. It became prudent, for the good of the empire, for Hattusilis to open peace talks with someone.

Peace and 'Friendship'

That someone turned out to be Ramesses II. Not wanting to deal with Assyria – a rogue province from the Hittite perspective – Hattusilis could at least secure his southern border and end one war, and that meant approaching Egypt – the lesser of two evils. There's no record of Ramesses' thoughts on this development, but he probably recognized a propaganda coup – a chance to present his foe as begging for peace. Immediately, envoys started travelling back and forward between the two empires, hammering out the details of a treaty. By the twenty-second year of Ramesses' reign, eighteen articles had been agreed, receiving the royal seals of both kings. Each kingdom kept an official version of the treaty on a silver tablet, both now lost, but three copies of the text still survive: two in Egyptian, at Karnak Temple and the Ramesseum, and one from Hattusa, written in cuneiform. Among the clauses, the Hittites and Egyptians agreed to extradite refugees; to help each other in times of crisis; to return fugitives unharmed; and made a pact of non-aggression and mutual assistance. The Egyptians also accepted Hattusilis as the true king of the Hittites, rather than as a usurper (accusations that seem to have particularly irked the Hittite king since his rise to power), and gave up any claim to Amurru and Qadesh, putting an end to a century of squabbling over this poor city.

The two warrior kings may have sealed a peace treaty, ending years of hostility, but this didn't mean that they'd put the past entirely behind them.

About fifteen to twenty years after the Battle of Qadesh, Hattusilis complained to Ramesses about the pharaoh's 'account' of the battle, questioning its veracity. In his reply, Ramesses simply explained how events had unfolded from his own perspective, repeating the 'official' version carved across Egypt's temple walls. He particularly emphasized how he'd won the battle single-handedly, away from his chariots and troops. Given that Hattusilis was physically present at Qadesh, Ramesses' reply can only have infuriated him further – perhaps this was the pharaoh's intention. It shouldn't be surprising then that this wasn't the only exchange about the battle. In another letter, Hattusilis expressed disbelief about Ramesses' claim to have fought alone, without his army and chariotry. Ramesses took offence, and insisted that it was the truth. One wonders, by this point, did Ramesses truly believe his own story? Or did he really just enjoy annoying Hattusilis.

Thirteen years after agreeing their peace treaty, the Egyptians and Hittites decided to solidify their relations further: one of Hattusilis' daughters would marry Ramesses II. The event was meant to bring the two families closer together, but ended up reigniting tensions. Angry about delays caused by the Hittites, Ramesses wrote to Queen Pudukhepa, wife of Hattusilis, to enquire about the whereabouts of promised royal gifts that had failed to materialize. Unfazed, in her reply, she told the pharaoh about difficulties at the palace, including a fire, and how what had been left was donated to the gods by Urhi-Teshub (Mursilis – the deposed and exiled Hittite king). For confirmation, she suggested that Ramesses go ask Urhi-Teshub about it – after all, he was there in Egypt!

Despite such arguments (and probable further digs about the Urhi-Teshub/Mursilis incident), Ramesses married Hattusilis' daughter as planned. The princess and her entourage were escorted from Hittite territory to Egypt by a high-level Egyptian charioteer (and later king's son of Kush) named Hori, and after her arrival, she became known as Queen Maathorneferure. She would go on to spend time at the royal harems in both Pi-Ramesses in the Delta, and Gurob in the Faiyum Oasis. At long last, a golden era of peaceful relations had truly begun – according to stelae erected by Ramesses to celebrate the marriage – when a person could travel through the Levant as far as the Hittite Empire without putting his life in danger.

Egypto-Hittite relations now blossomed, to the extent that sometime between years thirty-six and thirty-eight of Ramesses II's reign, the Hittite Crown Prince Hishmi-Sharrura (the future King Tudkhalia IV) visited Egypt during the winter months. And it's even possible that Hattusilis himself came to Egypt. Ramesses certainly invited him, offering to meet his 'brother' in the southern Levant, but the Hittite king seems not to have made the journey. Hattusilis had suffered from health problems his entire life, particularly with his eyes, and had now apparently been overcome by a condition known as 'fire of the feet' – some form of inflammation. (Perhaps he just didn't want to see the Qadesh battle scenes plastered across Ramesses' temple walls.) Even though Hattusilis probably didn't make it to Egypt in the end, it didn't affect diplomatic ties between the two kingdoms, for sometime between years forty to forty-five of Ramesses' reign, the pharaoh married a second Hittite princess.

Peace may have arrived, but key Egyptian garrisons continued to operate in the Levant, particularly those at Gaza, Dor, and Beth Shean, where soldiers lived in buildings constructed and decorated according to Egyptian architectural styles. There were Egyptian temples too, and hybrid temples that combined Egyptian and Levantine traditions. Soldiers created their own pottery anthropoid coffins, and some – perhaps even Asiatics – were mummified. Egyptians living in the Levant also married locals, adding to the mixing of cultures.

Egypt may have entered a new cosmopolitan age, with people freely moving to the country, but slaves, both Asiatic and Nubian, still entered in large numbers, some sent by Egypt's Asiatic vassals at the pharaoh's command; a lawsuit from the reign of Ramesses II mentions how one Egyptian paid four *deben* (about 91 g) and one *qite* (a tenth of a *deben*) of silver for a female slave; this slave girl, bought from merchants, was given the name Gemniherimentet, meaning 'I found her on the West (of Thebes).'

Tourism in Ancient Egypt

Travel for pleasure is hard to trace in the Egyptian record before the New Kingdom. Certainly there was a lot of movement: people constantly travelled up and down the Nile on business, and messengers, traders, and soldiers frequently passed beyond Egypt's borders. Such ancient travellers might have stopped at historic sites during their 'business trips' to marvel at the great monuments of the past as a perk of the job.

What could be called 'religious tourism' also existed; this is particularly noticeable in the Middle Kingdom, when people across the country hoped, at least once in their lives, to make the pilgrimage to Abydos and witness the annual festival of Osiris. By the early Middle Kingdom, the Egyptians regarded the 1st Dynasty tomb of King Djer at Abydos as the Tomb of Osiris, and used it to mark the final stop in the Osiris procession (it can perhaps be regarded as an early 'heritage attraction').

In the New Kingdom, tourists particularly enjoyed visiting the Old Kingdom pyramids – already over 1,000 years old by the time of Ramesses II. In year fifty of Ramesses II, a scribe named Ptahemwia left a graffito on the 5th Dynasty tomb of the Vizier Ptahshepses at Abu Sir, saying that he had travelled there with his father, the Scribe Yupa, 'to see the shadow of the pyramids.'[3] Similarly, the Scribe Aakheperkareseneb visited the Pyramid of Sneferu at Meidum in the forty-first year of Tuthmosis III's reign, exclaiming that he found it as if heaven were within it. But perhaps the most popular tourist site of all was the Step Pyramid of Djoser at Saqqara, where numerous people left graffiti in ink or hastily scratched into the walls. One such tourist, the Treasury Scribe Hednakht, arrived in year forty-seven of Ramesses II to 'walk about, and amuse himself on the west of Memphis'[4] and left a prayer to various gods.

A Cold Pint of Kizzuwatna in Pi-Ramesses?

Louis XIV had Versailles. Henry VIII loved Hampton Court. But for Ramesses II, a simple (royal) palace would not be enough: he wanted to build an entire city (and slap his name on it). Pi-Ramesses – 'The House of Ramesses' – was built over Ramesses' hometown in the north-eastern Delta. Scribes composed poems in honour of the new city's splendours: it boasted beautiful balconies, they said; was filled with flourishes of lapis-lazuli and malachite; and everyone wanted to move there – in fact, given that the poems were composed under Ramesses II, it all feels a little like they were trying to convince people to relocate.

If true, it worked. Due to the city's location, Pi-Ramesses quickly became a cultural melting pot, attracting traders from across the world. If you fancied some of that high-quality Amurru wine, it was the place to go. Tempted by the taste of Kizzuwatna's famous beer? Head to Pi-Ramesses, people would have told you. Pottery at Pi-Ramesses reflects the presence of traders or ambassadors from Cyprus, the Levant, and Anatolia. The chief of Sidon – an Egyptian vassal – even had a house at the city. Mycenaeans were also present: archaeologists have found the remains of their vessels, used to transport expensive oils, as well as a scale from a boar tusk – part of a Mycenaean helmet. Exotic animals came to Pi-Ramesses too – either alive or dead – including giraffes and elephants.

This multiculturalism is reflected in the city's main temples: according to Papyrus Anastasi III, the temple to Amun stood in the west; Seth in the south; Astarte (a Near Eastern goddess) in the east; and Wadjet in the north.

A block from the temple of Astarte has been uncovered during excavations, as well as a door lintel bearing the name of the Near Eastern god of war, Reshef. This isn't too surprising: Asiatic gods, such as Reshef, Baal, Hauron, Astarte, Anat, and Qadesh all started to be worshipped in Egypt during the New Kingdom. And with peace, this only increased; interestingly, their worship was not limited to the elite, for devotion to them is found at all levels in society. A northern suburb of Memphis even had a temple to Baal, and became an area where Canaanite merchants gathered.

Pi-Ramesses prospered for another reason too: with access to the Mediterranean Sea via a Nile tributary and located only a short distance by land from the Levant, it became the port for Egypt's military ships and a base for the army. This has dramatically been shown through excavations over the past thirty years at Qantir – the modern village now atop the remains of Pi-Ramesses. In one area, archaeologists revealed horse stables; these formed a massive structure, 15,000 metres squared, where the Egyptians kept at least 480 horses. Items of daily life, found in the stable areas, show that stable workers passed their time playing games. To the east of this area, the excavators uncovered an area of specialized workshops and a columned courtyard – probably an exercise court that once resounded with the clip-clopping of hooves, given that hoof prints, preserved in the earth, were found there.

At the workshops, chariots, and items used by charioteers, were produced and repaired. Like an assembly line, each workshop had a particular specialization: bronze casting, leatherwork, wood-working. One even created equipment from bone, such as arrowheads. Pi-Ramesses had faience factories, and glass-making and glass colouring workshops too. Excavations have revealed pieces of chariots, including a bronze nave cap, nails for holding chariots together, decorative elements, and even a bronze horse bit. There were also weapons, among them: bronze short swords, bronze lance-tips, and projectiles used to split open metal armour. Scales from armour were also found, some made of bone, others of yellow-glazed and red-glazed pottery. Egyptians, Hittites, and Mycenaeans were present in these workshops, probably putting their expertise to work.

One curious discovery at Pi-Ramesses was that the Egyptians were producing Hittite shields. Excavators found moulds for the bronze fittings of these shields, including a variation with a stylized bull's head as decoration; this was a symbol of the Hittite weather god. Why were the Egyptians producing Hittite military equipment? It's possible that a Hittite garrison was based at Pi-Ramesses, perhaps as a show of cooperation, but they may also have been troops serving the Hittite princess that had married Ramesses II.

Ramesses in Nubia: Divinity and War

In Nubia, Ramesses II initiated an ambitious construction campaign, creating seven new temples over the course of his life. His aim there, like Amenhotep III before him, was to present himself as a divinity to the Nubian people. At his temple at Wadi es-Sebua, Ramesses is depicted worshipping himself among the gods; and similarly, at the Great Temple at Abu Simbel, he offers to a divine image of himself and sits among the gods in the temple's sanctuary.

The two temples at Abu Simbel – the Great and Small Temples – were Ramesses' greatest monuments in Nubia; their location, close to the river, meant that all ships would see the four colossi of the king, carved into the rock, when sailing by. These temples were constructed using slave labour, brought from 'all foreign countries,' we're told, and people from Syria worked the temple land. Scenes of Nubian war decorate the interior of the Great Temple. Ramesses returned to Egypt from this campaign with prisoners (and brought his pet lion along too), sending captured Nubians north, Asiatics south, Shasu-Bedouin west, and Libyans to the hilltops, taking each group as far from their homelands as possible. At the temple of Derr, a further Nubian campaign is depicted, fought in the region of Irem sometime between Ramesses' years fifteen to twenty as king.

Many king's sons of Kush served during the long reign of Ramesses II. Among them was Paser, who restored Abu Simbel after an earthquake struck; although he repaired the interior of the Great Temple, and fixed one of the arms of a colossus outside, he was unable to rejoin the upper half of another colossus, which had fallen to the floor. The King's Son of Kush Setau, Paser's successor, is also well-known, mainly because he left many inscribed monuments in Nubia, including a stele from Wadi es-Sebua that mentions that he served as army commander during Ramesses' campaign in Irem. He also built Ramesses' temple at Wadi es-Sebua, using slaves captured in Libya (as reported on a stele belonging to an officer named Ramose).

The Reign of Merenptah

By the time of Ramesses II's death, Merenptah, the oldest surviving royal prince (the thirteenth!), was sixty to seventy years old, yet he still managed to reign for about twelve years. Although peace with the Hittites continued, fresh problems emerged to challenge the aging pharaoh. In particular, early in his reign, Merenptah was forced to send his army to quell rebellions at

Ashkelon, Gezer, and Yenoam in the Levant, fighting groups including the Shasu and the Israelites (their first mention on an Egyptian monument). Meanwhile, the Hittites were experiencing a period of decline; there was instability on the fringes of their territory and widespread famine, forcing them to turn to the Egyptians for help. And so, following the terms of the peace treaty sealed by his father, Merenptah sent ships filled with grain to the Hittite Empire.

There was also trouble with Libya. Egypt's relations with the people to its west had become increasingly tense since the start of the 19th Dynasty, when Seti I had campaigned in the region. Ramesses II witnessed this campaign firsthand, and during his own reign, aware of the growing threat, had constructed a series of fortresses, stretching from the western Delta at Kom el-Hisn, all the way to the coastline at Mersa Matruh, a distance of about 200 km. These forts defended the Delta, monitored the movement of people, and perhaps protected trade ships arriving from Crete. Due to the forts' proximity to one another, the troops could quickly relay messages between them, speeding up the Egyptians' reaction to any potentially threatening behaviour from passing Libyan groups. Given the clear and present danger posed by the Libyans, as well as the effort expended on constructing these western forts under Ramesses, it's odd then that Merenptah abandoned them.

Indeed, Merenptah probably wished that he'd kept the forts operational. In his fifth year on the throne, a coalition of Libyan groups – the Libu and Qeheq – along with the 'foreign peoples of the sea' or 'Sea Peoples' as they're better known today, attacked the Nile Valley. Quite unusually, the Egyptians recorded the name of the Libyan chief leading the campaign: he was Mariyu, son of Didi, and he'd brought his wife and children along with his warriors (who'd brought their families as well); this wasn't a rapid military raid on Egyptian territory, but a migration. Both the Libyans and the Sea Peoples – comprised of various groups from the Aegean and Turkey, including the Aqaiwasha, Tursha, Lukku, Sherden, and Shekelesh – were moving due to famine. Merenptah says that his enemies had been in Egypt for some months; by the time of the battle, they'd already reached Bahariya and Farafra Oases, entering Egypt in search of food. They may even have made it as far as Memphis and Heliopolis.

Merenptah gave his troops two weeks to prepare for the campaign, and was quite assured of success thanks to the god Ptah appearing to him in a dream and handing him the sword of victory. Once these two weeks had passed, perhaps on a date and location agreed with his enemies, the Egyptians set up camp. After waiting a full day, the Libyans and Sea Peoples arrived; it was a large coalition, 16,000 strong, including whole families hoping to settle in Egypt. The battle began at dawn the next day, and lasted for six hours. The Egyptians were ultimately victorious. According to the Egyptians, Mariyu was so afraid that he fled the battle, leaving his sandals, bow and quiver in his haste, as well as everything else that was with him (including his wife). The Egyptians captured all of these goods: silver and gold, weapons, and the chief's wife's adornments, and took them back to the palace with the prisoners.

The Egyptians pursued Mariyu, but he escaped, passing one of Egypt's remaining operational western forts during the night. The fort's commander later wrote to Merenptah saying, 'If he lives, he won't be raised up again. He is fallen, a rebel to his army.'5 As you can imagine, back at home, the surviving Libyans were furious at their chief for abandoning them, leading to infighting among their commanders and tents being burnt. The Egyptian commander goes on to say that the Libyans then appointed a new chief from among Mariyu's brothers, and that they fought Mariyu whenever they saw him, indicating that the ex-chief did at least make it home. Despite the political problems he now faced in Libya, being alive and away from Egyptian territory was a positive outcome for Mariyu, because the pharaoh had issued a kill-on-sight order to his officers if they ever came across him in Egypt again. The fortress commander's letter shows that the Egyptians were keeping an eye on the Libyans after the battle, and received intelligence on the activities of the Libyan leaders. And Mariyu wasn't the only Libyan to flee the battle: one of Merenptah's stele, – today known as 'The Israel Stele' – suggests that many others also made a run for it: the archers, for example, are said to have thrown down their bows, unbound their water-skins, and discarded their packs before fleeing.

After the battle, the Egyptian army returned home. Donkeys pulled carts filled with thousands of uncircumcised Libu phalli, while from the Sea Peoples, who were apparently circumcised, the Egyptians severed a hand from each body instead. This shows that the Egyptians brought the hands and uncircumcised phalli of defeated enemies back to Egypt, probably to be presented before the gods in heaps. Thousands of prisoners were also taken, the majority of whom were sent to work in the temples or made to fight for the Egyptian army. Others were impaled to the south of Memphis.

Before the battle, the Libyan coalition had tried to encourage an uprising in Nubia, but the ensuing rebellion began too late – the Egyptians had already dealt with the Libyans and were able to send their forces south without distraction. There is little detail about this Nubian campaign, other than the harsh punishments inflicted on the rebels of Wawat and Kush. Regarding the rebels of Wawat, one stele relates, 'their great ones have been set on fire, in the presence of their relatives(?) (As for) the remainder: their hands were cut off because of their crimes. Others had their ears and eyes carried off and taken to Kush. They were made into heaps in their towns.'[6]

Merenptah and Ugarit

According to a letter found at Ugarit, under Merenptah, the king of Ugarit asked for an Egyptian sculptor to be sent to his city, for he wanted a statue of the pharaoh to be erected in front of the Temple of Baal. Although Merenptah denied the request, he did send many other luxury goods in place of the sculptor, including ebony and textiles. A sword bearing Merenptah's name was found during excavations at Ugarit, and the king sent grain supplies to the city, in the same manner as he did for the Hittites; one letter, found in a house at Ugarit, mentions that this grain was to relieve a famine, probably a result of the increasing drought in the region.

Years of Intrigue

Following Merenptah's death, his eldest son, Seti II, came to the throne, but was challenged soon after by a man named Amenmessu, who was probably another son of Ramesses II or Merenptah. Partly successful in his bid (but far from being king of the north and south, as he claimed), Amenmessu ruled the Theban area from the second to fourth years of Seti II's reign, at which point the usurper suddenly vanishes from history. Afterwards, Amenmessu's name was removed from all monuments and Seti II's put in its place. Seti died only two years later, after having spent a chunk of his reign restoring royal authority across the country. He was only around twenty-five years old.

The throne then passed to Siptah, a young boy with a deformed left foot, who was probably the son of the usurper Amenmessu and a Syrian woman named Soteraja – with there being no surviving heirs of Seti II, he seems to have been the only choice left. Due to Siptah's young age, Tawosret – who had been the great royal wife of Seti II, and was probably a granddaughter of Ramesses II – acted as queen regent, becoming known as the great regent in all the land. At the same time, an intriguing figure suddenly rose to prominence: a man named Bay. Bay had been a royal scribe and butler under Seti II, and, like many royal butlers at the time, was of foreign descent, referring to himself on his monuments as 'a foreigner from that northern land.' This all changed under Siptah's rule: Bay would now serve as chancellor in the entire land – a rather epic rise.

Bay is also known from correspondence sent to the king of Ugarit, Ammurapi; in this letter, which for the most part cannot be read, Bay is referred to as Beya and holds the title, chief of the troops of the great king in the land of Egypt. The content of this letter is unexpected, not only because it shows that Bay held military power, but because letters are normally sent between kings, not from a named courtier to a king. Back in Egypt, equally unexpected are reliefs depicting Bay equal in size to the king and queen. Size mattered in Egyptian art, with rank communicated through each figure's stature. No commoner had ever been shown at the same scale as the king and queen before this time.

On monuments, Bay is also described as one 'who established the king upon the seat of his father,' indicating that he played some role in putting Siptah on the throne; some scholars speculate that he may have been related to Siptah's Syrian mother, a connection that would explain his sudden rise to power. Bay also began construction of a tomb for himself in the Valley of the Kings. Although various non-royals are buried in the Valley, their tombs tend to be rather small and undecorated – there, the tomb's proximity to a king's burial highlighted the individual's special status, not its decoration. Bay's tomb, however, was built and decorated in the royal style, being similar to those made for Siptah and Tawosret. More oddly, the foundation deposits within Siptah's mortuary temple bear Bay's name and titles.

Despite his unusual prominence, Bay's period of influence didn't last long. An ostracon, discovered at the village of Deir el-Medina – home of the artisans who excavated and decorated the royal tombs in the Valley of the Kings – records a message delivered by Paser, scribe of the tomb, to the workmen. Dated to year five of an un-named king, but almost certainly Siptah – the very pharaoh that Bay had helped put on the throne – it describes Bay as 'the great enemy,' and says that the king had killed him. Unfortunately, we don't know what events led to Bay's fall from grace.

Other events of interest from Siptah's reign derive from brief statements found on private monuments. One inscription at Abu Simbel, for example, mentions that the Royal Messenger to Every Country and Charioteer of His Majesty Rekhpehtuf travelled at the king's command in the first year of Siptah's reign to install the new King's Son of Kush Seti. Meanwhile, the Royal Messenger to Every Country Neferhor left a graffito at Buhen's south temple, saying that in the first year of Siptah's reign, he brought rewards for the governors of Nubia and conveyed the newly installed King's Son of Kush Seti on his first tour of inspection.

Siptah died in the sixth year of his reign – about a year after Bay's execution – leaving the throne without a male successor. Consequently, Queen Tawosret came to power as pharaoh, reigning for between eight and eleven years. Although the Near East had been experiencing instability during the last decades of the 19th Dynasty, Egypt's relations with the Levant continued to flourish. Two hoards of gold and silver found by archaeologists at Bubastis included precious items, seemingly of Syrian origin, inscribed with the names of Seti II and Tawosret, and her name as king has been found on artefacts from Sidon.

The events surrounding the end of Tawosret's reign – and with her the end of the 19th Dynasty – remain in shadow. The Elephantine Stele, inscribed at the start of the 20th Dynasty, refers to an 'Asiatic' taking control of Egypt, aided by others. In this text, Egypt is saved from a period of darkness by King Sethnakht, the first ruler of the 20th Dynasty, a man of unclear origins, who dedicated his first two years as pharaoh to restoring order across the country. Papyrus Harris I, from the reign of Ramesses IV, also mentions these complex times, making reference to an Asiatic named Irsu – meaning 'he made himself.' This man cannot currently be associated with any known individual (given that Bay was already dead), and so was perhaps an invader: the Asiatic mentioned on the Elephantine Stele.

Taken together, these texts say that before the rise of Sethnakht there had been a time of lawlessness, when temples were neglected and Egyptians fought one another. Then, during the 'empty years,' Irsu the Asiatic came to seize power and plunder Egypt. We're told that the Asiatics fled when Sethnakht arose to restore order, discarding gold, silver, and copper behind them. Through all of this, there's no reference to the fate of Tawosret, who simply vanishes from history. Perhaps she died without a successor and chaos ensued. Or perhaps she died during the Asiatic invasion. We may never know.

Chapter 9

Sea Peoples, Libyans, and the End of the New Kingdom (1187–1064 BCE)

W hen the curtain rises after the darkness at the end of the 19th Dynasty, a new king sits on Egypt's throne: Sethnakht, of the 20th Dynasty. There's no information about his origins, and he makes no claim to royal descent on any of his monuments. Still, it's possible that he was a descendant of Ramesses II, for his name includes mention of Seth, just like Seti I and II. And, as Seth was a popular deity in the northeast Delta, where the Ramesside family originated, there's at least some possible connection. Otherwise, the only other clue to the circumstances surrounding Sethnakht's rise to power is his statement that he was chosen by the gods from 'myriads,' suggesting competition for the throne. Yet even after his successful rise, problems remained: according to one source, his enemies were only quashed by the second year of his reign.

With order once again restored across the Two Lands, after only four short years, Sethnakht died, passing his crown to his son, Ramesses III, a man obsessed with Ramesses II. Like his idol, Ramesses III is known for his architectural achievements and his military campaigns. But unlike the second Ramesses, Ramesses III didn't need to go in search of war – it came to him. Over the thirty-two years of his reign, he faced two Libyan invasions and one by the Sea Peoples. He may have also dealt with a rebellion in Nubia, although the evidence for this is extremely limited. (Nubians are among the people said to have been captured by the king and given to the temple of Amun, and a Nubian war scene is depicted on the walls of the king's mortuary temple, among other slight sources.)

Ramesses' First Libyan Campaign

The first of the Libyan invasions faced by Ramesses III occurred during his fifth year on the throne, an event described in detail – like all his major campaigns – on the walls of his mortuary temple at Medinet Habu in Thebes. He fought this campaign against a coalition of various Libyan groups, namely the Libu, Soped, and Meshwesh. Unfortunately, no information is provided as to where the battle took place, though it most probably occurred in the western Delta. The texts do inform us, however, that the Libyans had been crossing Egypt's borders and were robbing the country on a daily basis.

Further unusual details are provided in the battle account's prelude: the Libyans had 'begged' Ramesses to appoint a chief to rule them – so the text relates – leaving the king no choice but to install a 'child of the Tjehenu' as chief. The Libyans, despite 'begging' for this to occur, then rejected the pharaoh's appointment, setting in motion the march to war. It's an odd detail, and perhaps indicates that the Egyptians wanted to impose some kind of central control over what was a tribal society – this would have given the Egyptians a representative among the Libyans to deal with during negotiations. A more compelling reason for the invasion, however, was the widespread famine affecting the eastern Mediterranean world at the time. We've already seen how Merenptah battled Libyans, who were fighting to gain access to food. And there's no reason to think that the situation in Libya had improved by the time of Ramesses III. A second mass movement towards the plentiful fields of Egypt was an inevitability.

As was normal, before launching his campaign, Ramesses III first secured divine sanction. Depictions at Medinet Habu show the king in the presence of the gods Ptah and Thoth, and being handed a *khepesh*-sword by the enthroned Amun – a symbol of Ramesses' inevitable success. From there, accompanied by the war god Montu, standard-carrying priests escorted him from the temple. Surrounded by his troops, who were armed with spears, bows, *khepesh*-swords, and shields, he stepped onto his chariot, while soldiers played bugles, sounding the start of war. The king and his charioteers then rode into battle, the infantry running alongside them. In the war scenes, Ramesses is presented as massive in scale, riding in his chariot, crushing his enemies beneath its wheels and the hooves of his horses. In contrast to the ordered, composed image of the pharaoh, the battle raging among the smaller figures is chaotic: Egyptians shoot their arrows at the Libyan enemies (each dressed in a long robe with pointed beards and a side-lock of hair), who collapse in pain, the arrows protruding from their bodies. Sea Peoples groups are also present, working with the Egyptians, fighting and capturing their enemies, presumably as mercenaries.

The Egyptians successfully defeated the Libyan invasion, and afterwards celebrated at a fortress modestly called 'Usermaatre Meriamun (Ramesses III) is the Repeller of the Tjemehu-Libyans.' There, standing at a balcony, Ramesses addressed the assembled elite, the heads of his soldiers bowed.

In front of them, three piles of hands and two piles of phalli were counted and recorded by scribes. A second celebratory scene shows Ramesses nonchalantly perched on the back of his chariot, watching as his men drag rows of bound Libyans before him. Three additional piles of enemy hands lie in heaps, and a further pile of phalli. The Egyptian troops and foreign mercenaries then marched home, dragging along the bound Libyan prisoners with them – the rope tied around their necks. Back in Egypt, the king presented his prisoners before the Theban triad: the gods Amun, Mut, and Khonsu.

Many of these Libyan prisoners were dealt with harshly; as the Medinet Habu inscriptions relate, leaders among the Libyans were burned to death and others had their hearts removed. I think it's safe to say that both forms of execution are particularly unpleasant, but from the Egyptian perspective, the sentence continued beyond the painful, physical act of death. According to Ancient Egyptian belief, a preserved body (or statue) was required for the soul to continue to exist in the afterlife, and without a heart, a person couldn't be judged by Osiris, for it was needed during the weighing of the heart ceremony in the god's judgement hall. No heart meant no chance of joining the blessed dead. To the Egyptians, they weren't simply wiping these Libyans from existence in this life, but from the next one too. In addition to the cruel punishments meted out to the captured Libyans, the Medinet Habu inscriptions also contain another unexpected detail: they provide the names of specific Libyan enemies, including a whole succession of Libu rulers, comprising Didi, Mishken, Mariyu, Wermer, and Tjetmer. Perhaps Ramesses wanted to emphasize that he'd defeated the family line that included Mariyu, the chief that had fled following Merenptah's campaign – a family line that would now cease with Tjetmer.

'The Sea Peoples' and the End of the Late Bronze Age

'The foreign countries made a conspiracy in their islands. All at once the lands were removed and scattered in the fray. No land could stand before their arms, from Hatti, Kode, Carchemish, Arzawa, and Alashiya (Cyprus) on, being cut off at [one time]. A camp [was set up] in one place in Amor (Amurru). They desolated its people, and its land was like that which has never come into being.'[1]

This is how the Sea Peoples are introduced in the Medinet Habu inscriptions. The ancient author paints a picture of scattered groups, originally islanders, pushing across the world, devastating every city in their path until they reach Egypt and face Ramesses III. At Medinet Habu, various groups are identified among them, including the Peleset, Tjekeru, Shekelesh, Danuna, and Washash. Despite these specific references, the question of the Sea Peoples' origins remains difficult to answer: all that scholars can suggest at present is that they were most probably displaced and disparate groups from the Aegean and southern Turkey, whose movements were motivated by famine and drought. As they progressed over a fifty year period, large parts of the eastern Mediterranean world, from Anatolia to Cyprus, and south through the Levant, were attacked and burned. This is the traditional picture, but it would be wrong to place the blame for this destruction solely on the Sea Peoples; take, for example, the fate of the Hittites.

During the period of the Sea Peoples' migration, the Hittite Empire, now under Suppiluliuma II, collapsed. Though this is sometimes said to be the fault of the Sea Peoples, some scholars now argue that the final death blow to the empire was a popular uprising. An archaeological analysis of the final destruction of Hattusa – the Hittite capital – shows that the attackers only targeted the city's royal and government buildings – effectively anything associated with the elite. In this reconstruction, these were specific attacks by people who knew the city, not the acts of rampaging, looting hordes, running amok in the streets. Another interpretation is that the buildings were emptied and abandoned before their destruction. The Hittite elite, led by their king, simply left the city, disappearing from history's spotlight. Hattusa, abandoned, was later burnt down.

In either scenario, what the Hittites experienced was not simply a sudden wave of unstoppable migrating enemies, but the effects of what is referred to as a 'systems collapse,' spreading across the eastern Mediterranean world. This was the end result of years of developing international problems: famine and drought had long afflicted the Hittites and other peoples of the eastern Mediterranean (remember that Merenptah had sent the Hittites grain supplies during his reign), increasing tensions between the ruling elite and the common people. And the Hittites had been fighting constant rebellions on the edges of their territory. With the ensuing instability, the flow of foreign luxury goods, so depended on by the elite to reflect their status and lifestyles, slowed. To be rich and powerful, you have to be seen to be rich and powerful – it's all about display. A member of the elite, lacking any acknowledged symbols of prestige, is just the same as anybody else. In the end, the Hittites were unable to adapt to these changing circumstances and disruptions. Drought, famine, disease, a series of massive earthquakes (an 'earthquake storm'), social tensions, rebellions, large scale migrations, and an inflexible political system, all came together to contribute to the State's collapse. For centuries, the Hittite elite had one way of viewing the world. Unfortunately for them, the world around them no longer shared it. This, of course, then affected every civilization connected with the Hittites, civilizations that were already experiencing their own similar problems. The 'systems collapse' continued to claim its victims.

The Sea Peoples were just part of this wider problem, but one that everyone could easily point the finger at and blame. Whatever the Egyptian scribes would later write about them, these displaced groups were a symptom of the eastern Mediterranean world's growing environmental, social, and political problems, not the cause. With instability in the air, major centres in Greece had already fortified their settlements well in advance of the destruction of Mycenae. They clearly saw it coming. Others no doubt did too. Famine had been afflicting the eastern Mediterranean for years, and desperate people were already searching for new fertile lands to settle in or risk starvation. Burning down symbols of the elite – palaces and government buildings – was just the latest emanation of the people's growing lack of faith and distrust of those in power. Living in these dire environmental times, populations within towns and cities, long exploited by the elite and now receiving little from them in return, were probably already rebelling of their own accord, without ever having met or heard of a 'sea person.'

When enough people are driven by desperation, not even the greatest state can stop them; symbols of wealth and prestige mean nothing if enough people reject their meaning. In such times, some will rise up, burn, and rebuild on the ashes. Others will leave. And so, in this time of instability, disease, violence, famine, and drought, the assorted 'Sea Peoples' took the second option: they travelled eastwards, bringing their families and possessions along with them, leaving their homelands behind. To support themselves or when attempting to settle, sometimes they turned to violence, probably supported by mercenaries, creating their legend.

During these uncertain times, a number of settlements across the eastern Mediterranean were destroyed, but it's often left unmentioned how many remained untouched and continued to develop. Despite what the Egyptians and subsequent writers say, not everything was burned to the ground (Cyprus even continued to prosper), and in some cases, even cities that had been destroyed were rebuilt, such as Megiddo. Ugarit, however, was one of the unlucky ones. In a letter found at the city, probably sent from the Hittite viceroy of Carchemish to the king of Ugarit, it says, 'Concerning that which you wrote (me): "enemy ships have been sighted at sea" – if it is true that ships have been sighted, then make yourself very strong … Surround your cities with walls. Bring (your) infantry and chariotry into (them). Be on the lookout for the enemy and make yourself very strong.'² The king of Ugarit then wrote to the king of Cyprus, saying, 'My father, now the ships of the enemy have been coming. They have been setting fire to my cities and have done harm to the land ... Now if other ships of the enemy turn up, send me a report somehow(?) so that I will know.'³ Although this all sounds rather 'Sea Peoplesy,' another letter, sent from Eshuwar, Cyprus' chief administrator, adds useful information: the enemy ships were in fact from Ugarit itself, suggesting that the culprits were pirates or angry traders – so perhaps another case of rioting locals – rather than the Sea Peoples. Recent archaeological investigations have also shown that these letters could have been written well before the city's final days, maybe even years before its destruction. Whatever the case, and whoever was responsible, when Ugarit was finally destroyed, it was violent: the city was burned and arrowheads were found among the ruins. Emar, another Syrian city, east of Ugarit, was also destroyed, with tablets describing 'hordes of enemies.'

The Cape Gelidonya Shipwreck

Like the Uluburun shipwreck during the Amarna Period, the Cape Gelidonya wreck, which sank just off the coast of Anatolia during the reign of Ramesses III, provides a snapshot of international trade. This vessel, either of Cypriote or Syrian origin, was 9 m in length, and carried 1,000 kg of cargo – goods from across the known world. At port in Cyprus, its crew had loaded it with large storage vessels, stirrup jars, and forty copper ingots, varying from 16 kg to 27 kg in weight. They had carefully wrapped each ingot in reed matting and stacked them in piles at the fore and aft to balance the ship. Twenty copper bun ingots, averaging almost 4 kg each, were nestled amongst them. Bronze tools, agricultural implements, weapons, and household utensils – including a mirror and a kebab spit – were stored in wicker baskets, stacked on a layer of brushwood to protect the planks. Many of these items were broken – scrap that would be sold on for the value of their metal. The ship also held assorted Egyptian paraphernalia, including scarabs and cylinder seals, glass, and crystals.

The Year Eight Campaign of Ramesses III

Ramesses III's inscriptions treat the arrival of the Sea Peoples as rather sudden, but with all the turmoil throughout his known world, you can't imagine it was *that* unexpected. The battle occurred in Ramesses' eighth year as king, and as with his earlier Libyan campaign, the events of the war are recounted and depicted on the walls of his mortuary temple at Medinet Habu. In preparation for battle, Ramesses armed his soldiers with various weapons, while scribes noted down each item handed out, including shields, helmets, spears, bows, and *khepesh*-swords. Though not depicted, the associated inscription makes clear that Nubians and Sherden warriors were among the troops. Afterwards, the king went to inspect his horses, before setting off for war, accompanied by his charioteers and infantry.

Ramesses fought his war against the Sea Peoples on two fronts: there was a land battle in the Levant and a waterborne conflict at the Nile mouths along the Mediterranean coast. On the walls of Medinet Habu, the king is depicted as present at both, which can either be taken as an ideological statement of royal power, or as showing that the battles weren't simultaneous (or that he can move really fast). For the land portion, we're told that those who arrived in Egypt were 'overthrown' and 'slain.' The accompanying scene depicts the king on a massive scale, riding upon his chariot, while all around, the tiny figures of Egyptians and Sea Peoples clash. The different Sea Peoples groups are carefully distinguished in the illustrations, each with particular identifying features: the Sherden with their round shields and horned bronze helmets, surmounted by a disc, and other groups, including the Peleset, wearing feathered headdresses. Meanwhile, carts dragged by oxen carry women and children – emphasizing that this wasn't simply a military invasion, but the migration of whole families, searching for better lives.

For the sea battle, the Sea Peoples entered Egypt via the Nile mouths. The depictions show a mass of boats, in which a mixture of Sea Peoples and Egyptians fall about chaotically, one over the other and some out of their boats. Arrows protrude from the bodies of many of the Sea Peoples – easily identifiable once again thanks to their differing headgear and weapons. Ramesses III is far from the action, standing upon a pile of dead enemies on the shore (giving him a little extra height). Despite his distance, he still shoots his arrows into the melee, killing his enemies. Ramesses' chariot driver stands patiently behind with his fan-bearer, as if waiting for the king to finish his work for the day so they can go home. In the accompanying inscription, Ramesses says how he caused his ships – each filled with warriors – to seal the mouths of the Nile like a 'strong wall.' It was like a net, he goes on to say, and those caught inside were pinioned and butchered. Nonetheless, the Egyptians still took many prisoners, tying them in excruciating positions and marching them away (as usual). After the battle, they held a celebration; this took place at a fortress of Ramesses III, where scribes recorded the numbers of prisoners and hands severed. The king presented many of the captives to the god Amun, and perhaps executed some of them. According to Papyrus Harris I, others were settled in 'strongholds' of Ramesses III across Egyptian controlled territory.

The Second Libyan Campaign

Ramesses' third and final campaign occurred in his eleventh year as king. Seemingly inspired by talks with the Rebu-Libyans, a Meshwesh-Libyan chief named Mesher, the son of Chief Kaper, led the Meshwesh eastwards (perhaps aided by Tjemehu- and Soped-Libyans), attacking the Tjehenu-Libyans along the way. They then entered Egyptian territory with the aim of settling there, perhaps in the region west of the Wadi Natrun. The war scenes at Medinet Habu again provide us with elaborate imagery of the king at war: Ramesses drags a Libyan chief by the head to his chariot, ties up others in excruciating positions, and tramples another beneath his chariot, all the while shooting arrows at his enemies. Archers line up, also ready to shoot their arrows at the Libyans. Some Egyptians carry spears, shields, and *khepesh*-swords. In the end, the Libyans fled the carnage, forcing the Egyptians to chase them between two fortresses. In the second of these scenes, Mesher is identified upon a chariot, attempting to flee, and Sea Peoples groups, including the Sherden, fight alongside the Egyptians.

Despite trying to escape, Mesher was captured. His father, Kaper, came to the Egyptians to beg for peace, laying down his weapons and crying to the sky whilst begging for his son. But this father's heartfelt plea for his son's safe return fell on Ramesses' deaf ears. The Egyptians seized Kaper and slaughtered his army. Afterwards, Kaper too was executed. Both Mesher and Kaper can be seen on the walls of Medinet Habu, their hands bound, as they're escorted into pharaoh's presence during the royal review of the spoils of war. Here, mounds of hands and phalli are once again piled up and counted by scribes. The Egyptians had killed over 2,000 Meshwesh, and seized their family members, along with their animals and belongings, including their swords and chariots. Certain prisoners were presented before the gods, but many were settled in 'strongholds,' where they were forced to learn Egyptian. The Egyptians trained these Libyans to fight, and assigned them to army divisions according to their tribe of origin (e.g. Meshwesh, Libu, Tjemehu), each overseen by an Egyptian commander and a Libyan chief. They then lived in settlements in Egypt, until summoned to fight for pharaoh.

Following Ramesses' two campaigns against them, the various Libyan groups of the Western Desert changed their approach to infiltrating Egyptian territory: the northern route, along which the previous battles had been fought, was abandoned. In response, the Egyptians fortified settlements at the entrance to the desert routes further south, such as at Asyut and Abydos. It didn't work. In Ramesses' year twenty-eight, enemies are described as arriving at western Thebes, a reference that almost certainly refers to a Libyan raid. It would be the first of many over the course of the 20th Dynasty.

From the Levant to Punt: Further Foreign Affairs under Ramesses III

From depictions at Medinet Habu, Ramesses III also fought wars in the Levant, notably against Ullaza, Tunip, and Amurru in the north. If actual events, it would seem that the king sent his troops into territory previously controlled by the (now collapsed) Hittite Empire. Not only was Amurru now up for grabs once again, but by taking Amurru, Ramesses III would have shown himself to be the true successor to his idol, Ramesses II. Ullaza and Tunip, similarly under Hittite control until their collapse, would also be a nice extension to his territory.

Items bearing Ramesses III's name are known from Byblos, Lachish, and Jaffa, and Egyptian soldiers and administrators were present at Megiddo, even though it wasn't an Egyptian garrison town. At Beth Shean, an Egyptian administrative centre and garrison town, Ramesses commanded a temple be built and a statue be erected. In a house there lived Ramessesuserkhepesh, one of the few Egyptian military men based in the Levant known from the reign of Ramesses III. Descended from a military family, he was a host commander and chief steward, serving as the town's chief administrator, overseeing the town and local security. Beth Shean primarily housed Egyptians, but there was also a small local population and perhaps a number of Cypriotes, acting as mercenaries. Egyptians and mercenaries alike were buried in clay anthropoid coffins in the local cemetery. Although some of Egypt's other permanent garrisons in the Levant had already been abandoned at the end of the 19th Dynasty, Beth Shean continued to operate under Ramesses III and afterwards too, until it was burned down at the end of the 20th Dynasty.

During the 20th Dynasty, the Egyptians constructed a redistribution centre at Tell es-Saidiyeh, complete with a large residence and a 'Western

Palace,' built according to Egyptian architectural norms. In one building, they kept storage jars in a pool, probably to keep the oils and wine within cool. Sea Peoples served alongside the Egyptians there; these were buried at the local cemetery, often in makeshift coffins formed from two large storage jars being put together. (Sea Peoples in the Levant could also be buried in 'slipper coffins' bearing fake hieroglyphic inscriptions.) Generally, Tell es-Saidiyeh's dead were wrapped in linen and covered in bitumen – seemingly an attempt to replicate the work of Egypt's embalmers – before burial. They were also sometimes accompanied into the afterlife with weapons, which were either individually wrapped like mummies, or placed among the mummy wrappings.

Meanwhile, Egypt's influence over the southern Levant was being challenged. Various Sea Peoples groups, such as the Peleset, Sherden, and Tjekeru had settled in the coastal areas. Some cities were destroyed, including Ashdod, while Gaza, Egypt's main headquarters in the region, now found it difficult to communicate with other Egyptian bases. To block any attempt at expansion, the Egyptians built new fortresses on the fringes of the Sea Peoples' territory and increased the numbers of their troops at existing garrisons. Egyptian control nonetheless began to wane, but for the time being, their administrators continued to collect grain taxes from the local population in order to pay for Egypt's military presence and bureaucracy in the region. Ramesses gave land in the Levant to the Temple of Amun at Karnak, the Temple of Re at Heliopolis, and the Temple of Ptah at Memphis. Turquoise continued to be mined in the Sinai, and copper ore at Timna in Eilat, from where it was brought to the king's Window of Appearance and presented during an official ceremony. At least until the end of Ramesses III's reign, life in the Levant was business as usual.

According to Papyrus Harris I, Ramesses III sent a mission to Punt, which brought myrrh to Egypt, along with the children of the chief of Punt, who returned with the expedition to meet the king. Ramesses is only recorded as building one temple in Nubia, though his eldest son, the Crown Prince Ramesses, did visit Soleb, where Amenhotep III had built a temple during the 18th Dynasty. The career of Ramesses' King's Son of Kush Hori is also well-known. Starting in the chariotry during the late 19th Dynasty, he worked his way up to become a royal messenger under Siptah, and by the reign of Ramesses III had become mayor of Buhen and king's son of Kush. His son, also called Hori, succeeded him as king's son of Kush in around Ramesses III's fifth year as king.

Foreigners at Deir el-Medina

The state-run village of Deir el-Medina in western Thebes is one of the best-known settlements from Ancient Egypt, primarily due to the vast amount of textual evidence discovered during excavations. Founded at the start of the New Kingdom, the village was home to the artisans who cut and decorated the royal tombs in the Valley of the Kings, and continued to operate until the end of the 20th Dynasty, when the Valley was abandoned. In addition to Egyptians, the village housed a number of foreign residents at various times during the New Kingdom. Some are referred to by their place of origin, such as two individuals called 'the Cypriote,' while others reveal their foreign origins through their names, for example, the Semitic name Deliliah, or Hurrian names, such as Tulpriya and Zilli. As it was unusual for Egyptians to give their children foreign names, it's probable that these individuals were immigrants. Nine of the women with foreign names at Deir el-Medina were housewives, married to the workmen, while another was a member of the workers' team. Most of the foreign men were workmen, though one was a necropolis guard and two were gardeners. Perhaps the most influential foreign individual was the Chapel Scribe Zabu, who held a position in the lower temple bureaucracy. Around seventeen Libyans also lived at Deir el-Medina in the New Kingdom; most were low-ranking in village society, but one did become a chief craftsman. Others held the positions of guardian of the tomb, scribe, and priest.

The Loss of Empire and Growing Instability

Despite these signs of continued prosperity, Egypt's economy started to slow. The country couldn't escape the effects of the wider 'systems collapse' forever. As a result, corruption was on the rise: the first workers' strike in history occurred under Ramesses III at Deir el-Medina, the state-run village housing the artisans who cut and decorated the royal tombs in the Valley of the Kings. These artisans hadn't been paid their food rations – their salaries – and downed tools in protest. But their lack of payment wasn't due to the state having run out of grain, it was because corrupt members of the local elite were diverting the supplies for their own use. Although this dispute was eventually settled, strikes continued to erupt throughout the 20th Dynasty. Eventually, local people would turn to robbing the temples and tombs to improve their situation.

As a bloodier sign of Egypt's growing instability, Ramesses III ended his reign with his throat slit – the victim of a large-scale harem conspiracy. This plot involved men and women from across the administration, including a Libu-Libyan butler named Yanini, and was led by a minor queen named Tiye. Though the attack was successful, the conspiracy's ultimate aim – to put a prince named Pentaweret on the throne – failed. The rightful successor, Ramesses IV, was crowned and those involved in the conspiracy were put on trial. The majority were executed or forced to commit suicide.

Having dealt with the conspirators, Ramesses IV got on with the business of running the country. Wanting to emulate his father's success as a builder, Ramesses continued to exploit the copper mines at Timna, the turquoise mines in Sinai, and sent a large-scale quarrying expedition into the Wadi Hammamat for stone. In the Levant, only a few objects bear Ramesses IV's names, and it was probably during this time that the Egyptians lost control of Gaza, their main headquarters in the region. Between Ramesses IV and the end of the New Kingdom, Egypt's other forts in the Levant would also be abandoned or destroyed. Indeed, the only slight evidence for a campaign in the Levant during Ramesses IV's reign comes from a fragmentary stele found at Amara West in Nubia. These fragments refer to a sea battle and combat on land during the night. In Nubia, Ramesses IV is also mentioned on monuments at Aniba, Buhen, and Kawa, but there's no evidence for military activity in the region.

Under Ramesses V, the copper mines at Timna were exploited for the last time, highlighting Egypt's loss of control in the region. Indeed, there's very little evidence for Ramesses V's activities outside of Egypt at all. Egypt itself, however, remained heavily militarized, and many foreigners continued to live there. A glimpse into the demography of Middle Egypt under Ramesses V is provided by the Wilbour Papyrus, a taxation document recording land-ownership. From this, we find that land was owned by Sherden warriors, Libyans, and Asiatics, probably the descendants of mercenaries, who were awarded these plots as thanks for their years of military service. Military settlements dotted the landscape, and Egyptian military men owned large portions of land. Meanwhile, in southern Egypt, Libyan incursions continued. On one occasion, the Deir el-Medina workmen refused to work for fear of the 'enemy,' most probably Libyans, who had attacked a nearby town called Per-Nebty and burned the population. Ramesses V died after only four years as king, probably happy that he didn't have to deal with the increasingly dire situation across his kingdom.

Though Egypt's influence in the Levant continued to wane, archaeologists have found objects made under Ramesses VI in the region: a ring bearing his name was discovered at Deir el-Balah; a scarab at Alalakh; and he had a bronze statue erected at Megiddo. At the same time, he was the last New Kingdom pharaoh to exploit the turquoise mines at Serabit el-Khadim – Egypt's expeditions now didn't even pass beyond the Sinai. Control of Nubia remained strong, however. As with his immediate predecessors, Ramesses VI's main aim was to secure his borders. A scene on the second pylon-gateway at Karnak Temple in Thebes shows the king victorious over the Libyans – perhaps indicating that combat occurred – and a statue, also from Karnak, presents him striding along, his pet lion at his side, holding an axe with his right hand, and gripping a bent over Libyan with his left. Despite such aggressive imagery, Libyans, either through migration, forced settlement, or as the descendants of mercenaries, were becoming an increasingly large and integral part of Egyptian society, and were even appointed to high-level military positions.

The Royal Tomb Robberies at Thebes

Little can be said about the reigns of Ramesses VII and VIII, but under their successors, the final kings of the 20th Dynasty, there were further Libyan incursions, and the number of tomb and temple robberies at Thebes increased. These robberies – serious offences against the king and gods – are recorded on various papyri dated to the reigns of Ramesses IX and XI, and describe teams of thieves breaking into the tombs in the Valley of the Kings, the Valley of the Queens, and the tombs of the nobles to steal any items of value that they could get their hands on. Thieves targeted the temples too, taking precious stones and metals. These papyri record the depositions of those caught, providing vivid accounts of their crimes, as well as of the State's efforts to investigate them. Among those mentioned in the papyri are foreigners living at Thebes.

From the reign of Ramesses IX, for example, a foreigner named Khallazi, seemingly a slave of the high priest of Amun, is among a list of people who had returned gold and silver to the authorities after realizing he'd received stolen goods. Others were not so honest. Papyrus Meyer B presents an account of a quarrel between thieves, who were arguing about how their loot should be divided. A 'foreigner' named Pais came across the thieves and blackmailed them into giving him a cut of the loot in return for his silence. He then joined the band of robbers, and was involved in the robbery of the tomb of King Ramesses VI.

Pakamun, another foreigner at Thebes, who worked for the land-survey of Amun, was interrogated by the authorities. He took an oath, like all those interrogated, saying that if he spoke falsehood, he would be mutilated and sent to Kush. His captors asked him about his role in the tomb robberies, and beat him with a staff, but he said nothing. He was then beaten with a staff and birch, and 'examined with the screw,' but still admitted nothing. Perhaps Pakamun was innocent after all. Other foreigners mentioned in the tomb robbery papyri include Ptah-khau, who stole precious items from the Ramesseum – the mortuary temple of King Ramesses II; the Craftsman Tjauenanuy, who worked at Deir el-Medina; Panehesy, who was a priest of Sobek of Pi-ankh; Peikamen, who lived in Armant; and Usihatnakht, who worked for the superintendent of the hunters of Amun. The authorities also interrogated the family members of thieves; the wife of one suspect was asked from where she and her husband, a foreigner, had received the silver that they'd used to buy their slaves.

The End of the New Kingdom

The events that led to the fall of the New Kingdom are far from clear, and can only be pieced together from scattered evidence. Here I present one possible scenario, starting with the actions of a certain king's son of Kush named Panehesy. First known from a papyrus in Turin – in which the king commands him to assist the Steward and Cupbearer of Pharaoh Yanusa during a mission to complete the construction of a portable shrine in Nubia – there's nothing in this early evidence to suggest that Panehesy would start a civil war. But with ongoing turmoil at Thebes, and a king with little influence, someone had to step in to restore order. Indeed, the situation had become so dire at Thebes that the Deir el-Medina artisans had abandoned their village, and moved within the fortified walls of Medinet Habu, seeking protection from the frequent Libyan raids.

It is probable that Panehesy originally marched with his troops from Nubia to Thebes to assist the High Priest of Amun Amenhotep, who due to some new outbreak of violence, had also been forced to hide within Medinet Habu for safety. He'd been there for eight or nine months by the time Panehesy arrived to end the siege. The problem was, afterwards Panehesy refused to leave, and in doing so, effectively took control of southern Egypt. Panehesy then tried to expand his influence north, looting Cynopolis along the way. But his march was halted by General Piankh, a man loyal to the king. Defeated, Panehesy fled south, chased by the king's army, and escaped into Nubia. Piankh, meanwhile, stopped at Thebes to restore order (again).

But perhaps inspired by Panehesy's earlier actions, Piankh (not so loyal after all) decided to take control of southern Egypt for himself, instigating a period known as the 'Repeating of Births,' in which the calendar was reset to 'year one.' Removing the recently re-installed High Priest Amenhotep, Piankh proclaimed himself high priest of Amun and vizier, and kept the title of general too. Libyans continued to be present at Thebes under the new regime, and perhaps served in Piankh's army (Piankh himself may even have been of Libyan descent).

Order restored, Piankh began to plan a Nubian campaign, his aim to kill Panehesy and take back the Nubian territory lost to the rebellious king's son of Kush. An insight into this campaign can be gained thanks to the survival of a series of letters written by the Scribe of the Tomb – the most important administrative office at Deir el-Medina – Djehutymose to his son, the Scribe Butehamun. From one letter, we learn that General Piankh had asked Djehutymose to meet him at Elephantine, and had sent a boat to bring him from Edfu. At this meeting, Piankh told Djehutymose about his plans to attack Panehesy in Nubia. Given that Djehutymose then asks Butehamun to pray to Amun for his safe return home, it seems that Piankh also commanded the scribe of the tomb to accompany him on the mission. Djehutymose then mentions military conscripts at Thebes, asking that food be provided for them (while also telling Butehamun to make sure that they don't run away). In another letter, Djehutymose, now in Nubia, once again asks his son to pray to Amun for his safe return, and refers to his location as 'Yar,' a word that some scholars translate as 'hellhole' (in one letter he says that he'd been 'abandoned' in Yar, and makes frequent references to being ill – an illness only relieved by beer).

Other letters refer to the movements of Medjay and Sherden warriors between Thebes and Nubia; rations for the Medjay; the manufacture and receipt of spears; and the use of cloth and rags as bandages for wrapping men – perhaps either for the wounded or to wrap mummies. Piankh also asks that two Medjay be interrogated in his house, in order to find out what they'd been saying to people; it isn't clear what these men were thought to have said, but Piankh ordered that if what he'd heard turned out to be true, then his men were to place the Medjay in two baskets and throw them into the river at night. (And nobody was to find out.) Piankh commands his men to find an intact royal tomb as well, presumably so they could empty it and use the treasures to fund his military campaign. But even with all this funding and power, Piankh failed to capture and kill Panehesy. The rogue king's son of Kush continued to rule in Nubia until his death, when he was buried beneath a small pyramid at Aniba. Afterwards, the Egyptians regained Lower Nubia up to the Second Cataract, and king's sons of Kush continued to control the region into the Third Intermediate Period.

After Piankh's death, he was succeeded as ruler of the south by a man named Herihor, who, as well as being high priest of Amun, went one step further and awarded himself royal titles at Thebes (and may have married Piankh's widow). Herihor also gave his children Libyan names suggesting that, although his own name was Egyptian, he might have had Libyan ancestry. Through all of this turmoil, Ramesses XI continued to rule in the Delta. His troops fought the Shasu-Bedouin near the Red Sea, and according to a broken obelisk now in the British Museum, he sent a crocodile and a monkey as royal gifts to King Ashur-bel-kala of Assyria, who put them on public display. When Ramesses XI died, he was succeeded in the north by a man named Smendes (Nesibanebdjedet), who had been governor of Tanis and may have married Tentamun, a daughter of Ramesses. The south, meanwhile, remained under the control of priest-kings – the descendants of Piankh – their decisions dictated by the oracle of Amun. Egypt was once again divided, and the Third Intermediate Period had begun.

Chapter 10

Libyan Pharaohs, the Kingdom of Kush, and the Assyrian Invasion
(1064–664 BCE)

A literary tale, known as 'The Report of Wenamun,' set during the period of political turmoil when the New Kingdom was transitioning into the Third Intermediate Period (and found on a 21st or 22nd Dynasty papyrus), neatly demonstrates how far Egypt's standing in the world had sunk by the turn of the First Millennium BCE. As the story begins, our unfortunate hero, Wenamun, has set sail from Tanis – the Egyptian royal family's new residence city in the Delta, replacing Pi-Ramesses – for Byblos, in order to collect wood for the Temple of Amun at Karnak. With his Syrian captain, Mengebet, they stopped at ports along the Levantine coast, including Dor, a town controlled by the Tjekeru – one of the Sea Peoples groups, who had settled in the region. There, a member of Wenamun's crew stole the gold and silver meant to pay for the wood in Byblos. Naturally upset, Wenamun visited a local prince, asking him to search for the thief. He received a less than sympathetic response: if the thief had been from Dor, living in the city, the prince said, he would have repaid Wenamun for his loss until the thief was found. But because the thief was among Wenamun's own crew, no such payment would be made. The prince would, however, help search for the thief.

After nine days waiting, and no doubt realizing that he was getting nowhere, Wenamun left Dor for Byblos, stopping along the way at Tyre. While at sea, he encountered a Tjekeru ship from Dor carrying roughly the same amount of silver as had been stolen from him. Seeing an opportunity to recoup his losses from the people he regarded as in league with the thief, Wenamun took the law into his own hands and seized the silver. He told the Tjekeru that he'd only return it if they either handed over the thief or his stolen goods. And with that, he left. Soon after, Wenamun arrived at Byblos, and erected his tent on the shore. Security conscious, he buried his possessions, including his portable divine statue: Amun-of-the-Road.

But the prince of Byblos refused to see Wenamun. By now rather angry, the Egyptian began a sit-in, refusing to move from the port, despite protestations from the prince of Byblos, who wrote to him daily, telling him to get out of his harbour! After twenty-nine days, Wenamun was about to give up, when his luck changed: a 'seer' at the court of Byblos told the prince that the god Amun had led Wenamun to travel to his city, and that the Egyptian should be brought to the court. Following the seer's advice, the prince sent the harbour master to fetch Wenamun. He arrived to find the Egyptian packing up his belongings and preparing to leave.

And so, five months after his departure from Thebes, Wenamun finally got to meet the prince of Byblos face to face. It didn't go well. First, the prince asked Wenamun for documentation, proving that he was on a mission from the Temple of Amun. It wasn't possible: Wenamun had given these documents to Smendes, the governor of Tanis (and later king), before departing from Egypt. Next, the prince asked why Wenamun was travelling with a Syrian ship and crew, did Smendes want to get him murdered? Wenamun's reply was blunt: if sailing on a ship representing Egypt, it is an Egyptian crew. The prince then asked Wenamun why he had travelled to Byblos, only to be told that the Egyptian had come to fetch lumber for the barque of Amun. By this point, Wenamun must have been tiring of the prince's interrogation, for he blurted out that the prince should do as his father had done, and as his father's father had done: supply Egypt with wood. The prince agreed that his family had always supplied Egypt with wood – but the Egyptians had always paid first. There were further negotiations, and eventually Wenamun agreed to send a letter to Smendes, requesting enough items to pay for the wood. These items were later received, and the prince finally agreed to supply the cedar.

Unfortunately, just as Wenamun was about to leave Byblos – his ship now fully loaded with timber – eleven Tjekeru ships were spotted sailing towards the port, their crews demanding that the prince apprehend the Egyptian. Uncharacteristically, the prince took pity on Wenamun, sending for two amphorae of wine, a sheep to eat, and an Egyptian songstress to sing for him that evening – anything to calm his guest's nerves. The prince said that he'd solve the problem the next day. And so, when morning came, the prince spoke with the Tjekeru, explaining that he couldn't apprehend an envoy of Amun in his territory, but if they'd let Wenamun sail away, they could pursue and apprehend him themselves.

Left with little choice, Wenamun sailed off towards Egypt, probably fearing for his life, but soon after, the wind blew him off course to Cyprus.

There, he found himself on a beach, surrounded by angry locals who wanted to kill him. Wenamun fought his way through the crowd to discover their princess, Hatiba, who – luckily – was accompanied by an interpreter fluent in Egyptian. No doubt choosing his words carefully, Wenamun explained that he was an envoy of Amun, and that if the townspeople killed him and his crew, the prince of Byblos would retaliate. She agreed, and summoned her people, reprimanding them for their behaviour. And this is where the text breaks off: the rest is lost.

The 'Report of Wenamun' reflects Egypt's failing importance on the world stage. Not only did traditional allies no longer show respect to envoys travelling in the name of Egypt, but the Egyptians didn't even have their own ships: they had to sail on Syrian ships instead. Interestingly, the tale also refers to Egyptians living abroad: in Byblos, a butler named Penamun and a singer called Tanetnot are mentioned, and Wenamun encounters people fluent in Egyptian in Dor, Byblos, and Cyprus. Although Egypt's influence was waning, its overall impact on the world was still very much evident.

Divisions in the 21st Dynasty

As we have already seen, by the end of the New Kingdom Egypt was once again divided. The priest-kings of Amun ruled in the south, exerting their influence from the region of el-Hiba down into Nubia (although it isn't clear how far); and the kings at Tanis, starting with Smendes (Nesibanebdjedet) – who had been governor of Tanis – ruled in the Delta as the 21st Dynasty. Nevertheless, despite Egypt appearing fractured, the divisions were not as strong as in previous intermediate periods. The ruling families in the north and south remained connected: the third king of the 21st Dynasty, Psusennes I, for example, was the son of Pinudjem I, a priest-king of Thebes; and Psusennes I's brother, Menkheperre, took over the office of priest-king at Thebes when their father died. For a time then, one brother ruled as king of the north and the other as king of the south.

With enough problems at home, the Egyptians had little contact with the Levant in the early Third Intermediate Period. However, pottery from the reign of Psusennes I is known from Tell Qasile, and this king is referred to as a 'seizer of cities,' suggesting that a foreign campaign of some kind occurred. Archaeologists have found Egyptian pottery at Dor (famous from the Wenamun tale), and a lapis lazuli bead, discovered in the burial of Psusennes I at Tanis, bears a cuneiform inscription for the eldest daughter of Ibashshi-ilu, an Assyrian vizier, reflecting the continuation of wider trading relations.

The Libyan Period

During the 21st Dynasty, a Libyan man ascended the throne of Egypt: this was Osorkon the Elder, a great chief of the Ma (better known as the Meshwesh tribe), who ruled for around six years. Osorkon the Elder's nephew, Shoshenk I, later became the first king of the 22nd Dynasty (a phase sometimes referred to as the Libyan Period). Unlike his predecessors in the Third Intermediate Period, who seemed quite content to live in a fractured country, Shoshenk I wanted to reunite Egypt under a single king. He installed one of his sons as high priest of Amun, removing the independence of the temple, and appointed loyal family members and supporters to high office. The importance of kinship and lineage was a key feature of Libyan rule, and powerful individuals across the land married into the Libyan family to reinforce their power. On temple walls, the Libyan kings presented themselves as traditional pharaohs and high priests of all the gods, whilst simultaneously emphasizing their heritage as great chiefs of the Meshwesh.

Shoshenk I attempted to reassert Egypt's power in the Levant, a territory that had changed significantly since its recent Egyptian-dominated past. The Philistines, descendants of the Peleset 'Sea Peoples,' now lived on the southern coast, with major centres at Gaza, Gath, Ekron, Ashkelon, and Ashdod. The Kingdom of Israel seems to have existed too, but in a more limited form than described in the Bible. (Beyond the Bible, there is only a small amount of evidence for Israel during this phase, but an Aramaic inscription from the city of Dan does mention a tribal leader called David, who in the Biblical tradition is the father of King Solomon.) Various tribal units, collectively referred to as the Canaanites, lived in city-states and kingdoms spread across the region and into southern Lebanon. The Phoenician cities, now free of Egyptian or Hittite control and protected by their fortified walls, prospered on the coast of modern Lebanon – particularly at Tyre, Byblos, and Sidon. And further north, in what had been Hittite territory in Syria, were now the Neo-Hittite kingdoms: at least fifteen simultaneous dynasties, some ruling over large territories, others small. Among the most important of these was the state centred on Carchemish, previously a major Hittite-controlled city in Syria. The Aramaeans of northern Syria had also founded kingdoms in the region, for example at Damascus, and later came to rule over some of the Neo-Hittite Kingdoms. Aramaic became the new language of diplomacy, replacing Akkadian. And because people preferred to write Aramaic in ink, it led to a growth in papyrus exports from Egypt.

Shoshenk's campaign in the southern Levant is recorded in the Bible, as well as in reliefs at Karnak Temple and a fragment from a stele at Megiddo. According to the Biblical account, a prophecy had foretold that a man named Jeroboam would come to control ten of the tribes ruled by King Solomon of Israel. To stop this, Solomon tried to kill Jeroboam, who – fearing for his life – fled to Shoshenk's court (presented in the Bible as Shishak). Following Solomon's death, and the accession of his son Rehoboam, Jeroboam returned to the Levant. But soon after, Jeroboam and ten of the tribes rebelled, incited by Rehoboam's continuing cruelty towards his people. Jeroboam took Rehoboam's northern territory, creating the Northern Kingdom of Israel, its capital at Samaria. Rehoboam was left to rule the Kingdom of Judah in the south, with its capital at Jerusalem. Then, in the fifth year of Rehoboam's reign (around 926 BCE), Shoshenk attacked Jerusalem, arriving with 1,200 chariots, 60,000 horsemen, and Libyan and Nubian troops. The pharaoh took away the treasures of the Temple of Solomon and of the royal palace. Given the Biblical account, some argue that Shoshenk's campaign was launched in support of Jeroboam's rebellion against Rehoboam.

However, the Biblical account, written hundreds of years after the events described, can be doubted in its details: for a start, Jerusalem isn't mentioned among the many cities in Shoshenk's Karnak Temple scenes, despite other nearby locations being cited. Archaeological evidence shows that a campaign did occur in the region during the tenth century BCE, but at this time Jerusalem was only a small and poor village. Indeed, Judah only truly began its journey to statehood in the ninth century BCE, and only became a fully realized state in the eighth century BCE. The first non-Biblical reference to Judah is found in an inscription of the Assyrian king Tiglath-Pileser III, who ruled from 745–727 BCE. So, when Shoshenk was campaigning, Judah was just a small chiefdom, centred on a tiny village; it certainly didn't have a large and wealthy temple, and probably cooperated with the pharaoh to escape destruction. The story built around the campaign was an invention of its author, meant to show punishment for Rehoboam's cruelty to his people.

The true aim of Shoshenk's campaign in the southern Levant was probably to re-establish Egyptian control in the region and to dominate its trade routes. It was perhaps provoked by a small-scale invasion of Egypt: Shoshenk's Victory Stele from Karnak Temple mentions the death of soldiers and leaders, and presents the king as consulting his advisors on how to proceed. The king then set off with his chariotry and made a great slaughter in the Bitter Lakes region on the isthmus of Suez. Enemies, it seems, had crossed Sinai and attacked the eastern Delta, provoking the king's violent response. Afterwards, Shoshenk probably decided to cross into the southern Levant, continuing his retaliation. A priest of Amun-Re and scribe, called Hor, also mentions that he followed Shoshenk I on campaign in the Levant.

Despite violence in the southern Levant, the Egyptians now resumed friendly relations with Byblos in the north. A statue base from Byblos bears Shoshenk's name, and its inscription says that the statue was brought from Egypt for Baalat-Gebal (the 'Lady of Byblos'). Contact with Byblos continued into the reign of Shoshenk's son and successor, Osorkon I, when Elibaal, king of Byblos, dedicated a statue of the pharaoh at the famous port city. Osorkon II also sent a statue to Byblos, and a large vessel, bearing his name, was found at Samaria, capital of the Northern Kingdom of Israel. It had probably been used to transport precious oil as a royal gift.

King Osorkon II kept a close eye on international affairs. He had no choice. The Assyrians had been on the rise since the tenth century BCE, expanding their empire over the course of a century to incorporate territory all the way from Babylon to the Syrian coastline. Ashurnasirpal II, ruling from 883–859 BCE, was primarily responsible for this expansion. He'd marched west of the River Euphrates to find that the region's city-states wanted no trouble: by paying tribute and supplying troops, weapons, and chariots to the Assyrians, they avoided destruction. Only the Kingdom of Luash fought back. So the Assyrians destroyed the kingdom's cities and impaled the captives taken. Diplomats they were not.

Under Ashurnasirpal II's successor, Shalmaneser III, campaigning continued even more aggressively than before (he left a pile of 300 corpses outside one city). But the Assyrian was met with resistance: the various kings of northern Syria had formed a coalition to oppose his armies. They fought a number of battles, but ultimately lost the war. Southern Syria was Shalmaneser's next target. Taking inspiration from the northern Syrian city-states, the kings of south Syria formed a coalition, but this time, they were supported by forces sent by kings from across the Levant and beyond, including Egypt. If the reading of 'Musri' as 'Egypt' on an Assyrian stele erected at Kurkh is correct, Osorkon II sent 1,000 troops to aid the Syrian kings in battle against Shalmaneser III at Qarqar (modern Tell Qarqur) in 853 BCE. These numbers are quite small compared to the others who joined the coalition: Damascus sent 20,000 troops and 1,200 chariots; Israel sent 10,000 troops; Byblos alone sent 500 troops. The coalition lost the battle, and the defeated kingdoms were forced to pay tribute to the Assyrians; nonetheless, they continued to resist Assyrian rule for decades. Interestingly, though Egypt was not invaded, the Black Obelisk of Shalmaneser III (found at Nimrud – ancient Kalhu), erected in 825 BCE, refers to 'Musri' sending tribute to Assyria, including elephants, a rhinoceros, and other exotic animals.

It was also under King Osorkon II that Egypt once again began to fragment. In around 867 BCE, the high priest of Amun at Thebes, Harsiese, declared himself king, founding a separate royal line, known today as the 23rd Dynasty. This set in motion a series of violent clashes: various individuals competed not just for the throne of Thebes, but for rule of the Nile Valley from Herakleopolis down into Nubia. On one of his monuments, Prince Osorkon, high priest of Amun during the reign of Takelot II (a king of the 23rd Dynasty, ruling from 841–815 BCE), talks of violence in the south: Hermopolis was cleansed; people were arrested at Karnak Temple and executed; and various rebellions forced Osorkon (who actually lived in the north) to travel to Thebes to restore order. The image presented is one of the Theban region in chaos, and perhaps even of civil war.

At the same time, the Delta fragmented too: a patchwork of individual kingdoms came into existence during the middle of the 22nd Dynasty, each overseen by its own 'mini-king.' These were relatives of the 22nd Dynasty family, but acted independently. Since the start of the Libyan Period, important positions across the administration had been given to members of the royal family, reflecting the Libyans' interest in kinship – their inscriptions sometimes include genealogies reaching back generations. But these same individuals now regarded themselves as powerful enough to call themselves kings. And by 735 BCE, contemporary with Shoshenk V of the 22nd Dynasty, yet another prominent family line had emerged: the 24th Dynasty, ruling from the city of Sais in the western Delta. These were of Libu-Libyan descent and slowly expanded their territory to take over most of the Delta. As a result of all this, the 22nd and 23rd Dynasties overlap for much of their existence, with the 24th Dynasty then overlapping too from around 735 BCE. By now you're probably thinking: this is a mess. And you'd be right. The concept of a singular king of Upper and Lower Egypt was increasingly nothing more than a memory. If Egypt were to once again unify as a kingdom, it was time for a change.

The Origins of the Kings of Kush

During the early Third Intermediate Period, there's little information about events in Nubia, though Egyptian control appears to have continued, perhaps as far south as the Second Cataract. Some New Kingdom Egyptian temple towns were abandoned. Others continued to serve as major local centres. The same local elite probably remained in power either side of the fall of the New Kingdom. The office of king's son of Kush continued to exist, with each king's son simultaneously (and curiously) holding an office in the cult of Khnum at Elephantine. One of these individuals is the only woman known to have become king's son of Kush: Nesikhons.

But around 850 BCE (or earlier, in around 1000 BCE, depending on the chronology used), a new ruling elite emerged between the Third and Fourth Cataracts of the Nile, their graves at el-Kurru, near Gebel Barkal. Their descendants, the kings of Kush, would later become the 25th Dynasty pharaohs of Egypt, a royal line with a particular devotion to the god Amun and Egyptian tradition. Given these strong Egyptian associations, what is interesting about this new line of Kushite rulers is that, at first, beyond the presence of Egyptian imports, their burials show no Egyptian influence at all. Each burial is of a type typical in Upper Nubia – a pit with a side chamber – topped by a circular mound with a cylindrical stone wall (similar in style to those used by the C-Group). Later burials at el-Kurru then start to show increased signs of Egyptian contact: for example, *wedjat*-eye amulets, and a gold nugget bearing an inscription in honour of Amun (perhaps indicative of contact with the high priests of Amun at Thebes). There's also smashed red pots, used in Egyptian execration rituals. Shortly afterwards, a tomb with a mud-brick chapel was built (also with smashed red pots), and tombs surmounted by small pyramids. Egyptian hieroglyphs are then found, as the burials become increasingly Egyptianized. Given the speed and extent of Egyptianization witnessed at el-Kurru, this new ruling family may have used Egyptian religion to associate themselves with Nubia's New Kingdom past, perhaps to provide a sense of continuity and legitimacy.

The kings of Kush traded widely: their graves at el-Kurru contained lapis lazuli, Red Sea shells, ivory goods, and obsidian; at Hillat el-Arab, close to el-Kurru, Egyptian vessels used for transporting wine and oil show that trade with Egypt continued; and items from Sudan are mentioned in Assyrian accounts, such as ebony, ivory, and elephant skins, brought to Nineveh via the Levantine city-states and Egypt. Horses may also have been sent to Nineveh. To protect the northward movement of these goods, the Kushites seem to have built fortifications at Qasr Ibrim, north-east of Abu Simbel. Such trade connections may explain how this new dynasty managed to become so powerful so quickly.

The Kushite dynasty's first steps north towards Egypt may be reflected in a text at Semna West. This is the earliest preserved Kushite royal inscription. Written in Egyptian using hieroglyphs, it mentions a rebellion against an un-named Kushite king – possibly one of the rulers buried at el-Kurru – and was made by a queen named Katimala, who is depicted in an Egyptian style: a tight linen dress, holding a flail, with a broad collar around her neck. On her head, she wears a wig, with a vulture crown, its wings hanging over her ears. Above the vulture is a solar disc and double plumes. At about the same time, at Debeira East, just north of the Second Cataract, Nubians were constructing graves similar to those at el-Kurru. Among the grave goods were Egyptian imports, showing continuing trade interactions with their northern neighbours. The influence of the Kushite dynasty at el-Kurru thus reached far north of their home, even at this early stage in the Third Intermediate Period.

The first named king of the Kushite line is Alara, who was probably buried in one of the tombs at el-Kurru and ruled from around 780–760 BCE. When mentioning Alara, his successors placed his name in a royal cartouche, normally reserved for a pharaoh, and describe him as a 'son of Re' and 'king.' He is also depicted on a stele offering to Amun. Alara was succeeded by Kashta, the first of the Kushite kings to enter Egypt. Kashta expanded Kushite influence to Thebes, and installed his daughter, Amenirdis I, as successor to the god's wife of Amun at the Temple of Amun at Karnak – by this time, the god's wife was a position normally held by the king's daughter, and had become one of the most important roles in the temple. Kashta erected a stele at Elephantine proclaiming himself 'king of Upper and Lower Egypt' and showing him worshipping the god Khnum. The last known king's son of Kush, Pamiu, held office at this time. The disappearance of this position, after nearly 800 years of existence, probably marks the moment that the 23rd Dynasty – the Thebans, ruling Upper Egypt – lost control of Lower Nubia; with the death of the 23rd Dynasty King Rudamun in around 739 BCE, this dynasty's power base shifted further north into Middle Egypt. The Kushites now controlled, or at least had strong influence over, southern Egypt. Thebes had fallen without a single drop of blood being spilled.

The Wars of King Piye

Kashta was succeeded by Piye, a son-in-law of Alara. His reign was far less peaceful. On a stele, probably dated to his third year as king, Piye says that Amun of Napata had made him ruler of every foreign country, and Amun of Thebes had made him king of Egypt. He emphasizes that he is above all kings and chiefs in these lands, promoting his supremacy over the Delta rulers. To prove his case, in his fourth year on the throne, Piye travelled to Thebes with his army for the Opet Festival, before heading north to engage in battle with one or more of the Delta rulers. This began his push to control the whole of Egypt.

Years later, due to the expanding influence of Tefnakht of Sais (of the 24th Dynasty) – who had by now seized half of the Delta for himself and was threatening Herakleopolis – Piye again despatched his army north, led by two generals. He gave them specific instructions on how to behave during the campaign: 'Do not attack by night in the manner of draughts-playing; fight when one can see. Challenge him to battle from afar. If he proposes to await the infantry and chariotry of another town, then sit still until his troops come. Fight when he proposes. Also if he has allies in another town, let them be awaited.'[1] Piye added that upon arrival at Karnak Temple, they should wash themselves in the river, put on their finest linen, and place down their weapons, before kissing the ground in front of Amun. After following the king's commands, the army sailed north of Thebes. They fought their first successful battle on the river, against a Delta coalition heading south, after which they faced another army further north. This time, many of the leaders of the coalition were killed, but some managed to flee to Lower Egypt.

Piye, angered that his enemies had escaped, decided to travel north himself. With the king present on campaign (after he'd stopped at Thebes to celebrate the Opet Festival), success arrived too. His army seized Hermopolis, saved Herakleopolis from a siege, and after enjoying further victories even captured Memphis (Tefnakht had apparently fled on horseback before Piye's army arrived). Throughout the campaign, Piye was careful to show himself as a true king: he wanted to ensure the safety of innocent people, protected the temples from pillage, and did not take into his harem the female family members of defeated enemies. Finally, at Athribis, the Delta rulers (and everyone else around) submitted to Piye, although Tefnakht, fearful apparently, just sent a messenger. Piye then sent two officials to receive Tefnakht's submission in person. Successful in his mission, Piye returned south, leaving the chastised Delta rulers in their positions. As far as we're aware, he never returned to Egypt. Before his campaign, Piye had spent his time expanding the Temple of Amun at Gebel Barkal – he even brought the statuary of earlier kings from across Nubia to its sacred domain – and he seems to have returned to this project after arriving back home. After twenty-six years as king, Piye was buried at el-Kurru.

But Piye's campaign didn't put a stop to Tefnakht's royal aspirations. Afterwards, Tefnakht simply continued as before, and even awarded himself royal titles. He then passed his 'crown' to his son, Bakenrenef (a famous law-maker according to the first century BCE Greek historian Diodorus Siculus), making him the second king of the 24th Dynasty. Bakenrenef continued his father's expansionist policy, provoking Piye's successor, Shabaka, to move his base of operations from Nubia to Memphis. According to the Ptolemaic Period writer Manetho, Shabaka then captured Bakenrenef and burnt him alive, allowing the Kushite king to take full control of Sais' extensive domain. A commemorative scarab tells us that Shabaka also slaughtered rebels in the north and south of Egypt, and that the foreigners and 'sand-dwellers' (those living on the coastal shore of the Levant or Sinai) were weak. It's probable that he strengthened Egypt's control of the eastern border. Under Shabaka, the Libyan 'mini-kings' of the Delta remained in their positions, but were overseen by the Kushite pharaoh. Egypt, now fully controlled by the Kushites, was once again united under a single strong ruler. For this reason, most scholars begin Egypt's 25th Dynasty with Shabaka.

The 25th Dynasty and Assyria

While Piye and Tefnakht were fighting over control of Egypt, the Assyrian King Tiglath-Pilaser III (ruling from roughly 745–727 BCE) was aggres-sively expanding his empire. Famously brutal to conquered states, he slaugh-tered people in their thousands and deported others from their homelands to reduce the risk of rebellions. Any territory seized by the Assyrians became a province of the empire, and large provinces were divided into more man-ageable pieces. Slowly, the Assyrians were redrawing the political map of the Near East.

Tiglath-Pilaser's army took Gaza in 734 BCE, pushing Assyrian con-trol right up to the Egyptian border. Hanun, king of Gaza, fled to Egypt, but eventually returned home to take his place as an Assyrian vassal. The Assyrian king then erected a stele, marking his border at the 'Brook of Egypt,' and established a customs base for any trade between the two pow-ers. He next appointed a man named Idibi'ilu as 'gatekeeper,' to monitor the movement of people and goods from Egypt into Assyrian territory. Sinai became a buffer zone. The scene was set for conflict.

Which brings us back to Shabaka. In 720 BCE, a year after Shabaka had ascended the Egyptian throne, the king of Hamath, a city in the Levant, formed a coalition of city-states (including Gaza under Hanun) and rebelled against Assyria, itself now under King Sargon II. To support them, the Egyptians/Kushites sent a military force, led by a general called Re'e (in Akkadian, Raia in Egyptian). It was another failure. The Assyrians crushed part of the rebellion at Qarqar (modern Tell Qarqur), and then defeated the Egyptians at Raphia. Afterwards, in 716 BCE, an Egyptian king (either the pharaoh or one of the Delta 'mini-kings') sent tribute to Sargon II, and Osorkon IV (one of these 'mini-kings') sent twelve horses as a diplomatic gift. Intriguingly, a seal found at Nineveh, once attached to correspondence sent from Shabaka to Sargon II, shows that the two kings were in contact with each other. Was this an attempt to improve diplomatic relations between the two great powers?

In 712 BCE, relations between Egypt and Assyria were further strained. Iamani, king of Ashdod, led a revolt against Sargon II. It failed, and with his city plundered by the Assyrians, Iamani fled to Egypt. Sympathizing with the king's plight, Shabaka granted him asylum. Things were looking up for Iamani – that is until Shabaka died and Shabataka ascended Egypt's throne. In 706 BCE, close to the start of his reign, Shabataka agreed to send Iamani to Sargon II, leading to the ex-king of Ashdod being bound and despatched into his enemy's presence. It isn't clear why Shabataka suddenly decided to expel Iamani, but perhaps it was another attempt to improve Egypt's relations with the Assyrians. Shabataka also sent a diplomatic mission to the Assyrian court.

Sargon II died in battle in 705 BCE, leaving the throne to his son Sennacherib. Irrespective of the diplomatic progress Shabataka may have made, this signalled another violent turn in Egypt's relations with Assyria. Revolts were breaking out across the Assyrian Empire and, in 701 BCE, a coalition of Levantine city-states requested Egypt's help in a planned rebellion against Sennacherib. Shabataka duly summoned his brother Taharka – aged only twenty – from Nubia, asking that he bring his army. The ensuing battle was fought at Eltekeh, probably north of Ashdod. From Sennacherib's account, we're told that the Egyptians were defeated, and that many of the Kushite and Egyptian charioteers were killed by the Assyrian army, but this may not be the whole truth. In fact, the Assyrian campaign probably ended in a stalemate: Taharka promoted the campaign on one of his monuments, something that we wouldn't expect if it had been a total defeat; and the Assyrians failed to take Jerusalem, seemingly due to plague breaking out among their soldiers (this was lucky for the people of Jerusalem, because Taharka seems to have abandoned his attempt to save the city).

Taharka succeeded his brother on the throne in 690 BCE. During the first decade of his reign, there was an increase in trade with the Levant: high-quality wood and Asiatic bronze was sent to Taharka's temple at Kawa, and Asiatic gardeners went to work at the vineyards of the Temple of Amun. The Temple of Mut at Karnak also received wood from Lebanon (significant because a few decades earlier, in the 730s BCE, the Assyrians had banned the sale of timber from the Phoenician cities to Egypt). This may show that the Egyptians were re-asserting their claim over the Levantine territory, particularly as in a later inscription, Taharka laments the loss of tribute from the Levant. Meanwhile, the king also reoccupied some of the Middle Kingdom fortresses in Nubia, such as Buhen and Semna, probably to protect transport vessels. He also built for the gods in various locations. At Kawa, Taharka constructed a temple following New Kingdom architectural styles: a rectangular building with a pylon-gateway, courtyard, hypostyle hall, and sanctuary. On its walls, his artisans carved a scene of Libyan defeat copied from the Old Kingdom pyramid complex of Sahure at Abu Sir, to the extent that the captured Libyans shown even have the same names as those in the already ancient original. The temple also had Tjehenu-Libyan staff and gardeners from Bahariya Oasis.

Taharka had a good relationship with his army. A stele records that his troops ran daily as training, and that the king was so impressed by them, he decided to organize a competition: they would run from Memphis to the Faiyum Oasis, about 50 km, and the first to finish would dine with the royal bodyguard as reward (though the runners-up received rewards too). Apparently, so the text says, Taharka accompanied the runners on his chariot, inspiring them, but ran part of the way on foot too.

All in all, it was a period of surprising calm and prosperity. But everything changed again in 681 BCE when the brutal (yet frequently ill) Esarhaddon became king of Assyria. Marching west with his army, he brought the Levant firmly back under Assyrian control (beheading a couple of its kings along the way). Then, in 673 BCE, he launched the Assyrians' first invasion of Egypt. The Egyptians successfully fought off the invaders, but it would only buy them a couple more years of freedom.

The Assyrian Occupation

After consulting their oracles about the best time to attack (the god's response interpreted through the condition of sacrificed rams' livers), in the summer of 671 BCE, the Assyrians returned to Egypt. Three pitched battles were fought over the course of fifteen days, culminating with the sack of Memphis, the corpses of its inhabitants piled up in the streets. The Egyptians were no match for the Assyrians' stronger iron weaponry and sophisticated siege equipment. And whereas the Egyptians still used chariots, the Assyrians now preferred cavalry. King Taharka, wounded by five arrows in the fighting, abandoned his family and fled south, leaving the Assyrians to seize control of Lower Egypt. Esarhaddon swiftly installed new government officials – some Egyptian and some Assyrian – and imposed an annual tribute on his newly won cities, some of which were assigned Assyrian names. Most of the 'mini-kings' of the Delta were allowed to remain on their 'thrones.'

The Assyrians deported Egyptians and Kushites to far-flung parts of the empire. Certain people, particularly those with useful skills, such as artisans, were taken to Assyria. Taharka's queen, the Crown Prince Ushanhuru, and the king's other sons, daughters, and secondary wives were likewise all sent to Assyria. The Kushite crown prince is depicted on one of Esarhaddon's stelae, a rope piercing his lips as he kneels in the presence of the king. An inscription from Karnak Temple, inscribed under Taharka after his defeat, describes his distress at the loss of his family. Addressing the god, the king says, 'Oh Amun, [... ... m]y wives, let my children live. Keep death away from them for me.'[2]

In the years that followed his defeat, Taharka continued to oppose Assyrian rule from southern Egypt. In the north, effective power now rested in the hands of Necho I of Sais (installed by the Assyrians, and probably a descendant of the 24th Dynasty kings Tefnakht and Bakenrenef of Sais), who controlled the western Delta and part of its centre, and a man identified as Sarru-lu-dari, who oversaw the eastern Delta. Beneath them in the hierarchy, the established 'mini-kings' continued to exert their influence, just as they'd done throughout the Third Intermediate Period. Occasional visits by the *turtanu* and *rab-shaqeh* – the highest level Assyrian officials below the king – and the chief eunuch, kept everything in check. But Assyrian control was shaky (Esarhaddon even asked the oracle whether his chief eunuch would be safe in Egypt), and Taharka eventually returned north to retake his throne. His actions prompted Esarhaddon to march back to Egypt with his army in 669 BCE; but the Assyrian king died en route, causing the campaign to be postponed.

This left the task of reinstating Assyrian control over Egypt to Ashurbanipal, Esarhaddon's successor. He arrived in 667 BCE, and fought a pitched battle against Taharka. The Kushite king was once again defeated, and fled south, chased by his enemies. But it wasn't all bad news: according to a fragmentary stele from Karnak Temple, Taharka's army prevailed over the pursuing Assyrians at Thebes. During this doomed attempt to reassert Kushite control, Necho of Sais, Sarru-lu-dari, and a ruler from the east Delta named Paqrur had joined the rebellion against the Assyrians. Retribution was swift: Necho and Sarru-lu-dari were taken as prisoners to Nineveh, and there were mass executions at Sais, Mendes, and Se'nu, their city walls hung with flayed skin. Unexpectedly, Paqrur, for whatever reason, was let off. And in a further unexpected twist, Ashurbanipal showed mercy to Necho too. Not only did the Assyrian spare Necho's life, but he sent him back to Egypt to rule over Sais, and perhaps also over the even more powerful city of Memphis, previously directly controlled by the Assyrians. Sarru-lu-dari, on the other hand, was executed. Meanwhile, Taharka continued to rule as king of Upper Egypt and Nubia, having successfully stopped the Assyrians from seizing the south. Upon his death in 664 BCE, he was buried beneath a pyramid at Nuri near Gebel Barkal in Nubia. The Assyrians bluntly recorded, 'The sacred weapon of the god Assur and the might of Ashurbanipal overwhelmed him and he died.'[3]

Taharka was succeeded by his nephew Tanutamun. Like his predecessor, the new pharaoh sought to reassert Kushite control over the Delta, his campaign inspired by a dream, in which he held two snakes, representing Egypt and Kush. Eager to fight, after his coronation, Tanutamun sailed to Memphis to face a coalition of Egyptians loyal to the Assyrians, Necho I among them. A fierce battle raged at the ancient city, and in the end, Necho lay among the dead. Tanutamun had succeeded where Taharka had failed: Memphis, the administrative heart of Egypt, was back under Kushite control. Afterwards, the king crisscrossed the Delta, challenging the region's 'mini-kings' to face him in battle. According to the pharaoh, they fled and hid behind their walls, like rats into holes. None would come out to fight. Tanutamun had shown his bravery on the battlefield, but to really consolidate his control over the Delta, he'd need to show some diplomacy too. So, back at court in Memphis, Tanutamun received the various Delta kinglets, and in return for their submission to his rule, allowed them to return to their cities.

As might be expected, Tanutamun's actions enraged Ashurbanipal. The Assyrian king immediately despatched his army to Egypt, where a battle was fought. The Kushites were defeated and Tanutamun, like Taharka before him, was chased south. But unlike under Taharka, this time, Thebes did not escape the Assyrians' wrath. The invaders seized and sacked the sacred city, or as Ashurbanipal says: 'They (his army) conquered this city completely, smashed (it as if by) a floodstorm.'[4] Gold and silver, the royal treasures, horses, male and female servants, and even monkeys were all taken back to Nineveh as booty. Ashurbanipal also mentions that his army brought away two heavy obelisks. Archaeologists have found an Assyrian helmet and iron tools during excavations on the west bank of Thebes, no doubt left from this time. The Assyrian king commemorated the event on the walls of his palace at Nineveh: fortresses are captured, gates set on fire, and Nubians are marched away, to be relocated elsewhere in the empire.

Tanutamun never returned to Egypt – he was laid to rest in 653 BCE at el-Kurru – but his successors continued to rule over their homeland in Kush. Ashurbanipal, meanwhile, satisfied that Egypt was once again subjugated, got on with the task of managing his empire. And in Egypt, with Necho of Sais dead, his son, Psamtik – a man known to the Assyrians as Nabusezibanni, who had probably grown up at the Assyrian court – received a promotion: previously ruler of Athribis, Psamtik was now appointed overseer of all Assyria's interests in the Delta, with his power base at Sais. In retrospect, this was a very bad move.

Chapter 11

Vive La Resistance
(664–332 BCE)

It's hard to figure out what was going through Psamtik's head. This is a man who'd probably been brought up at the Assyrian court, had been installed by the Assyrians as king of Sais, and now, decided to fight to regain Egypt's independence. Did he hate the Assyrians all along? Was it a long game of deception? Or did he actually have a soft spot for his old masters? After all, for the rest of his long reign, he never engaged with them in direct battle, and it's possible that Assyria had simply acknowledged that Egypt was just too far away and too much trouble to bother ruling directly. For them, Psamtik – even if he got away with calling himself King Psamtik I – was a good plan B: someone talented enough to ensure order in Egypt, but perhaps capable of being manipulated when the situation demanded it.

It's also worth remembering that it wasn't the Assyrians that were Psamtik's main challengers for the throne, and not even the Kushites, but the Delta 'mini-kings,' ever ready to – perhaps literally – stab each other in the back. Given the lack of evidence, it isn't clear how Psamtik managed to get these famously unruly rulers to submit to his kingship, but it was probably a combination of approaches. Certain Delta rulers disappear under Psamtik, replaced by men loyal to the new king. Others accepted his rule, and went on to advise him as members of a high-level council of nobles – sometimes it's smart to be diplomatic.

Meanwhile, in the south, the Temple of Amun continued to hold considerable power. By Psamtik's reign, the most influential man in the region was Montuemhat, fourth priest of Amun, mayor of Thebes, and overseer of southern Egypt. But again – somehow – seemingly without a single drop of blood being spilled, Psamtik managed to convince Montuemhat to ally himself with the north. To formalize the south's acceptance of his rule, Psamtik had his daughter Nitocris adopted as successor to the God's Wife of Amun Shepenwepet II, a daughter of King Piye, transferring authority at the temple from the Kushites to the Saites (people from Sais). And so, with Psamtik ruling Egypt from Sais, a new line of kings was founded – the 26th Dynasty – and the Late Period (664–332 BCE) began.

Although there's no evidence for conflict between Psamtik I and the Delta rulers, according to classical writers, Psamtik backed his diplomacy with a powerful hired army: Carian and Ionian mercenaries – from south-western Anatolia and central coastal Anatolia respectively – sent to Egypt by Gyges of Lydia, a region in south-western Anatolia. Whether Gyges sent these mercenaries as support against the Assyrians, or purely to help Psamtik 'influence' the Delta rulers and Thebans cannot be known. Indeed, we can also question whether the classical accounts should be trusted: only a single statuette ascribed to Psamtik's reign suggests the presence of foreign mercenaries in Egypt at the time. Belonging to Pedon, son of Amphinneos, this traditional Egyptian block-statue (so-named because they're shaped like blocks), found near Priene in Turkey, and perhaps once placed in an Ionian temple, bears a Greek inscription saying that it had been brought from Egypt, and that Psamtik had given Pedon a golden bracelet in reward for his valour. If Greek mercenaries did arrive in Egypt at this time, however, they would have stepped from their boats wearing gleaming bronze armour and versed in modern military tactics, exactly what Psamtik needed to aid his Egyptian (and perhaps Asiatic) troops.

The Oases and Libya in the Late Period

After neglecting the region for centuries, the Egyptians developed an interest in the western oases during the Third Intermediate Period: notably, Shoshenk I made a register of the wells and orchards of Dakhla and Kharga, and also restored order at Dakhla Oasis in his fifth year as king. This newfound interest developed further in the Late Period. Kings Psamtik I, Necho II, Psamtik II, and Ahmose II each left their mark on temples at Kharga and Dakhla, and from the reign of Apries onwards, there was an Egyptian presence at Bahariya Oasis too. Bahariya now received its own governor and temples, and began to flourish as a centre for trade. Further north, the famous temple of Amun at Siwa Oasis was built under Ahmose II (or possibly a little earlier). Siwa had previously been ruled by Libyans, who now became subject to the Egyptians. Herodotus talks of a king of Siwa called Etearchus, and relates a story in which the Persian king Cambyses sent 50,000 men to the oasis; these vanished in the desert, sometime after leaving Kharga Oasis.

Foreign Affairs Under King Psamtik I

After consolidating his power in Egypt, Psamtik I turned his attention to the world beyond his borders. In Nubia, since Tanutamun's departure from Egypt, a phase known as the Napatan Period had begun – named after the Kushite capital city of Napata, beside Gebel Barkal. Despite having lost Egypt, Kushite territory was still extensive, stretching from Lower Nubia down to Sennar on the Blue Nile, 300 km beyond modern Khartoum. Nuri, near Napata, was now the royal burial ground, replacing el-Kurru, and Gebel Barkal remained the main religious capital, centred on its Temple of Amun. Meroe, a city between the Fifth and Sixth Cataracts of the Nile, probably held political importance too.

The Kushites continued to prosper thanks to their key position in the African trade network: luxury goods – gold, ivory, ebony – as well as slaves, travelled from central Africa to the Mediterranean, probably as a state run enterprise. Egyptian goods entered Nubia (some are even found in Kushite royal graves, perhaps sent as diplomatic gifts), and Kushite goods entered Egypt. Few of the Napatan kings are known beyond their names, but Psamtik's Kushite counterpart in the later years of his reign was Anlamani (623–593 BCE), who erected various statues, and, at Kawa, mentions a small-scale campaign against nomads called the Bulahau. Herodotus – the famous Greek historian, writing in the fifth century BCE – relates that Psamtik I's Elephantine garrison revolted and moved south; perhaps they joined Anlamani's forces?

In his tenth or eleventh year as king, when Libyan groups were attempting to enter Egypt, Psamtik campaigned in Libya, raising troops from across Egypt to face the threat. Psamtik also expanded eastwards into the Levant, entering territory traditionally held by his royal predecessors, and more recently had been controlled by the Assyrians. A stele, dated to 613 BCE – Psamtik's fifty-second year on the throne – mentions a coffin of Lebanese wood, and says that the chiefs of the Lebanese people were overseen by an Egyptian administrator and taxed as if Egyptians. This inscription shows that parts of the Levant were directly under Egyptian control by the later years of Psamtik's reign. Statuary, probably made under Psamtik, has also been found in the region, as have other items of Egyptian origin, particularly at Ashkelon and Ekron on the Levantine coast (although these may have ended up there through trade). Adding to the evidence for an Egyptian presence, Herodotus says that Psamtik I bribed invading Scythians (a nomadic people) in the Levant, saying that the king met them in Palestine and offered them gifts and prayers to stop them from moving closer to Egypt.

One of the reasons for Assyria's sudden weakness in the east was the rise of the Neo-Babylonian Empire, founded by Nabopolassar in 626 BCE. Rebellion had spread across the Assyrian Empire after Ashurbanipal's death in 627 BCE, and Nabopolassar had used the opportunity to announce himself king of Assyria's Chaldean region. From there, he had expanded his influence. Faced with this political reality, in around 620 BCE, when Nabopolassar seized Babylon, the Assyrians – now led by Sinsharishkun, a son of Ashurbanipal – made an alliance with the Egyptians. (You have to wonder what Psamtik's first reaction was to this plea for assistance.) By 616 BCE, Psamtik's fighting force was at Gablini in the Middle Euphrates, attempting to aid their new Assyrian allies and block the Babylonian advance. It didn't work. Four years later, Nineveh fell to the Babylonians, supported by other rebellious groups, forcing the Assyrian elite to retreat from their home territory to Harran, 370 km further west, where they established their new capital. This was only a short distance east of Carchemish, where the Egyptians had installed a garrison in 616 BCE, meant to protect Egypt's Levantine territory from invasion.

Carian Mercenaries and Egyptianization

Among the foreign peoples entering Egypt to fight for the pharaohs in the 26th Dynasty were the Carians. These were from south-west Anatolia and are little known, except for their fame as warriors – in fact, there's more evidence for them in Egypt than in their Anatolian homeland. Many Carians settled in Egypt during the Late Period, rather than returning home after their campaigns, and their inscriptions (still being deciphered) are found across the country, from Buhen and Abu Simbel in Nubia, to Sais in the north. Herodotus says that during the festival of Bubastis, the Carians cut their own foreheads to show everyone present that they weren't Egyptian – a rather dramatic way of emphasizing their separate ethnic identity. But this reported need to highlight their foreign origin is at odds with what is found in the archaeological record: notably, at Saqqara, Carians adopted the use of Egyptian funerary stelae for their burials. One stele even displays Egyptian, Greek, and Carian iconography (with one mourner even shown cutting his forehead). Although present at Bubastis for a time, Egypt's Carian mercenaries moved to Memphis under King Ahmose II; it was no doubt these individuals that were buried at nearby Saqqara.

The Reign of King Necho II

Psamtik I died in the Levant in 610 BCE – during a lunar eclipse apparently – and was brought back to Egypt for burial. When Necho II, his son, came to power, he inherited a united Egypt and the Levantine territory taken by his father, but also the problems posed by the expansion of the Babylonian Empire. Only six months after ascending the throne, Necho II marched against the Babylonians in support of Assyria, the Assyrians' increasingly diminishing empire now ruled by King Ashuruballit II. But Harran, Assyria's temporary capital, was lost, and with the city abandoned, the Babylonians looted its temple. The following year, in 609 BCE, Necho returned to the northern Levant (killing Josiah of Judah at Megiddo along the way, perhaps due to the vassal's non-payment of taxes – harsh). Arriving at Harran, the Egyptians and Assyrians tried to retake the city. But again the campaign was a failure. Necho II returned to Egypt and Ashuruballit vanished from history.

Assyria's leadership now retreated 100 km further west, to Carchemish, where the Egyptians already had a garrison. But it was a futile move. In 605 BCE, the Babylonians, led by Crown Prince Nebuchadnezzar, forced their way into the city and slaughtered everyone. The Egyptian garrison was defeated. At Hamath, further south, a second Babylonian victory then brought Egypt's renewed control of the northern Levant to an end. Worse, the Babylonians were getting closer and closer to Egypt itself. The possibility of renewed foreign occupation must have weighed heavy on Necho's mind.

Four years later, in 601 BCE, the Babylonians made their move. Nebuchadnezzar, now king, tried to enter Egypt at Pelusium in the eastern Delta, but the Egyptians forced his troops to retreat. Hot on their heels, Necho's army pursued them into the Levant and retook Gaza. Despite this initial success, the Babylonian threat continued to loom large on the horizon. Nebuchadnezzar seized Jerusalem in 598 BCE, and a planned revolt by local leaders amounted to nothing. It was perhaps in this time that Necho took Migdol in the southern Levant, as reported by Herodotus, but there is little evidence for the pharaoh's presence in the region. A period of calm followed, thanks to Babylon's attention being directed elsewhere.

Meanwhile, late in his reign, Necho II launched a campaign south against the 'Nubian bowmen.' Recorded at Elephantine, the campaign included horses and chariots, and a fleet of eighteen vessels, including the king's own ship, which probably travelled as far as the Second Cataract. Necho's Kushite rival at the time was Anlamani (623–593 BCE), whose death, soon after the campaign, would provide another opportunity for the Egyptians to attack Kush and weaken their southern rival.

Saites at Sea

For much of the Pharaonic Period, it cannot be said that Egypt had a true navy. Ships were primarily used for transporting infantry along the Nile, or for trading or expeditionary activities. It was only in the Late Period that the navy became an important aspect of Egypt's military machine, a change that can be attributed to the Egyptians' increased reliance on Greek mercenaries, including sailors. Under Necho II, Egypt created two sets of seafaring forces: one for the Mediterranean, and the other for the Red Sea. According to Herodotus, Necho II also introduced triremes into the Egyptian navy: ships built for battle, with three levels of oarsmen on each side of the ship, capable of fast manoeuvres and ramming enemies. These were invented in the seventh century BCE in Corinth, and so were cutting edge in Necho's day. Using them, the Egyptians once again took control of important trade routes. One man who would have known these vessels well was Hor (nicknamed Psamtik); Hor was overseer of the royal combat vessels in the Mediterranean under Psamtik II (Necho II's successor) and commander of Aegean troops, suggesting that it was Greek crews that manned these combat vessels. Herodotus also says that Necho II attempted to dig a canal between the Red Sea and the Mediterranean, and sent a Phoenician vessel to circumnavigate Africa.

The Destruction of Napata

With Babylon distracted, in his third regnal year (593 BCE), Psamtik II – Necho II's successor – decided to launch a campaign into Nubia. This attack may have coincided with succession problems in Nubia following the death of the Kushite King Anlamani. Monuments belonging to King Aspelta, Anlamani's successor, have been attacked and restored, and during his reign, various priests were put to death by burning, seemingly either because they'd planned regicide or had manipulated the oracle against the king (perhaps to install another ruler on the throne).

According to his Victory Stele, Psamtik II didn't personally accompany this campaign beyond Shellal, just south of Asawn (where this stele was inscribed). Taking a relaxed attitude to campaigning, he was roaming the marshes at Lake Neferibre (seemingly in the Aswan area), when a messenger arrived to tell him that his troops had reached 'Pnubs' (probably Kerma).

The Kushites had attacked the pharaoh's army there, but the Egyptians were ultimately victorious, taking 4,200 captives. After the battle, the names of the Kushite 25th Dynasty kings were attacked across Egypt, reflecting a violent shift in attitude towards these pharaohs and their reigns, and the Egyptians seized territory between the First and Second Cataracts.

Extra detail about this campaign can be gleaned from a stele of Psamtik II, erected at Tanis, and from graffiti left by the king's army at Abu Simbel during their march. According to the Tanis stele, the Egyptians learnt of an impending Kushite attack, and decided to act first, sending the army to Napata. There, they burned the Kushite king in his palace. Archaeological evidence backs up this account: the Napatan palace and nearby temples were indeed burned down. Excavators also found ten royal statues fallen and smashed. The soldiers' graffiti, meanwhile, found on the legs of the seated colossi in front of the Great Temple at Abu Simbel, reveal the presence of Greek, Carian, and Phoenician soldiers on the campaign. They were led by the Commander of Foreign Mercenaries, Padisematawy, better known today as Potasimto, while the Egyptian Division was led by Ahmose – probably the later King Ahmose II. A man named Psamtik, son of Theocles, served under Potasimto. His father, Theocles, must have earlier settled in Egypt and, despite his foreign origin, named his son in honour of the Egyptian king. A letter, written centuries after the campaign, suggests that Judean troops were also present. It was a truly multicultural force.

The Phoenicians in Egypt

During the first millennium BCE, the Phoenicians – living along the northern Levantine coast – were renowned for their maritime activities, and enjoyed good relations with Egypt, transporting Egyptian goods across the known world. Their most important city-states were at Byblos, Sidon, and Tyre, but there were also Phoenician trading stations along the Mediterranean coastline, both in north Africa and southern Europe (in fact, it was through the Phoenicians that the alphabet entered Greece). In the Late Period, Phoenicians, some acting as mercenaries, lived in the eastern Delta and Memphis too. But due to Egypt's long-standing interactions with the northern Levant, many were already Egyptianized to some degree before their arrival: the Phoenicians already used Egyptian-style scarab seals, and their art had long been influenced by Egypt. During the 27th Dynasty, important Phoenicians were even buried in Egyptian-inspired stone sarcophagi.

The Wars of Apries and Ahmose

In 588 BCE, the Babylonians marched west to crush a rebellion in Judah, placing Jerusalem under siege. Apries, son and successor of Psamtik II, sent his troops to the city's defence, but it fell to the Babylonians two years later. Apries also sent a force to assist the cities of Sidon and Tyre against the Babylonians, but with equally little success. Once again, the Babylonians directly threatened the Egyptians, who reacted by launching campaigns against Cyprus and the northern Levant, attempting to bolster their power in the eastern Mediterranean. Cypriote mercenaries would now fight for Egypt, leaving their graffiti on the Great Pyramid at Giza, at Abydos, and Karnak Temple, and dedicating their sculptures in the sanctuary of Aphrodite at Naukratis.

But this was only the start of Apries' problems. According to Herodotus, late in Apries' reign, the king sent a force of *machimoi* – Egyptian warriors, mainly of Libyan descent – against Cyrene, a Greek kingdom in Libya, probably at the request of a local Libyan ruler. For this reason, Egypt's Greek mercenaries were kept behind, for they might have had mixed allegiances. The campaign was a disaster and the Egyptian *machimoi* were decimated. The survivors accused Apries of favouring his foreign troops over the Egyptians, arguing that he was happy to send them to their deaths. To ease tensions, the king suggested that the troops speak with General Ahmose, a high-level Egyptian military man. It's safe to say that this didn't have the desired result: the Egyptian troops quickly decided that it was time for a revolution and Ahmose was the man to lead them, proclaiming him king in 570 BCE. But this wasn't the end of Apries. After launching a failed attempt at retaking the throne, Apries fled to Babylon, seeking the assistance of the Babylonian king in his bid to regain his kingship. He returned to Egypt four years later backed by a Babylonian fighting force. Fierce battles raged on land and at sea, with the Egyptian army supported by Carian and Ionian warriors, as well as Greeks from Cyrenaica (north-east Libya). This time, Apries was defeated and killed.

Now unchallenged in Egypt, Ahmose II resumed contact with Kush, sending a probable trading mission under military escort in his forty-first year as king. Prosperity should have followed, but new developments in the east would change the political landscape once again: the rapid and violent expansion of Persia. The Persians had arrived in south-west Iran in around 1000 BCE, and under Cyrus II, 450 years later, were aggressively expanding their territory. They conquered Babylon in 539 BCE, defeating its king, Nabonidus, bringing about the collapse of the Babylonian Empire. Assimilating Babylonian territory, the newly established Persian Empire (also known as the Achaemenid Empire) now stretched all the way from Central Asia to the Levant. It was only a matter of time before they would attempt to invade Egypt.

Seeing this growing threat, Ahmose II had earlier reached out to Croesus of Lydia, and the leaders of Babylon and Sparta to form a coalition against the Persians, but Cyrus had seized Lydia and Babylon before any action could be taken. Unwilling to give up, Ahmose tried to forge other alliances among the Greek city-states, sending gifts and contributing to the reconstruction of Delphi. He even married a Greek princess named Ladice, according to Herodotus.

War loomed nonetheless, and Ahmose began to make preparations. Among the foreign mercenaries hired to fight for Egypt was Phanes of Halicarnassus, a man described by Herodotus as brave and intelligent. For some unexplained reason, however, Phanes deserted the Egyptian army and joined the Persians, providing them with information on how best to cross the desert into Egypt. This left the Egyptians in a weakened position. Luckily for Ahmose, he wouldn't have to deal with the fallout: he died in 526 BCE, leaving the impending crisis in the hands of his son, Psamtik III.

Trading with the Greeks: The Cities of Naukratis and Thonis-Heracleion

During the Late Period, ships carrying Greek trade goods were forced to enter Egypt through the thriving port and customs station of Thonis-Heracleion. From there, they passed along the Canopic Branch of the Nile to Naukratis in the western Delta, where taxes were imposed on precious goods, providing extra income for the temple of the goddess Neith. From Naukratis, ships could then sail onwards to Memphis, or along a canal to Sais. Both Naukratis and Thonis-Heracleion housed large Greek populations, with Naukratis eventually awarded the status of *polis* and Greek trading post; Herodotus says that the people of twelve Greek city-states and islands lived there. Traders sold Egyptian grain, papyrus, and perfume to their foreign counterparts, and workshops at Naukratis produced Egyptian scarabs, popular among the Greeks and Phoenicians as protective amulets. Foreign traders brought copper, tin, iron, wine, wool, oils, and lead ingots into Egypt, and left offerings from their homelands in the sanctuaries of their gods at Naukratis. Temples to Apollo, Aphrodite, and Hera, as well as other foreign gods, were constructed there, near temples to traditional Egyptian gods, such as Amun-Re of Naukratis. Thonis-Heracleion was also home to Greek mercenaries: Greek armour has been found there, as was a bronze mould, probably used to produce lead sling 'bullets' for the Greeks.

The Persian Invasion and Occupation

In 525 BCE, the Persians, now led by Cambyses II, launched their invasion of Egypt. The Egyptian army met them at Pelusium, in the eastern Delta. There, according to Herodotus, the Greeks and Carians, angry with Phanes of Halicarnassus for turning traitor, brought Phanes' sons (apparently left behind in Egypt) to their camp, making sure that Phanes could see them from across the battlefield. The mercenaries then slit each son's throat, draining the blood into a bowl and mixing it with water and wine. Only after drinking this grisly concoction did they go into battle. But their gruesome show made no difference to the outcome: the Persians were still the better fighting force and the Egyptians fell back to Memphis. The city was besieged for ten days, and in the end, Psamtik was taken prisoner. The Persians enslaved Psamtik's daughter, executed his son, and paraded 2,000 Egyptians, condemned to execution, before the captured pharaoh. Later, as a prisoner of Cambyses, Psamtik planned an uprising against his captors, but was discovered. According to Herodotus, as punishment, the Persians forced Psamtik to drink bull's blood, causing his death. And so, bathed in enough blood to keep a vampire happy for decades, the 26th Dynasty ended, and the 27th Dynasty – better known as the Persian Period – began. Egyptians were now forced to fight for the Persian army and the country's naval fleet was seized. Egypt's Greek mercenaries were sent home.

Accounts describing the Persian occupation of Egypt are strikingly at odds with one another. Classical sources present Cambyses II's rule as one of horrors and Persian atrocities, whereas Egyptian texts portray Cambyses as at pains to understand Egyptian customs. The most detailed description of life during this intriguing period was left by a man named Udjahorresnet. Udjahorresnet had served as admiral of Egypt's naval fleet under Ahmose II and Psamtik III, but shifted career quite dramatically after the Persian invasion: Cambyses appointed the former admiral controller of his palace, asked him to compose the royal titulary, and made him chief physician. In his account, Udjahorresnet goes on to say that Cambyses removed Persian squatters from the Temple of Neith at Sais, re-established the temple's offerings and festivals, and visited the temple himself to make offerings. In short, he presents Cambyses as a foreign king trying his best to follow Egyptian traditions and be accepted as a true pharaoh.

This is all at odds with Herodotus' account, in which Cambyses is described as cruel to Egypt's priests and temples, to the extent that he even murdered the sacred Apis bull. It's true that an Apis bull was buried under Cambyses, but the associated inscription presents the Persian pharaoh as a true king (rather than a bull killer). At the same time, however, Cambyses did limit the revenues of the temples, an act that would surely have made him unpopular among Egypt's priests. This probably led to people inventing stories about the Persian's impiety. Whatever the case may be, with rebellion back home in Persia, Cambyses left Egypt in 522 BCE, but died en route after being wounded in Syria. Following news of his death, the Egyptians revolted. Their uprising was quashed by Cambyses' successor, Darius I.

Darius I is remembered in classical writings as less cruel than Cambyses: he commanded the compilation of Egypt's laws from ancient times through to the reign of Ahmose II, for example – an interest in law that's commented on by the first century BCE Greek historian Diodorus Siculus – and just like any true pharaoh, his name is found on monuments across Egypt (but particularly at el-Qab and Kharga Oasis, continuing the Late Period interest in the region). A statue of Darius, carved in Egypt and covered in hiero-glyphic texts (but wearing Persian clothing), was even erected at Susa, the Persian capital. And Darius had one of his palaces at Susa decorated with ivory provided by the kings of Kush, who sent new supplies of elephant ivory every three years, according to Herodotus.

Darius placed Egypt under a satrap (provincial governor) named Aryandes, who was based at Memphis along with an Assyrian garrison (all paid for by Egyptian taxes and tribute, of course). And Persian governors and commanders were sent out to different parts of the country: among them was Parnu, commander of Aswan, and Atiyawahy, governor of Coptos from 524 to 473 BCE. Atiyawahy oversaw the despatch of stone from the Wadi Hammamat to Kharga Oasis for construction projects (and intriguingly, also invoked Egyptian gods in his inscriptions). And like Udjahorresnet, some Egyptians supported the Persian administration during the occupation. One such man, a treasurer named Ptahhotep, may have been rewarded by the Persian king, for he wears a Persian torque on one of his statues (although he may have just been fashion conscious). Udjahorresnet's life story also con-tinues under Darius: towards the end of Cambyses' reign, he had travelled abroad, but returned home under Darius to restore a House of Life (a place of learning), where he taught medicine at the request of the king. (Egyptian doctors also helped Darius when he sprained himself when dismounting from his horse, according to Herodotus.)

The reigns of Cambyses and Darius were brief periods of calm during the Persian occupation. The rulers that succeeded them were far more brutal, leading to repeated rebellions across Egypt. One revolt was led against Darius I in the early 480s BCE, only to be crushed by Xerxes I, his successor in 486 BCE. In response, Xerxes intensified the Persianification of Egypt's administration. Later, in the mid-460s BCE, upon Xerxes' death, another revolt broke out, led by a man named Inarus. Proclaimed king of Egypt by his followers, Inarus – apparently from the western Delta, and perhaps a descendant of Psamtik I – raised an army of Egyptians and Athenian mercenaries against the Persians, who were distracted by succession problems at home. At first, Inarus' movement was successful: the Egyptians defeated a Persian force, led by the Satrap Achaemenes (who himself was killed), and marched on Memphis, placing the Persian garrison there under siege. But two years later, the city remained under siege, and a second Persian fighting force had arrived to restore order, led by the famous commanders Artabazus and Megabyzus. The Egyptians and Athenians fled north, but were pursued and defeated. Inarus, apparently betrayed, was crucified. His revolt had lasted only six or seven years. Egypt would not regain independence for another six decades.

The Jewish Garrison at Elephantine

Egypt's Persian occupation led to a new influx of foreigners into the country, including the establishment of Jewish garrisons at Hermopolis and Memphis. But a Temple to Yahweh, and a garrison of Jewish mercenaries, had already existed at Elephantine before this time. Aramaic papyri provide a snapshot of life at this temple during the 27th Dynasty, notably recording that the local priests of Khnum destroyed the Temple of Yahweh in 410 BCE. No reason is given for this attack, and the temple was later rebuilt. These documents also reveal that the Jewish settlers received rations from the local storehouse, and married Egyptians.

Egypt is Freed and Kush Expands

The king that freed Egypt from the Persians was Amyrtaeus of Sais, the first and only pharaoh of the 28th Dynasty. He began his revolt in 405 BCE, probably in the Delta. At the time, Cyrus, younger brother of the Persian King

Artaxerxes II, was hoping to secure Persia's crown for himself. Although Cyrus' bid for the throne failed (he was killed in battle), it all worked out rather nicely for Amyrtaeus: for one, Artaxerxes' troops had been on their way to quash the rebellion in Egypt when they were redirected to fight against Cyrus, distracting them from the uprising; and two, after Cyrus lost the battle, his admiral, Tamos, fled to Egypt with thirty ships. Seeing this readymade fleet, Amyrtaeus executed Tamos, along with his children, and kept the ships for himself. Meanwhile, forgetting about Egypt for the moment, Artaxerxes travelled back to Susa, having realized the pressing need to secure his rule at home. So, for the time being at least, Egypt was free.

Armed with a fleet of ships and backed by an army of Egyptian warriors, Amyrtaeus now probably marched on Memphis, where a garrison of Persian troops was stationed. Knowing that no backup was on the way, these surrendered and switched allegiance to the Egyptians. It was probably the same in Upper Egypt, where further Persian garrisons were posted. And so, after securing the country, upon the death of Darius II in 404 BCE, Amyrtaeus formally declared independence from the Persian Empire. Taking the throne, he changed his name to Psamtik, either to highlight his descent from the illustrious founder of the 26th Dynasty, or to create an association with him. Things were looking up, both for Egypt and Amyrtaeus, until the newly minted pharaoh's reign was suddenly cut short by a man from Mendes named Nepherites. The usurper fought and captured Amyrtaeus, and then had him executed in Memphis – not the best reward for liberating your country, I'm sure you'll agree.

Meanwhile, in Nubia, the Kushites under King Harsiyotef (404–369 BCE) were also fighting rebellions and incursions across their territory. Over Harsiyotef's long reign, he fought nine campaigns, battling nomads called Rehrehes in the northern Butana and in Meroe, and the Medjay in the Eastern Desert. Some of his campaigns were fought in Lower Nubia. Harsiyotef's troops pursued one group of enemies as far as Aswan – the first evidence for the Kushites campaigning this far north since the 25th Dynasty – and fought 'rebels' at Mirgissa, capturing the town. This repeated need to campaign in Lower Nubia could show that the region was resistant to Kushite control, and wanted to be independent of both the Kushites and the Egyptians.

The Final Years of Independence

Now under Nepherites I of the 29th Dynasty, the Egyptians, faced with the threat of impending Persian (re-)invasion, set out to make life as difficult as possible for their former overlords. Probably using Tamos' captured fleet, they attacked coastal cities in the Levant, reducing the chance of a seaborne Persian attack, and probably constructed new ships to add to their numbers. In 396 BCE, they also sent grain and equipment for 100 ships to support the Spartan fleet at Rhodes (they were intercepted along the way, but it's the thought that counts). Three years later, in 393 BCE, Hakor (called Achoris by the Greeks) succeeded Nepherites, and ruled for the next thirteen years. Continuing the spirit of defiance, he sent fifty triremes to support Evagoras, the king of Salamis in Cyprus, Egypt's ally in the fight against Persia. Evagoras successfully repelled the Persians, and even seized Tyre, but was later forced to surrender Cyprus in 380 BCE. Persia's attempts to retake Egypt in 385 and 383 BCE failed. Hakor was then succeeded by Nepherites II, who only reigned for four months before being deposed by his general, Nectanebo – now King Nectanebo I.

Nectanebo's act of usurpation founded the 30th Dynasty, the family that would rule over the final four decades of Egyptian independence (380–342 BCE). Like their predecessors in the 26th Dynasty, the 30th Dynasty relied on foreign mercenaries for their power and strength, particularly Greek mercenaries, and foreign allies, such as the Phoenicians. But unlike in earlier times, these mercenaries predominantly came from mainland Greece, and only travelled to Egypt when needed. The Egyptians also hired famous foreign generals to support them. Expecting the Persians to invade at any time, Nectanebo fortified the north-east Delta and coast, and had soldiers monitor all routes into Egypt. The anticipated attack came in 373 BCE, when the Persian Satrap of Syria Pharanabazos led his army to the Mendesian branch of the Nile. Nectanebo's defences held strong. The Egyptians forced Pharanabazos to retreat. A second invasion, in 372 BCE, was also thwarted. Artaxerxes II now turned his attention to rebellions at home, leaving Nectanebo I to end his life in peace.

Upon taking the throne, Nectanebo's son Teos sought to take advantage of widespread unrest across the Persian Empire: parts of Anatolia were already revolting, and the empire had only a limited military presence in the Levant. It was the perfect time to launch a campaign. The Egyptians hired the Athenian General Chabrias to oversee the construction of ships and to train Egyptian naval officers. Chabrias also advised Teos to implement a system of heavy taxation across the country, particularly aimed at the temples, to raise funds for the campaign. It worked, but wasn't a particularly popular move among the people or priests. In the end, Teos managed to raise a force of 80,000 Egyptian troops, 10,000 Greek mercenaries, and 200 triremes. He also hired the veteran general and king of Sparta Agesilaus II, who arrived with 1,000 troops and thirty advisors. Egypt was ready for war.

The Egyptian army entered Phoenicia in 361 BCE, led by Teos himself. Below him, Agesilaus oversaw the Greek mercenaries, Chabrias the naval fleet, and Nectanebo – Teos' nephew – the Egyptian troops. The forces of Teos and Agesilaus remained in Phoenicia, securing the area, while Nectanebo and the Egyptian troops marched into Syria. The scene was set for a great battle, but it wasn't to be. Back in Egypt, Teos' brother, Tjahapimau, revolted, and sent a message to Nectanebo, asking him to seize the kingship. At the same time, a man from Mendes – home of the earlier 29th Dynasty – also claimed the throne. The Delta was falling into chaos. Back in the Levant, the Egyptian troops pledged their allegiance to Nectanebo, who then approached Chabrias and Agesilaus for their support. Agesilaus consulted with his authorities in Sparta, and was advised to make the decision alone; he sided with Nectanebo. Chabrias, meanwhile, remained loyal to Teos, but it was a futile move. Realizing his dire situation – all of the Egyptian and mercenary troops had turned against him – Teos fled to the Persian court, where he was received by Artaxerxes II. (A planned Persian assault on Egypt, seemingly involving Teos, would later be abandoned due to Artaxerxes' death in 358 BCE.) Meanwhile, Nectanebo and his Egyptian troops, aided by Agesilaus, left the Levant for Egypt and defeated the Mendesian usurper during a siege. No one now stood in the way of Nectanebo becoming King Nectanebo II.

Back in Persia, the newly crowned King Artaxerxes III had been left with the challenge of invading Egypt. First of all though, he had to dispose of any pesky rivals for his throne (killing eighty brothers in a single day, according to the first century AD Roman historian Quintus Curtius Rufus), and assert his right to rule at home. Only later, in 351 BCE, having re-established Persian control over the Levant, did he unleash his massive fighting force on Egypt. The assault ended in failure. Egypt's defenses – guarding vulnerable access points to the country and strengthened over recent decades – were more than a match for the Persian troops. The experienced Greek generals, Lamius the Spartan and Diophantus the Athenian, hired by Nectanebo, also ensured that the Egyptians could defend themselves from the Persian army.

After the battle, the Egyptians sent 4,000 mercenaries to aid a revolt at Sidon, inspiring the city and others in the region, as well as Cyprus, to throw off the Persian yoke. Artaxerxes' response was swift and brutal: he executed the rebels, burned down most of Sidon, and sent many of its inhabitants to Babylon and Susa as prisoners. The Persian king had sent a clear message:

rebellion would not be tolerated. Egypt's 4,000 mercenaries, led by Mentor of Rhodes, defected to the Persians, and Nectanebo sent no further troops to assist the Phoenician cities. By 345 BCE, the revolt was over. Persia's domination of the Levant was renewed. Egypt had abandoned its allies, and now, once again, faced the prospect of invasion.

Still, by now, Egypt had become pretty good at preparing for Persian invasions – they'd had a lot of experience. Nectanebo posted 5,000 men at Pelusium in the eastern Delta, and sent many others to protect the Nile mouths. In total, Egypt's army consisted of 60,000 Egyptians, 20,000 Greek mercenaries and 20,000 Libyans, all trained and ready to fight. But the Persians too had assembled a massive army, and arrived at Egypt's borders in 343 BCE with siege machines. They also had a secret weapon: Mentor of Rhodes' knowledge of Egypt's defences and strategies. Perhaps due to Mentor's intelligence, the Persian commanders divided their attack force into three divisions of Greeks and Persians (one division led by Mentor), and assigned each its own target: one attacked Pelusium, another Bubastis, and the third another city, unnamed in the sources. Overwhelmed, Nectanebo retreated to Memphis (where according to the fictional 'Romance of Alexander,' he used magic to manipulate and sink model boats, attempting to harm his very real enemies). It was a tactical miscalculation: hearing of the king's retreat, the Greek mercenaries defending Pelusium handed over the city in return for safe passage back to Greece. The people of Bubastis also surrendered, fearing that the Persians would burn their city down. Other cities followed suit. The door had been opened to the Persians. It could no longer be shut.

Accepting defeat, Nectanebo II, king of Egypt, gathered up his possessions and fled to Nubia. He then vanishes from history, except for a single mention of him as king on the walls of Edfu Temple a year after the Persian invasion. This raises the possibility that he made an attempt to reclaim his lost kingdom (or that the priests at Edfu were woefully behind on current affairs). Artaxerxes III, meanwhile, became the first Persian king in sixty years to sit on the throne of Egypt. It was probably still warm.

The Second Persian Period

Egypt's fall in 342 BCE brought about a renewed period of Persian rule, sometimes referred to as the 31st Dynasty or simply The Second Persian Period (342–332 BCE). Artaxerxes treated his reclaimed kingdom with immense brutality: first, the Persians demolished the fortifications of Egypt's main cities, ensuring that their inhabitants couldn't protect themselves from any future Persian attack (just in case anyone thought about rebelling again), and Persian garrisons were placed at important centres, including Pelusium. The king then robbed Egypt's sacred shrines of gold and silver, and took away the temples' sacred texts, which were later sold back to the priests by the Persian Vizier Bagoas. Some temples and tombs were destroyed entirely. Artaxerxes then installed a satrap at Memphis to rule in his name, and left the country for Babylon, taking one of Nectanebo's sons and other captives along with him.

Over the decade that followed, Egyptian rebellions were frequent. The best-known was led by a shadowy figure called Khababash, who perhaps came from Sais. According to Diodorus Siculus, Bagoas, the aforementioned Persian vizier, poisoned Artaxerxes III in 338 BCE, bringing about a crisis at the Persian court – it was the perfect time for Khababash to seize Egypt for himself. For the two year period of his kingship, roughly from 338–336 BCE, Khababash is known from a variety of small artefacts, as well as a marriage contract from Thebes, and an Apis bull sarcophagus from Memphis. He is also mentioned on the Satrap Stele, dated to the Ptolemaic Period; this mentions that the rebel pharaoh donated land in the Delta to the Temple of Buto, and inspected all the branches of the Nile that flowed into the Mediterranean – he must have known that the Persians wouldn't be distracted for long. And he was right. Darius III became king of Persia in 336 BCE, and soon after was back in control of Egypt. The new satrap, Sabaces, perhaps led the force that restored power, for he is attested in his position by 334 BCE. Nothing is known about the fate of Khababash.

But Sabaces wouldn't get to enjoy his new job for long. In 333 BCE, he travelled to Issus in southern Anatolia to fight alongside Darius III against Alexander the Great, leaving a man named Mazaces as satrap of Egypt in his place. Away from the action, Mazaces was probably as shocked as anyone when a fleet of ships turned up one day, along with 4,000 Greek mercenaries. Their leader, a Macedonian named Amyntas, had fought for Darius III at Issus, but had deserted the Persian king. Travelling to Egypt via Cyprus, Amyntas had taken Pelusium before continuing on to Memphis. There, he announced news of Sabaces' death at Issus and how Darius had made him – Amyntas – commander in Egypt. Mazaces must have been sceptical, for a battle was fought outside Memphis. Amyntas was the victor, but while his troops plundered the countryside around the city, a new wave of Egyptians left the safety of Memphis to attack them, killing each man, Amyntas among them. Mazaces, unexpectedly, had won the war, and remained satrap of Egypt. But his tenure would only last for one more year: Alexander the Great was on his way.

When Alexander entered Egypt in 332 BCE, welcomed by the Egyptians at Pelusium and having already taken the Levant, Mazaces was left in a difficult position: unpopular among the Egyptians, outmatched by Alexander's forces, and with no hope of Persian support arriving, how could he retain control of Egypt? The simple answer: he couldn't. Surrender was his only option. So Mazaces left his palace at Memphis and met Alexander at Heliopolis to formally hand over control of Egypt to the Macedonian. After decades of turmoil, suffering, and death, Persia's quest to dominate Egypt ended with a simple meeting, probably somewhere in the shadow of the Temple of Re.

A New Age: Ptolemies, Meroites, and Seleucids

Alexander only remained in Egypt for a short time, but it was long enough for him to assume the titles of a pharaoh, visit the Temple of Amun at Siwa Oasis (and be proclaimed the son of Amun), and found Alexandria. Nobody can accuse him of lazing around. Before continuing his wars in the east, Alexander left Egypt under new management, installing a variety of officers in government and leaving behind a large army to ensure control. After Alexander's death in the Palace of Nebuchadnezzar II at Babylon in 323 BCE, his generals carved up his empire, with Egypt and the southern Levant passing into the hands of General – later Pharaoh – Ptolemy.

Ptolemy's rule of Egypt initiated the Ptolemaic Period, a time of Greek-Macedonian pharaohs, from Ptolemy I to the death of Cleopatra VII in 30 BCE. Over the course of roughly 300 years, Egyptian and Greek culture would fuse and become known across the Mediterranean world. The Ptolemaic Kingdom stretched from Cyrene in modern Libya, through Egypt and into the Levant, where the Ptolemies competed for control with the Seleucid Empire, founded by Seleucus, another of Alexander's generals. Seleucus had been awarded control of Babylon in 312 BCE, and from there ruled Alexander's eastern empire. Over time, he had spread westward, eventually taking Anatolia and moving into Syria. This threatened the Ptolemaic Kingdom, and so, over the course of 100 years, the Ptolemies and Seleucids fought six wars (known as the Syrian Wars) for control of the Levant, continuing the unending tug-of-war for dominance over this much abused territory.

A new phase of history had begun in Nubia too. King Nastasen (335–315 BCE) was the final Kushite king to be buried at Nuri, and also commissioned the last Kushite royal inscription using Egyptian hieroglyphs. Within fifty years of his death, Kushite royal burials had moved from the region of Napata to Meroe, between the Fifth and Sixth Cataracts of the Nile, marking the end of the Napatan Period and the start of the Meroitic Period. This was a phase of fifty-seven kings, and a number of ruling queens, that lasted until around AD 350. The Meroites wrote in Meroitic (a writing system still not fully deciphered), introduced Kushite gods into their pantheon – such as the lion god Apedemak, often associated with warfare – and enjoyed good relations with the Ptolemies to the north. Exotic goods flowed between the two civilizations: in a palace storeroom at Wad Ben Naqa, archaeologists discovered stockpiles of ebony and ivory, probably meant for export; and the Treasury of Sanam was filled with elephant tusks. Traders carried wine, olive oil, and honey to Meroe from Egypt, along with ceramics and metalwork from across the Mediterranean world. The Meroites and Ptolemies also jointly built temples at Dakka – between the First and Second Cataracts – and on Philae Island at Aswan.

A new era of cultural interactions had begun across Nubia and Egypt, the Levant, and the wider eastern Mediterranean world. Just as in the preceding millennia, there would be wars, diplomacy, trade, and travel. People would interact, sharing technology and ideas. There would be innovations, and religious developments, great ideas realized and great ideas forgotten. Over successive centuries, the Ptolemaic Kingdom, the Meroitic Kushites, and the Seleucid Empire would interact, expand, contract, and end, their experiences always intertwined. And then would come the Romans.

But this is a story for another time.

Endnotes

Chapter 2: Building Foreign Relations (and Pyramids) (2584–2117 BCE)

1. Author's translation. For the scene, see Borchardt, L. (1913) *Das Grabdenkmal des Königs Sahu-re, Band II: Die Wandbilder*. Leipzig: J.C Hinrichs: pls. 12 and 13.
2. Author's translation. For the hieroglyphic text, see Sethe, K. (1933) *Urkunden des Alten Reichs*. Leipzig: J.C. Hinrichs: 130, 7-15.

Chapter 3: A Country Divided (2117–2066 BCE)

1. Translation from Manetho, *Aegyptiaca*. Translated by Waddell, W.G. (1940) *Manetho, With An English Translation by W.G. Waddell*. London: Heinemann: 61 (Fr 27).
2. Author's translation. For the hieroglyphic text, see Vandier, J. (1950) *Mo'alla: la tombe d'Ankhtifi et la tombe de Sébekhotep*. Cairo: Imprimerie de l'Institut français d'archéologie orientale: 185-186.
3. Author's translation. For the hieroglyphic text, see Vandier, J. (1950) *Mo'alla: la tombe d'Ankhtifi et la tombe de Sébekhotep*. Cairo: Imprimerie de l'Institut français d'archéologie orientale: 163.
4. Translation after Lichtheim, M. (1973) *Ancient Egyptian Literature*. Vol. I. Berkeley: University of California Press: 90.

Chapter 4: An Expanding World (2066–1781 BCE)

1. Author's translation. For the original hieroglyphic text, see Newberry, P.E. (1893) *Beni Hasan*, Part I. London: Kegan Paul, Trench, Trübner and co. Pl. 26, lines 157-158. My translation closely follows Allen, J.P. (2008) The Historical Inscription of Khnumhotep at Dahshur: Preliminary Report. *Bulletin of the American Schools of Oriental Research* 352: 29.
2. Authors' translation. For the original hieroglyphic text, see: Sethe, K. (1928) *Aegyptische Lesestücke zum Gebrauch im akademischen Unterricht: Texte des mittleren Reiches* (2nd edition). Leipzig: J.C. Hinrichs: 84, 3-4.

Chapter 5: The Hyksos and the Kermans: Their Rise and Fall (1781–1549 BCE)

1. Author's translation. For the original hieroglyphic text, see Helck, W. (1975) *Historisch-biographische Texte der 2. Zwischenzeit und neue Texte der 18. Dynastie*. Wiesbaden: Harrassowitz: 81, 4.

2. Author's translation. For the original hieroglyphic text, see Helck, W. (1975) *Historisch-biographische Texte der 2. Zwischenzeit und neue Texte der 18. Dynastie.* Wiesbaden: Harrassowitz: 80, 9-11.

3. Author's translation. For the original hieroglyphic text, see Helck, W. (1975) *Historisch-biographische Texte der 2. Zwischenzeit und neue Texte der 18. Dynastie.* Wiesbaden: Harrassowitz: 45, 16-19.

4. Translation after Simpson, W.K. *et al.* (2003) *The Literature of Ancient Egypt.* Cairo: The American University in Cairo Press: 346.

Chapter 6: Meeting the Mitanni and Assimilating Kush (1549–1388 BCE)

1. Translation after Shaw, I. (1991) *Egyptian Warfare and Weapons.* Princes Risborough: Shire Publications: 41-42.

2. Author's translation. For the original hieroglyphic text, see: Sethe, K. (1904-1909) *Urkunden der 18. dynastie.* Leipzig: J.C. Hinrichs: 324, 8-12.

3. Author's translation. For the original hieroglyphic text, see: Sethe, K. (1904-1909) *Urkunden der 18. dynastie.* Leipzig: J.C. Hinrichs: 657.

4. Author's translation. For the original hieroglyphic text, see: Sethe, K. (1904-1909) *Urkunden der 18. dynastie.* Leipzig: J.C. Hinrichs: 657, 16 - 658, 2.

5. Author's translation. For the original hieroglyphic text, see: Sethe, K. (1904-1909) *Urkunden der 18. dynastie.* Leipzig: J.C. Hinrichs: 660.

6. Author's translation. For the original hieroglyphic text, see: Sethe, K. (1904-1909) *Urkunden der 18. dynastie.* Leipzig: J.C. Hinrichs: 700, 12-14.

7. Author's translation. For the original hieroglyphic text, see: Helck, W. (1955-1958) *Urkunden der 18. dynastie.* Fascicles 17-22. Berlin: Akademie-Verlag: 1297, 1-1298, 2.

8. Author's translation. For the original hieroglyphic text, see the Memphis stele in: Helck, W. (1955-1958) *Urkunden der 18. dynastie.* Fascicles 17-22. Berlin: Akademie-Verlag: 1304, 10-14.

9. Author's translation. For the original hieroglyphic text, see the Memphis stele in: Helck, W. (1955-1958) *Urkunden der 18. dynastie.* Fascicles 17-22. Berlin: Akademie-Verlag: 1307, 6-1307, 17.

Chapter 7: Heresy and Diplomacy (1388–1298 BCE)

1. Author's translation. For the original hieroglyphic text, see: Helck, W. (1955-1958) *Urkunden der 18. dynastie.* Fascicles 17-22. Berlin: Akademie-Verlag: 1666, 3-18.

2. Translation after Bryce, T. (2003) *Letters of the Great Kings of the Ancient Near East: The Royal Correspondence of the Late Bronze Age.* Oxford and New York: Routledge: 179.

Chapter 8: The Hittites and the Ramessides (1298–1187 BCE)

1. Author's translation. For the original hieroglyphic text, see: Kitchen, K.A. (1979) *Ramesside Inscriptions: Historical and Biographical.* Vol. 2. Oxford: Blackwell: 81, 13-84, 5.
2. Author's translation. For the original hieroglyphic text, see: Kitchen, K.A. (1979) *Ramesside Inscriptions: Historical and Biographical.* Vol. 2. Oxford: Blackwell: 93, 16-94, 1.
3. Author's translation. For the original hieroglyphic text, see: Kitchen, K.A. (1980) *Ramesside Inscriptions: Historical and Biographical.* Vol. 3. Oxford: Blackwell: 437, 4.
4. Author's translation. For the original hieroglyphic text, see: Kitchen, K.A. (1980) *Ramesside Inscriptions: Historical and Biographical.* Vol. 3. Oxford: Blackwell: 148, 5-7.
5. Author's translation. For the original hieroglyphic text, see: Kitchen, K.A. (1982) *Ramesside Inscriptions: Historical and Biographical.* Vol. 4. Oxford: Blackwell: 7, 7-8.
6. Author's translation. For the original hieroglyphic text, see: Kitchen, K.A. (1982) *Ramesside Inscriptions: Historical and Biographical.* Vol. 4. Oxford: Blackwell: 1, 15-2,1.

Chapter 9: Sea Peoples, Libyans, and the End of the New Kingdom (1187–1064 BCE)

1. Translation after Pritchard, J.B. (1969) *Ancient Near Eastern Texts Relating to the Old Testament, Third Edition, with Supplement.* Princeton, New Jersey: Princeton University Press: 262.
2. Translation after Cline, E.H. and O'Connor, D.B. (2012) The Sea Peoples. In E.H. Cline and D. O'Connor (eds) (2012) *Ramesses III: The Life and Times of Egypt's Last Hero.* Ann Arbor, Mich: University of Michigan Press: 204.
3. Translation after Cline, E.H. and O'Connor, D.B. (2012) The Sea Peoples. In E.H. Cline and D. O'Connor (eds) (2012) *Ramesses III: The Life and Times of Egypt's Last Hero.* Ann Arbor, Mich: University of Michigan Press: 204-205.

Chapter 10: Libyan Pharaohs, the Kingdom of Kush, and the Assyrian Invasion (1064–664 BCE)

1. Translation after Lichtheim, M. (1980) *Ancient Egyptian Literature.* Vol. 3. Berkeley: University of California Press: 69.
2. Translation after Kahn, D. (2004) Taharqa, King of Kush and the Assyrians. *The Journal of the Society for the Study of Egyptian Antiquities* 31: 115.

3. Translation after Kahn, D. (2006) The Assyrian Invasions of Egypt (673–663 B.C.) and the Final Expulsion of the Kushites. *Studien zur Altägyptischen Kultur* 34: 261.
4. Translation after Pritchard, J.B. (1969) *Ancient Near Eastern Texts Relating to the Old Testament, Third Edition, with Supplement*. Princeton, New Jersey: Princeton University Press: 297.

Bibliography

Ancient Egyptian Foreign Relations – General

Abdalla, M.A. (2005) The Amputated Hands in Ancient Egypt. In K. Daoud, S. Bedier, and S. abd el-Fatah (eds) (2005) *Studies in Honor of Ali Radwan*. Vol. I. Cairo: Conseil Suprême des Antiquités de l'Égypte: 25–34.

Bárta, M. (2010) Borderland Dynamics in the Era of the Pyramid Builders in Egypt. In I.W. Zartman (ed.) (2010) *Understanding Life in the Borderlands: Boundaries in Depth and Motion*. Athens, Georgia: University of Georgia Press: 21–39.

Ben-Tor, A. (ed.) (1994) *The Archaeology of Ancient Israel*. Yale: Yale University Press.

Bresciani, E. (1997) Foreigners. in S. Donadoni (ed.) (1997) *The Egyptians*. Chicago and London: Chicago University Press: 221–253.

Bryce, T. (2003) *Letters of the Great Kings of the Ancient Near East: The Royal Correspondence of the Late Bronze Age*. Oxford and New York: Routledge.

Bryce, T. (2006) *The Kingdom of the Hittites*. 2nd edition. Oxford: Oxford University Press.

Bryce, T. (2014) *Ancient Syria: A Three Thousand Year History*. Oxford: Oxford University Press.

Cohen, R. and Westbrook, R. (eds) (2000) *Amarna Diplomacy: The Beginnings of International Relations*. Baltimore and London: The Johns Hopkins University Press.

Cooney, W.A. (2011) *Egypt's Encounter with the West: Race, Culture and Identity*. Unpublished PhD thesis, University of Durham.

Dodson, A. and Hilton, D. (2004) *The Complete Royal Families of Ancient Egypt*. London and New York: Thames and Hudson.

Faulkner, R.O. (1953) Egyptian Military Organization. *Journal of Egyptian Archaeology* 39: 32–47.

Gnirs, A.M. (1996) *Militär und Gesellschaft. Ein Beitrag zur Sozialgeschichte des Neuen Reiches*. Heidelberg: Heidelberger Orientverlag.

Hakimian, S. (2008) Byblos. In J. Aruz, K. Benzel and J.M. Evans (eds) (2008) *Beyond Babylon: Art, Trade, and Diplomacy in the Second Millennium B.C.* New York: Metropolitan Museum of Art; New Haven and London: Yale University Press: 49–50.

Hamblin, W.J. (2006) *Warfare in the Ancient Near East to 1600 BC: Holy Warriors at the Dawn of History.* London: Routledge.

Heinz, S.C. (2001) *Die Feldzugsdarstellungen des Neuen Reiches: eine Bildanalyse.* Vienna: Österreichischen Akademie der Wissenschaften.

Kemp, B. (1989) *Ancient Egypt: Anatomy of a Civilization.* London: Routledge.

Kitchen, K.A (1969–1990) *Ramesside Inscriptions: Historical and Biographical.* 8 Vols. Oxford: Blackwell.

Kitchen, K.A. (1996) *Ramesside Inscriptions. Translated and Annotated: Translations Vol. 2. Ramesses II, Royal Inscriptions.* Oxford: Blackwell.

Kitchen, K.A. (1999) *Ramesside Inscriptions. Translated and Annotated, Notes and Comments. Ramesses II, Royal Inscriptions.* Oxford: Blackwell.

Kitchen, K.A. (2000) *Ramesside Inscriptions. Translated and Annotated: Translations Vol. 3, Ramesses II, His Contemporaries.* Oxford: Blackwell.

Kitchen, K.A. (2003) *Ramesside Inscriptions. Translated and Annotated: Translations Vol. 4. Merenptah and the Late Nineteenth Dynasty.* Oxford: Blackwell.

Kitchen, K.A. (2004) The Elusive Land of Punt Revisited. In P. Lunde and A. Porter (eds) (2004) *Trade and Travel in the Red Sea Region.* Oxford: Archaeopress: 25–31.

Lichtheim, M. (1973–1980) *Ancient Egyptian Literature.* 3 Vols. Berkeley: University of California Press.

Liverani, M. (1990) *Prestige and Interest, International Relations in the Near East ca. 1600 – 1100 B.C.* Padova: Sargon.

Liverani, M. (2001) *International Relations in the Ancient Near East.* Basingstoke: Palgrave.

Lorton, D. (1974) *The Juridical Terminology of International Relations in Egyptian Texts through Dynasty XVIII.* Baltimore and London: The John Hopkins University Press.

Lundh, P. (2002) *Actor and Event, Military Activity in Ancient Egyptian Narrative Texts from Tuthmosis II to Merenptah.* Uppsala: Department of Archaeology and Ancient History, Uppsala University.

Meeks, D. (2003) Locating Punt. In D. O'Connor and S. Quirke (eds) (2003) *Mysterious Lands.* London: UCL Press: 53–80.

Moreno García, J.C. (ed.) (2013) *Ancient Egyptian Administration*. Leiden and Boston: Brill.

Morkot, R. (2000) *The Black Pharaohs: Egypt's Nubian Rulers*. London: Rubicon.

O'Connor, D. (1993) *Ancient Nubia: Egypt's Rival in Africa*. Philadelphia: University of Pennsylvania Press.

O'Connor, D. and Quirke, S. (eds) (2003) *Mysterious Lands*. London: UCL Press.

Podany, A.H. (2010) *Brotherhood of Kings: How International Relations Shaped the Ancient Near East*. New York and Oxford: Oxford University Press.

Pritchard, J.B. (1969) *Ancient Near Eastern Texts Relating to the Old Testament, Third Edition, with Supplement*. Princeton, New Jersey: Princeton University Press.

Redford, D. (1992) *Egypt, Canaan and Israel in Ancient Times*. Princeton, New Jersey: Princeton University Press.

Schneider, T. (2003) Foreign Egypt: Egyptology and the Concept of Cultural Appropriation. *Ägypten und Levante* 13: 155–161.

Schneider, T. (2008) Foreigners in Egypt. In W. Wendrich (ed.) (2008) *Egyptian Archaeology*. Malden, Oxford and Chichester: Wiley-Blackwell: 143–163.

Schneider, T. (2008) Egypt and the Levant. In J. Aruz, K. Benzel and J.M. Evans (eds) (2008) *Beyond Babylon: Art, Trade, and Diplomacy in the Second Millennium B.C.* New York: Metropolitan Museum of Art; New Haven and London: Yale University Press: 61–62.

Schulman, A.R. (1964) *Military Rank, Title and Organization in the Egyptian New Kingdom*. Berlin: B. Hessling.

Shaw, I. (1991) *Egyptian Warfare and Weapons*. Princes Risborough: Shire Publications.

Shaw, I. (ed.) (2000) *The Oxford History of Ancient Egypt*. Oxford: Oxford University Press.

Simpson, W.K. *et al.* (2003) *The Literature of Ancient Egypt*. Cairo: The American University in Cairo Press.

Smith, S. (2003) *Wretched Kush: Ethnic Identities and Boundaries in Egypt's Nubian Empire*. London: Routledge.

Spalinger, A. (1982) *Aspects of the Military Documents of the Ancient Egyptians*. New Haven: Yale University Press.

Spalinger, A. (2005) *War in Ancient Egypt*. Malden, Oxford and Chichester: Wiley-Blackwell.

Spalinger, A. (2013) The Organisation of the Pharaonic Army (Old to New Kingdom). In Moreno García, J.C. (ed.) (2013) *Ancient Egyptian Administration*. Leiden and Boston: Brill: 393–478.

Steiner, M.L. and Killebrew, A.E. (eds) (2013) *The Oxford Handbook of the Archaeology of the Levant: c. 8000-332 BCE*. Oxford: Oxford University Press.

Swan Hall, E. (1986) *The Pharaoh Smites his Enemies*. Munich: Deutscher Kunstverlag.

Taylor, J.H. *Egypt and Nubia*. London: British Museum Press.

Tőrők. L. (2009) *Between Two Worlds: The Frontier Region Between Ancient Nubia and Egypt, 3700 BC – 500 AD*. Leiden and Boston: Brill.

Van de Mieroop, M. (2007) *The Eastern Mediterranean in the Age of Ramesses II*. Malden, Oxford and Chichester: Wiley-Blackwell.

Waddell, W.G. (1940) *Manetho, With An English Translation by W.G. Waddell*. London: Heinemann.

Wilkinson, T. (2010) *The Rise and Fall of Ancient Egypt*. London, Berlin, New York and Sydney: Bloomsbury.

Preface: Crossroads

Galán, J.M. (1995) *Victory and Border: Terminology Related to the Egyptian Imperialism in the XVIIIth Dynasty*. Hildesheim: Gerstenberg Verlag.

Hornung, E. (1992) *Idea into Image: Essays on Egyptian Thought*. Translated by E. Bredeck. New York: Timken.

1. Another World

Adamski, B. and Rosińska-Balik, K. (2014) Brewing technology in Early Egypt. Invention of Upper or Lower Egyptians? In A. Maczynska (ed.) (2014) *The Nile Delta as a Centre of Cultural Interactions Between Upper Egypt and the Southern Levant in the 4th millennium BC*. Poznań: Poznań Archaeological Museum: 23–36.

Bárta, M. (2010) *Swimmers in the Sand: On the Neolithic Origins of Ancient Egyptian Mythology and Symbolism*. Prague: Dryada.

Bárta, M. (2013) Kings, Viziers, and Courtiers: Executive Power in the Third Millennium B.C. In Moreno García, J.C. (ed.) (2013) *Ancient Egyptian Administration*. Leiden and Boston: Brill: 153–175.

Baud, M. and Dobrev, V. (1995) De nouvelles annales de l'Ancien Empire égyptien. Une 'Pierre de Palerme' pour la VIe dynastie. *Bulletin de l'Institut Français d'Archéologie Orientale* 95: 23–92.

Braun, E. (2009) South Levantine Early Bronze Age chronological correlations with Egypt in light of the Narmer serekhs from Tel Erani and Arad: New interpretations. *British Museum Studies in Ancient Egypt and Sudan* 13: 25–48.

Braun, E. (2014) Reflections on the Context of a Late Dynasty 0 Egyptian Colony in the Southern Levant: Interpreting Some Evidence of Nilotic Material Culture at Select Sites in the Southern Levant (ca. 3150 BCE - ca. 2950 BCE). In A. Maczynska (ed.) (2014) *The Nile Delta as a Centre of Cultural Interactions Between Upper Egypt and the Southern Levant in the 4th millennium BC.* Poznań: Poznań Archaeological Museum: 37–56.

Chłodnicki, M., Ciałowicz, K.M. and Mączyńska, A. (2012) *Tell el-Farkha I: Excavation 1998–2011.* Poznan: Poznan Archaeological Museum.

Ciałowicz, K.M. (2009) The Early Dynastic Administrative-cultic Centre at Tell el-Farkha. *British Museum Studies in Ancient Egypt and Sudan* 13: 83–123.

Dębowska-Ludwin, J., Rosińska-Balik, K., Czarnowicz, M. and Ochał-Czarnowicz, A. (2012) Trade or Conquest? The Nature of Egyptian-South Levantine Relations in Early Bronze I from the Perspective of Tell el-Farkha, Egypt and Tel Erani, Israel. In *Recherches Archéologiques Nouvelle Serie* 4: 113–122.

De Miroschedji, P. and Sadek, M. (2001) Gaza et l'Égypte de l'époque prédynastique à l'Ancien Empire: Premiers résultats des fouilles de Tell es-Sakan. *Bulletin de la Société Française d'Égyptologie* 152: 28–52.

Gatto, M.C. (2006) The Early A-Group in Upper Lower Nubia, Upper Egypt and the Surrounding Deserts. In M. Chlodnicki, K. Kroeper, M. Kobusiewicz (eds) (2006) *Archaeology of the Earliest Northeastern Africa, Volume Dedicated to the Memory of Lech Krzyzaniak.* Poznan: Poznan Archaeological Museum: 223–234.

Gatto, M.C. (2009) Egypt and Nubia in the 5th–4th millennia BCE: A View From the First Cataract and Its Surroundings. *British Museum Studies in Ancient Egypt and Sudan* 13: 125–45.

Gatto, M.C. (2011) The Nubia Pastoral Culture as Link Between Egypt and Africa: A View from the Archaeological Record. In K. Exell (ed.) (2011) *Egypt in its African Context: Proceedings of the Conference Held at The Manchester Museum, University of Manchester, 2–4 October 2009.* Oxford: Archaeopress: 21–29.

Gophna, R. (1978) 'En Besor: An Egyptian First Dynasty Staging Post in the Northern Negev. *Expedition* 20: 4–7.

Hartung, U. (2003) Predynastic Subterranean Dwellers in Maadi, Cairo. *Egyptian Archaeology* 22: 7–9.

Hikade, T. (2012) Egypt and the Near East in Prehistoric Times. In D.T. Potts (ed.) (2012) *A Companion to the Archaeology of the Ancient Near East.* Vol 2. Chichester: Wiley-Blackwell: 833–850.

Lange, M. and Nordström, H-A., (2006) Abkan Connections. The Relationship between the Abkan Culture in the Nile Valley and Early Nubian Sites from the Laqiya Region (Eastern Sahara, Northwest-Sudan). In Karla Kroeper, Marek Chłodnicki, Michał Kobusiewicz (eds) (2006) *Archaeology of Early Northeastern Africa: In Memory of Lech Krzyżaniak.* Poznań: 297–312.

Mączyńska, A. (2013) *Lower Egyptian Communities and their Interactions with Southern Levant in the 4th millennium BC.* Poznań: Poznań Archaeological Museum.

Ochał-Czarnowicz, A. (2012) Trade or Conquest? The Nature of Egyptian-South Levantine Relations in Early Bronze I from the Perspective of Tell el-Farkha, Egypt and Tel Erani, Israel. *Recherches Archeologiques Nouvelle Serie 4:* 113–122.

Raue, D. (2002) Nubians on Elephantine Island. *Sudan and Nubia* 6: 20–24.

Somaglino, C. and Tallet, P. (2015) Gebel Sheikh Suleiman: A First Dynasty Relief After All... *Archéo-Nil* 25: 123–134.

Tristant, Y. and Midant-Reynes, B. (2011) The Predynastic Cultures of the Nile Delta. In E. Teeter (ed.) (2011) *Before the Pyramids, The Origins of Egyptian Civilization.* Chicago: Oriental Institute of the University of Chicago: 45–54.

Wengrow, D. (2006) *The Archaeology of Early Egypt: Social Transformations in North-East Africa, 10,000 to 2650 BC.* Cambridge: Cambridge University Press.

Wilkinson, T. (1999) *Early Dynastic Egypt.* London: Routledge.

Wilkinson, T. (2002) Reality Versus Ideology: The Evidence for 'Asiatics' in Predynastic and Early Dynastic Egypt. In Van den Brink, E.C.M. and Levy T.E. (eds) (2002) *Egypt and the Levant: Interrelations from the 4th through the Early 3rd Millennium BCE.* London: Leicester University Press: 514–520.

Williams, B.B. (2011) Relations Between Egypt and Nubia in the Naqada Period. In E. Teeter (ed.) (2011) *Before the Pyramids, The Origins of Egyptian Civilization.* Chicago: Oriental Institute of the University of Chicago: 83–92.

2. Building Foreign Relations (and Pyramids)

Bell, L. (1976) *Interpreters and Egyptianized Nubians in Ancient Egyptian Foreign Policy: Aspects of the History of Egypt and Nubia*. Unpublished PhD dissertation, University of Pennsylvania.

Borchardt, L. (1913) *Das Grabdenkmal des Königs Sahu-re, Band II: Die Wandbilder*. Leipzig: J.C Hinrichs.

Bradbury, L. (1996) Kpn-boats, Punt Trade, and a Lost Emporium. *Journal of the American Research Center in Egypt* 33: 37–60.

Dixon, D.M. (1958) The Land of Yam. *Journal of Egyptian Archaeology* 44: 40–55.

El Awady, T. (2009) *Abusir XVI: Sahure – The Pyramid Causeway: History and Decoration Program in the Old Kingdom*. Prague: Charles University in Prague.

Förster, F. (2007) With Donkeys, Jars and Water Bags into the Libyan Desert: The Abu Ballas Trail in the Late Old Kingdom/First Intermediate Period. *British Museum Studies in Ancient Egypt and Sudan* 7: 1–39.

Grajetzki, W. (2013) Setting a State Anew: The Central Administration from the End of the Old Kingdom to the End of the Middle Kingdom. In Moreno García, J.C. (ed.) (2013) *Ancient Egyptian Administration*. Leiden and Boston: Brill: 215–258.

Marcolin, M. (2006) 'Iny, a Much-traveled Official of the Sixth Dynasty: Unpublished Reliefs in Japan. In M. Bárta; F. Coppens, and J. Krejčí (eds) (2006) *Abu Sir and Saqqara in the Year 2005: Proceedings of the Conference Held in Prague (June 27–July 5, 2005)*. Prague: Czech Institute of Egyptology, Faculty of Arts, Charles University in Prague: 282–310.

Marcolin, M. and Espinel, A.D. (2011) The Sixth Dynasty Biographic Inscription of Iny: More Pieces to the Puzzle. In M. Bárta, F. Coppens and J. Krejčí (eds) (2011) *Abu Sir and Saqqara in the Year 2010*. Vol. 2. Prague: Czech Institute of Egyptology, Faculty of Arts, Charles University in Prague: 570–615.

Miroschedji, P. de. (2012) Egypt and Southern Canaan in the Third Millennium BCE: Uni's Asiatic Campaigns Revisited. In M. Gruber, S.A. Aḥituv, G. Lehmann and Z. Talshir (eds) (2012) *All the Wisdom of the East: Studies in Near Eastern Archaeology and History in Honor of Eliezer D. Oren*. Fribourg: Academic Press Fribourg; Göttingen: Vandenhoeck & Ruprecht: 265–292.

Moreno Garcia, J.C. (2010) War in Old Kingdom Egypt (2686–2125 BCE). In J. Vidal (ed.) (2010) *Studies on War in the Ancient Near East. Collected Essays on Military History.* Münster: Ugarit Verlag: 5–41.

Mumford, G. (2006) Tell Ras Budran (Site 345): Defining Egypt's Eastern Frontier and Mining Operations in South Sinai During the Late Old Kingdom (Early EB IV/MB I). *Bulletin of the American Schools of Oriental Research* 342: 1–55.

O'Connor, D. (1986) The Locations of Yam and Kush and Their Historical Implications. *Journal of the American Research Center in Egypt* 23: 27–50.

O'Connor, D. (2014) *The Old Kingdom Town at Buhen.* London: Egypt Exploration Society.

Pantalacci, L. (2010) Organisation et contrôle du travail dans la province oasite à la fin de l'Ancien Empire: Le cas des grands chantiers de construction à Balat. In B. Menu (ed.) (2010) *L'organisation du travail en Égypte ancienne et en Mésopotamie: Colloque Aidea, Nice 4–5 Octobre 2004.* Cairo: Institut français d'archéologie orientale: 139–153.

Phillips, J. (1997) Punt and Aksum: Egypt and the Horn of Africa. *Journal of African History* 38: 423–457.

Sethe, K. (1933) *Urkunden des Alten Reichs.* Leipzig: J.C. Hinrichs.

Shapland, A.L. (2010) In Pursuit of Punt: Egyptian Relations with a Lost Land. *Journal of Near and Middle Eastern Studies* 2010: 10–16.

Sowada, K.N. (2009) *Egypt in the Eastern Mediterranean During the Old Kingdom: A Re-Appraisal of the Archaeological Evidence.* Fribourg: Academic Press Fribourg.

Strudwick, N. (2005) *Texts from the Pyramid Age.* Atlanta: Society of Biblical Literature.

Tallet, P. (2012) Ayn Sukhna and Wadi el-Jarf: Two Newly Discovered Pharaonic Harbours on the Suez Gulf. *British Museum Studies in Ancient Egypt and Sudan* 18: 147–68.

3. A Country Divided

Bietak, M. (1987) The C-Group and the Pan-Grave Culture in Nuybia. In T. Hagg (ed.) (1987) *Nubian Culture: Past and Present: Main Papers Presented at the Sixth International Conference for Nubian Studies in Uppsala, 11–16 August, 1986.* Stockholm: Kungl. Vitterhets Historie och Antikvitets Akademien: Almqvist & Wiksell distributor: 113–128.

Brovarski, E. and Murnane, W.J. (1969) Inscriptions from the Time of Nebhepetre Mentuhotep II at Abisko. *Serapis* 1: 11–33.

Darnell, J.C. (1997) New Inscriptions of the Late First Intermediate Period from the Theban Western Desert and the Beginnings of the Northern Expansion of the Eleventh Dynasty. *Journal of Near Eastern Studies* 56: 241–258.

Darnell, J.C. and Darnell, D. (2002) *Theban Desert Road Survey in the Egyptian Western Desert, Volume 1: Gebel Tjauti Rock Inscriptions 1-45 and Wadi el-Hol Rock Inscriptions 1-45.* Chicago: Oriental Institute of the University of Chicago.

Darnell, J.C. (2003) The Rock Inscriptions of Tjehemau at Abisko. *Zeitschrift für Ägyptische Sprache und Altertumskunde* 130: 31–48.

Darnell, J.C. (2004) The Route of the Eleventh Dynasty Expansion into Nubia: An Interpretation Based on the Rock Inscriptions of Tjehemau at Abisko. *Zeitschrift für Ägyptische Sprache und Altertumskunde* 131:23–37.

Darnell, J.C. (2008) The Eleventh Dynasty Royal Inscription from Deir el-Ballas. *Revue d'Égyptologie* 59: 81–110.

Demidchik, A. (2003) The Reign of Merikare Khety. *Göttinger Miszellen* 192: 25–36.

El-Khadragy, M. (2004) The First Intermediate Period Tombs at Asyut Revisited. *Studien zur Altägyptischen Kultur* 32: 233–243.

El-Khadragy, M. (2006) The Northern Soldiers-Tomb at Asyut. *Studien zur Altägyptischen Kultur* 35: 147–164.

El-Khadragy, M. (2007) Some Significant Features in the Decoration of the Chapel of Iti-ibi-iqer at Asyut. *Studien zur Altägyptischen Kultur* 36: 105–135.

El-Khadragy, M. (2008) The Decoration of the Rock-cut Chapel of Khety II at Asyut. *Studien zur Altägyptischen Kultur* 37: 219–241.

Fischer, H.G. (1961) The Nubian Mercenaries of Gebelein During the First Intermediate Period. *Kush* 9: 44–80.

Fischer, H.G. (1963) Varia Aegyptiaca. *Journal of the American Research Center in Egypt* 2: 15–51.

Hayes, W.C. (1949) Career of the Great Steward Henenu under Nebhepetrē' Mentuhotpe. *Journal of Egyptian Archaeology* 35: 43–49.

Jansen-Winkeln, K. (2010) Der Untergang des Alten Reiches. *Orientalia Nova Series* 79: 273–303.

Moeller, N. (2005) The First Intermediate Period: A Time of Famine and Climate Change? *Ägypten und Levante* 15: 153–167.

Redford, D.B. (2010) *City of the Ram-man: The Story of Ancient Mendes.* Princeton; Oxford: Princeton University Press.

Seidlmayer, S. (2000) The First Intermediate Period (*c.* 2160–2055). In I. Shaw (ed.) (2000) *The Oxford History of Ancient Egypt.* Oxford: Oxford University Press: 108–136.

Silverman, D.P. (2008) A Reference to Warfare at Dendereh, Prior to the Unification of Egypt in the Eleventh Dynasty. In S.E. Thompson and P. Der Manuelian (eds) (2008) *Egypt and Beyond: Essays Presented to Leonard H. Lesko Upon His Retirement from the Wilbour Chair of Egyptology at Brown University June 2005*. Providence, R.I.: Dept. of Egyptology and Ancient Western Asian Studies, Brown University: 319–331.

Spanel, D.B. (1989) The Herakleopolitan Tombs of Kheti I, Jt(.j)jb(.j), and Kheti II at Asyut. *Orientalia* 58: 301–14.

Vandier, J. (1950) *Mo'alla: la tombe d'Ankhtifi et la tombe de Sébekhotep*. Cairo: Imprimerie de l'Institut français d'archéologie orientale.

Willems, H. (2014) *Historical and Archaeological Aspects of Egyptian Funerary Culture: Religious Ideas and Ritual Practice in Middle Kingdom Elite Cemeteries*. Leiden: Brill.

4. An Expanding World

Allen, J.P. (2008) The Historical Inscription of Khnumhotep at Dahshur: Preliminary Report. *Bulletin of the American Schools of Oriental Research* 352: 29–39.

Arnold, D. (2009) Foreign and Female. In S. D'Auria (ed.) (2009) *Offerings to the Discerning Eye: An Egyptological Medley in Honor of Jack A. Josephson*. Leiden and Boston: Brill: 17–32.

Baines, J. (1987) The Stela of Khusobek: Private and Royal Military Narrative and Values. In G. Dreyer and G. Fecht (1987) *Form und Mass: Beiträge zur Literatur, Sprache und Kunst des alten Ägypten: Festschrift für Gerhard Fecht zum 65. Geburtstag am 6. Februar 1987*. Wiesbaden: Harrassowitz: 43–61.

Bard, K. (2013) Seafaring in Ancient Egypt: Cedar Ships, Incense, and Long-Distance Voyaging. In J. Aruz, S.B. Graff, Y. Rakic (eds) (2013) *Cultures in Contact: From Mesopotamia to the Mediterranean in the Second Millennium B.C.* New York: The Metropolitan Museum of Art: 46–53.

Ben-Tor, D. (2011) Egyptian-Canaanite Relations in the Middle and Late Bronze Ages as Reflected by Scarabs. In S. Bar, D. Kahn, and J.J. Shirley (eds) (2011) *Egypt, Canaan and Israel: History, Imperialism, Ideology and Literature*. Leiden and Boston: Brill: 23–43.

Bradbury, L. (1988) Reflections on Traveling to 'God's Land' and Punt in the Middle Kingdom. *Journal of the American Research Center in Egypt* 25: 127–156.

Darnell, J.C. (1997) A New Middle Egyptian Literary Text from the Wadi el-Ḥôl. *Journal of the American Research Center in Egypt* 34: 85–100.

Darnell, J.C., Dobbs-Allsopp, F.W., Lundberg, M.J., McCarter, P.K. Zuckerman, B. and Manassa, C. (2005) Two Early Alphabetic Inscriptions from the Wadi el-Ḥôl: New Evidence for the Origin of the Alphabet from the Western Desert of Egypt. *The Annual of the American Schools of Oriental Research* 59: 67–124.

Dunham, D. & Janssen, J. (1960) *Second Cataract Forts. Vol I: Semna-Kumma*. Boston: Museum of Fine Arts.

Fattovich, R. and Bard, K.A. (2012) Archaeological Investigations at Wadi/ Mersa Gawasis, Egypt 2006–2007, 2007–2008 and 2009 Field Seasons. In P. Tallet and El-S. Mahfouz (eds) (2012) *The Red Sea in Pharaonic Times. Recent Discoveries Along the Red Sea Coast. Proceedings of the Colloquium Held in Cairo/Ayn Soukhna, 11th-12th January 2009*. Cairo: Institut français d'archéologie orientale: 21–26.

Fattovich, R. and Bard, K.A. (2012) Ships Bound for Punt. In P. Tallet and El-S. Mahfouz (eds) (2012) *The Red Sea in Pharaonic Times. Recent Discoveries Along the Red Sea Coast. Proceedings of the Colloquium Held in Cairo/Ayn Soukhna, 11th-12th January 2009*. Cairo: Institut français d'archéologie orientale: 27–33.

Fitton, L., Hughes, M., and Quirke, S. (1998) Northerners at Lahun, Neuron Activation Analysis of Minoan and Related Pottery in the British Museum. In S. Quirke (ed.) (1998) *Lahun Studies*. New Malden: SIA Publications: 112–140.

Gardiner, A.H. and Peet, T.E. (1952) *The Inscriptions of Sinai. Part I, Introduction and Plates*. London: Egypt Exploration Society. Part II = *Translation and Commentary* (1955) edited and compiled by Černý, J.

Hierakonpolis Expedition Website (accessed 2016) HK27C: The Nubian C Group Cemetery. http://www.hierakonpolis-online.org/index.php/explore-the-nubian-cemeteries/hk27c-c-group

Hierakonpolis Expedition Website (accessed 2016) Pan Graves – HK47. http://www.hierakonpolis-online.org/index.php/explore-the-nubian-cemeteries/hk47-pan-graves

Hikade, T. (2007) Crossing the Frontier into the Desert: Egyptian Expeditions to the Sinai Peninsula. *Ancient West and East* 6: 1–22.

Hoffmeier, J.K. (2006) 'The Walls of the Ruler' in Egyptian Literature and the Archaeological Record: Investigating Egypt's Eastern Frontier in the Bronze Age. *Bulletin of the American Schools of Oriental Research* 343:1–20.

Kamrin, J. (2009) The Aamu of Shu in the Tomb of Khnumhotep II at Beni Hassan. *Journal of Ancient Egyptian Interconnections* 1: 22–36.

Kitchen, K. (1961) An Unusual Stela from Abydos. *Journal of Egyptian Archaeology* 47: 10–18.

Kitchen, K. (1990) Early Canaanites in Rio de Janeiro and a 'Corrupt' Ramesside Land-Sale. In S. Israelit-Groll (ed.) (1990) *Studies in Egyptology Presented to Miriam Lichtheim*, Vol. 2. Jerusalem: Magnes Press, Hebrew University: 635–645.

Kitchen, K. (1991) Non-Egyptians Recorded on Middle-Kingdom Stelae in Rio de Janeiro. In S. Quirke (ed.) (1991) *Middle Kingdom Studies*. New Malden: SIA Publications: 87–90.

Marcus, E.S. (2007) Amenemhet II and the Sea: Maritime Aspects of the Mit Rahina (Memphis) Inscription. *Ägypten und Levante* 17: 137–190.

Marochetti, E.F. (2010) *The Reliefs of the Chapel of Nebhepetre Mentuhotep at Gebelein (CGT 7003/1-277)*. Transl. by K. Hurry. Leiden and Boston: Brill.

Newberry, P.E. (1893) *Beni Hasan*, Part I. London: Kegan Paul, Trench, Trübner and co.

Posener, G. (1957) Les asiatiques en Egypte sous les XIIe et XIIIe dynasties. *Syria* 34: 145–163.

Quirke, S. (1990) *The Administration of Egypt in the Late Middle Kingdom: The Hieratic Documents*. New Malden: SIA Publications.

Saretta, P. (2016) *Asiatics in Middle Kingdom Egypt: Perceptions and Reality*. London: Bloomsbury.

Schulman, A.R. (1982) The Battle Scenes of the Middle Kingdom. *Journal of the Society for the Study of Egyptian Antiquities* 12: 165–183.

Sethe, K. (1928) *Aegyptische Lesestücke zum Gebrauch im akademischen Unterricht: Texte des mittleren Reiches* (2nd edition). Leipzig: J.C. Hinrichs.

Smith, H.S. (1976) *The Fortress of Buhen: the Inscriptions*. London: Egypt Exploration Society.

Sparks, R. (2004) Canaan in Egypt: Archaeological Evidence for a Social Phenomenon. In J. Bourriau and J. Phillips (eds) (2004) *Invention and Innovation. The Social Context of Technological Change 2: Egypt, the Aegean and Near East, 1650-1150 B.C.* Oxford: Oxbow Books: 25–54.

Weinstein, J.M. (1975) Egyptian Relations with Palestine in the Middle Kingdom. *Bulletin of the American Schools of Oriental Research* 217: 1–16.

Wiener, M. H. (2013) Contacts: Crete, Egypt, and the Near East circa 2000 B.C. In J. Aruz, S.B. Graff, Y. Rakic (eds) (2013) *Cultures in Contact: From Mesopotamia to the Mediterranean in the Second Millennium B.C.* New York: The Metropolitan Museum of Art: 34–43.

5. The Hyksos and the Kermans: Their Rise and Fall

Ahrens, A. (2011) A 'Hyksos' Connection? Thoughts on the Date of Dispatch of Some of the Middle Kingdom Objects Found in the Northern Levant. In J. Mynářová (ed.) (2011) *Egypt and the Near East - The Crossroads*. Prague: Charles University in Prague: 21–40.

Bader, B. (2011) Contacts Between Egypt and Syria-Palestine as Seen in a Grown Settlement of the Late Middle Kingdom at Tell el-Dab'a/ Egypt. In J. Mynářová (ed.) (2011) *Egypt and the Near East – The Crossroads, Proceedings of the International Workshop on the Relations between Egypt and the Near East in the Bronze Age September 1–3, 2010.* Prague: Charles University in Prague: 41–72.

Baines, J. (1986) The Stela of Emhab: Innovation, Tradition, Hierarchy. *Journal of Egyptian Archaeology* 72: 41–53.

Bietak, M. (1996) *Avaris: The Capital of the Hyksos; Recent Excavations at Tell el-Daba*. London: British Museum Press.

Davies, W.V. (2003) Kush in Egypt: A New Historical Inscription. *Sudan and Nubia* 7: 52–54.

Gardiner, A.H. (1916) The Defeat of the Hyksos by Kamose: The Carnarvon Tablet, No. 1. *Journal of Egyptian Archaeology* 3: 95–110.

Helck, W. (1975) *Historisch-biographische Texte der 2. Zwischenzeit und neue Texte der 18. Dynastie.* Wiesbaden: Harrassowitz.

Morenz, L.D. and Popko, L. (2010) The Second Intermediate Period and the New Kingdom. In A.B. Lloyd (ed.) (2010) *A Companion to Ancient Egypt*. Vol 1. Malden, Oxford and Chichester: Wiley-Blackwell: 101–119.

Nigro, L. (2009) The Eighteenth Century BC Princes of Byblos and Ebla and the Chronology of the Middle Bronze Age. In A.M. Maila Afeiche (ed.) (2009) *Interconnections in the Eastern Mediterranean. Lebanon in the Bronze and Iron Ages. Proceedings of the International Symposium – Beirut 2008*: Beyrouth: Minstère de la culture, Direction Générale des Antiquités: 159–175.

Oren, E.D. (ed.) (1997) *The Hyksos: New Historical and Archaeological Perspectives.* Philadelphia: University Museum, University of Pennsylvania.

Redford, D.B. (1997) Textual Sources for the Hyksos Period. In E.D. Oren (ed.) (1997) *The Hyksos: New Historical and Archaeological Perspectives.* Philadelphia: University Museum, University of Pennsylvania: 1–44.

Ryholt, K.S.B. (1997) *The Political Situation in Egypt During the Second Intermediate Period, c. 1800-1550 B.C.* Copenhagen: Museum Tusculanum Press.

Säve-Söderbergh, T. (1949) A Buhen Stela from the Second Intermediate Period (Kharṭūm No. 18). *Journal of Egyptian Archaeology* 35: 50–58.

Shaw, G.J. (2009) The Death of King Seqenenre Tao. *Journal of the American Research Center in Egypt* 45: 159–176.

Shirley, J.J. (2013) Crisis and Restructuring of the State: From the Second Intermediate Period to the Advent of the Ramesses. In J.C. Moreno García (ed.) (2013) *Ancient Egyptian Administration*. Leiden and Boston: Brill: 521–606.

Smith, H.S. and Smith, A. (1976) A Reconsideration of the Kamose Texts. *Zeitschrift für Ägyptische Sprache und Altertumskunde* 103: 48–76.

Vandersleyen, C. (1971) *Les guerres d'Amosis; fondateur de la XVIIIe dynastie*. Brussels: Fondation Égyptologique Reine Élisabeth.

Weinstein, J.M. (1974) A Statuette of the Princess Sobeknefru at Tell Gezer. *Bulletin of the American Schools of Oriental Research* 213: 49–57.

6. Meeting the Mitanni and Assimilating Kush

Beylage, P. (2002) *Aufbau der königlichen Stelentexte vom Beginn der 18. Dynastie bis zur Amarnazeit*. Wiesbaden: Harrassowitz.

Botti, G. (1955) A Fragment of the Story of a Military Expedition of Tuthmosis III to Syria (P. Turin 1940 – 1941). *Journal of Egyptian Archaeology* 41: 64–71.

Bradbury, L. (1984–1985) The Tombos Inscription: A New Interpretation. *Serapis* 8: 1–20.

Bryan, B.M. (1991) *The Reign of Thutmose IV*. Baltimore, Maryland: The John Hopkins University Press.

Cochavi-Rainey, Z. (1990) Egyptian Influences in the Akkadian Texts Written by Egyptian Scribes in the Fourteenth and Fifteenth Centuries B.C.E. *Journal of Near Eastern Studies* 49: 57–65.

Davies, N. de. G., and Faulkner, R.O. (1947). A Syrian Trading Venture to Egypt. *Journal of Egyptian Archaeology* 33: 40–46.

Edel, E. (1953) Die Stelen Amenophis' II. aus Karnak und Memphis mit dem Bericht über die asiatischen Feldzüge des Königs. *Zeitschrift des deutschen Palästina-Vereins* 69: 97–176; addendum in (1954) *Zeitschrift des deutschen Palästina-Vereins* 70: 87.

Faulkner, R.O. (1942) The Battle of Megiddo. *Journal of Egyptian Archaeology* 28: 2–15.

Faulkner, R.O. (1955) A Possible Royal Visit to Punt. In Università di Pisa (1955) *Studi in memoria di Ippolito Rosellini nel primo centenario della morte (4 giugno 1843)*. Vol. II. Pisa: V. Lischi: 84–90.

Habachi, L. (1957) Two Graffiti at Sehel from the Reign of Queen Hatshepsut. *Journal of Near Eastern Studies* 16: 88–104.

Helck, W. (1955–1958) *Urkunden der 18. dynastie.* Fascicles 17-22. Berlin: Akademie-Verlag.

Klug, A. (2002) *Königliche Stelen in der Zeit von Ahmose bis Amenophis III.* Brussels: Fondation Égyptologique Reine Elisabeth.

Kuentz, Ch. (1925) *Deux Stèle d'Aménophis II (Stèles d'Amada et d'Elephantine).* Cairo: Institut Français d'Archéologie Orientale.

Lorton, D. (1990) The Aswan/Philae Inscription of Thutmosis II. In S. Israelit Groll and P. Magnes (eds) (1990) *Studies in Egyptology Presented to Miriam Lichtheim.* Vol. II. Jerusalem: Hebrew University: 668–679.

Manuelian, P. Der (1987) *Studies in the Reign of Amenophis II.* Hildesheim: Gerstenberg Verlag.

Panagiotopoulos, D. (2006) Foreigners in Egypt in the Time of Hatshepsut and Thutmose III. In E. Cline and D. O'Connor (eds) (2006) *Thutmose III: A New Biography.* Ann Arbor, Mich.: University of Michigan Press: 370–412.

Rainey, A.F. (1973) Amenhotep II's Campaign to Takhsi. *Journal of the American Research Center in Egypt* 10: 71–75.

Redford, D.B. (1973) New Light on the Asiatic Campaigning of Horemheb. *Bulletin of the American Schools of Oriental Research* 211: 36–49.

Redford, D.B. (2003) *The Wars in Syria and Palestine of Thutmose III.* Leiden: Brill.

Reineke, W-F. (1977) Ein Nubienfeldzug unter Königin Hatshepsut. In E. Endesfelder et al. (eds.) (1977) *Ägypten und Kusch.* Berlin: Akademie Verlag: 369–376.

Schulman, A.R. (1963) The Egyptian Chariotry: A Reexamination. *Journal of the American Research Center in Egypt* 2: 75–98.

Schulman, A.R. (1957) Egyptian Representations of Horsemen and Riding in the New Kingdom. *Journal of Near Eastern Studies* 16: 263–271.

Sethe, K. (1904–1909) *Urkunden der 18. dynastie.* Fascicles 1–16. Leipzig: J.C. Hinrichs.

Shaw, G.J. (2008) *Royal Authority in Egypt's Eighteenth Dynasty.* Oxford: Archaeopress.

Topozada, Z. (1988) Les Deux Campagnes d'Amenhotep III en Nubie. *Bulletin de l'Institut Français d'Archéologie Orientale* 88: 153–165.

Weinstein, J.M. (1981) The Egyptian Empire in Palestine: A Reassessment. *Bulletin of the American Schools of Oriental Research* 241: 1–28.

7. Heresy and Diplomacy

Baines, J. (2003) On the Genre and Purpose of the 'Large Commemorative Scarabs' of Amenhotep III. In N. Grimal, A. Kamel, and C.M. Sheikholeslami (eds) (2003) *Hommages à Fayza Haikal*. Cairo: Institut Français d'Archéologie Orientale: 29–43.

Berridge, G. (2002) Amarna Diplomacy: A Full-fledged Diplomatic System? In R. Cohen and R. Westbrook (eds) (2002) *Amarna Diplomacy: The Beginnings of International Relations*. Baltimore and London: The John Hopkins University Press: 212–224.

Cohen, R. and Westbrook, R. (eds) (2002) *Amarna Diplomacy: The Beginnings of International Relations*. Baltimore and London: The John Hopkins University Press.

Cohen, R. and Westbrook, R. (2002) Conclusion: The Beginnings of International Relations. In R. Cohen and R. Westbrook (eds) (2002) *Amarna Diplomacy: The Beginnings of International Relations*. Baltimore and London: The John Hopkins University Press: 225–236.

Darnell, J.C. and Manassa, C. (2007) *Tutankhamun's Armies: Battle and Conquest During Ancient Egypt's Late Eighteenth Dynasty*. Hoboken, N.J.: Wiley.

Davies, W.V. and Schofield, L. (eds) (1995) *Egypt, the Aegean and the Levant: Interconnections in the Second Millennium BC*. London: British Museum Press.

Moran, W.L. (1992) *The Amarna Letters*. Baltimore: The John Hopkins University Press.

Schulman, A.R. (1964) Some Observations on the Military Background of the Amarna Period. *Journal of the American Research Center in Egypt* 3: 51–69.

Schulman, A.R. (1982) The Nubian War of Akhenaton. In J. Leclant (ed.) (1982) *L'Égyptologie en 1979: Axes Prioritaires de Recherches*. Vol. 2. Paris: Editions du Centre National de la Recherche Scientifique: 299–316.

Westbrook, R. (2000) Babylonian Diplomacy in the Amarna Letters. *Journal of the American Oriental Society* 120: 377–382.

Yalçin, Ü. (2006) *The Ship of Uluburun: A Comprehensive Compendium of the Exhibition Catalogue 'The Ship of Uluburun: World Trade 3000 Years Ago.'* Bochum: Deutsches Bergbau-Museum.

Zaccagnini, C. (2002) The Interdependence of the Great Powers. In R. Cohen and R. Westbrook (eds) (2002) *Amarna Diplomacy: The Beginnings of International Relations*. Baltimore and London: The John Hopkins University Press: 141–153.

8. The Hittites and the Ramessides

Abbas, M.R. (2013) A Survey of the Diplomatic Role of the Charioteers in the Ramesside Period. In A.J. Veldmeijer and S. Ikram (eds) (2013) *Chasing Chariots: Proceedings of the First International Chariot Conference (Cairo 2012)*. Leiden: Sidestone Press: 17–27.

Gardiner, A.H. (1911) *Egyptian Hieratic Texts, Literary Texts of the New Kingdom*. Part 1. Leipzig: Hinrichs.

Kitchen, K. (1964) Some New Light on the Wars of Ramesses II. *Journal of Egyptian Archaeology* 50: 47–70.

Kitchen, K. (1982) *Pharaoh Triumphant: The Life and Times of Ramesses II, King of Egypt*. Warminster: Aris & Phillips.

Murnane, W.J. (1985) *The Road to Kadesh: A Historical Interpretation of the Battle Reliefs of King Sety I at Karnak*. Chicago: University of Chicago Press.

Ockinga, B. (1987) On the Interpretation of the Kadesh Record. *Chronique d'Égypte* 62: 38–48.

Pusch, E.B. (1996) 'Pi-Ramesses-Beloved-of-Amun, Headquarters of Thy Chariotry' Egyptians and Hittites in the Delta Residence of the Ramessides. In *Pelizaeus-Museum Hildesheim Guidebook, The Egyptian Collection*. Mainz: Von Zabern: 126–144.

Pusch, E.B. and Herold, A. (1999) Qantir/Pi-Ramesses. In K.A. Bard (ed.) (1999) *Encyclopedia of the Archaeology of Ancient Egypt*. London: Routledge: 787–790.

Prell, S. (2013) A Glimpse into the Workshops of the Chariotry of Qantir-Piramesse – Stone and Metal Tools of Site Q I. In A.J. Veldmeijer and S. Ikram (eds) (2013) *Chasing Chariots: Proceedings of the First International Chariot Conference (Cairo 2012)*. Leiden: Sidestone Press: 157–174.

Spalinger, A.J. (1979a) Traces of the Early Career of Ramesses II. *Journal of Near Eastern Studies* 38: 271–286.

Spalinger, A.J. (1979b) The Northern Wars of Seti I: An Integrative Study. *Journal of the American Research Center in Egypt* 16: 29–47.

Spalinger, A.J. (1980) Historical Observations on the Military Reliefs of Abu Simbel and Other Ramesside Temples in Nubia. *Journal of Egyptian Archaeology* 66: 83–99.

Yurco, F.J. (1986) Merenptah's Canaanite Campaign. *Journal of the American Research Center in Egypt* 23: 189–215.

Wilkinson, R.H. (ed.) (2012) *Tausret: Forgotten Queen and Pharaoh of Egypt.* Oxford: Oxford University Press.

9. Sea Peoples, Libyans, and the End of the New Kingdom

Cline, E.H. and O'Connor, D.B. (eds) (2012) *Ramesses III: The Life and Times of Egypt's Last Hero.* Ann Arbor, Mich: University of Michigan Press.

Cline, E.H. and O'Connor, D.B. (2012) The Sea Peoples. In E.H. Cline and D. O'Connor (eds) (2012) *Ramesses III: The Life and Times of Egypt's Last Hero.* Ann Arbor, Mich: University of Michigan Press: 180–208.

Epigraphic Survey, The (1930) *Earlier Historical Records of Ramses III. Medinet Habu Vol. I. Plates 1-54.* Chicago: The University of Chicago Press.

O'Connor, D. (1990) The Nature of Tjemhu (Libyan) Society in the Later New Kingdom. In A. Leahy (ed.) (1990), *Libya and Egypt c.1300–750 BC.* London: SOAS Centre of Near and Middle Eastern Studies and the Society for Libyan Studies: 29–114.

Oren, E. (2000) *The Sea Peoples and Their World: A Reassessment.* Philadelphia: University of Pennsylvania.

Peden, A.J. (1994) *The Reign of Ramesses IV.* Warminster: Aris and Phillips.

Peet, T.E. (1930) *The Great Tomb-robberies of the Twentieth Egyptian Dynasty: Being a Critical Study, with Translations and Commentaries, of the Papyri in which these are Recorded.* Oxford: Clarendon Press.

Porten, B. (2011) *The Elephantine Papyri in English: Three Millennia of Cross-cultural Continuity and Change.* 2nd Revised Edition. Atlanta: Society of Biblical Literature.

Schwartz, M. (2010) Darkness Descends: The End of the Bronze Age Empires. *Ancient Warfare* 4: 2–5.

Snape, S. (2012) The Legacy of Ramesses III and the Libyan Ascendancy. In E.H. Cline and D. O'Connor (eds) (2012) *Ramesses III: The Life and Times of Egypt's Last Hero.* Ann Arbor, Mich: University of Michigan Press: 404–441.

Vernus, P. (2003) *Affairs and Scandals in Ancient Egypt.* (Trans. Lorton, D.). Ithaca and London: Cornell University Press.

Ward, W.A. (1994) Foreigners Living in the Village. In L.H. Lesko (ed.) (1994) *Pharaoh's Workers: The Village of Deir el-Medina.* Ithaca and London: Cornell University Press: 61–85.

Wente, E.F. (1967) *Late Ramesside Letters.* Chicago: University of Chicago Press.

10. Libyan Pharaohs, the Kingdom of Kush, and the Assyrian Invasion

Caminos, R.A. (1959) *The Chronicle of Prince Osorkon*. Rome: Pontificium Institutum Biblicum.

Finkelstein, I. (2002) The Campaign of Shoshenq I to Palestine: A Guide to the 10th Century BCE Polity. *Zeitschrift des Deutschen Palästina-Vereins* 118: 109–135.

Gardiner, A.H. (1932) *Late-Egyptian Stories*. Brussels: Fondation égyptologique reine Élisabeth.

Kahn, D. (1999) Did Tefnakht I Rule as King? *Göttinger Miszellen* 173: 123–125.

Kahn, D. (2001) The Inscription of Sargon II at Tang-i Var and the Chronology of Dynasty 25. *Orientalia, Nova Series* 70: 1–18.

Kahn, D. (2004) Taharqa, King of Kush and the Assyrians. *Journal of the Society for the Study of Egyptian Antiquities* 31: 109–128.

Kahn, D. (2006) The Assyrian Invasions of Egypt (673-663 B.C.) and the Final Expulsion of the Kushites. *Studien zur Altägyptischen Kultur* 34: 251–267.

Kahn, D. (2015) Why Did Necho II Kill Josiah? In J. Mynářová, P. Onderka and P. Pavúk (eds) (2015) *There and Back Again – The Crossroads II, Proceedings of an International Conference Held in Prague, September 15–18, 2014*. Prague: Charles University in Prague: 511–528.

Kitchen, K. (1986) *The Third Intermediate Period in Egypt* (1100-650 B.C.). 2nd Edition. Warminster: Aris & Phillips.

Sass, B. (2002) Wenamun and His Levant – 1075 or 925 BC? *Ägypten und Levante* 12: 247–255.

Schäfer, H. (1905–1908) *Urkunden der älteren Äthiopenkönige*. 2 Vols. Leipzig: J.C. Hinrichs.

Vernus, P. (1975) Inscriptions de la Troisième Période Intermédiaire (I). *Bulletin de l'Institut Français d'Archéologie Orientale* 75: 1–66.

Zamazalová, S. (2011) Before the Assyrian Conquest in 671 B.C.E.: Relations between Egypt, Kush and Assyria. In J. Mynářová (ed.) (2011) *Egypt and the Near East - The Crossroads: Proceedings of an International Conference on the Relations of Egypt and the Near East in the Bronze Age, Prague, September 1–3, 2010*. Prague: Czech Institute of Egyptology: 297–328.

11. Vive La Resistance

Agut-Labordère, D. (2013) The Emergence of a Mediterranean Power: The Saite Period. In J.C. Moreno García (ed.) (2013) *Ancient Egyptian Administration*. Leiden and Boston: Brill: 965–1027.

Fischer-Bovet, C. (2014) *Army and Society in Ptolemaic Egypt*. Cambridge: Cambridge University Press.

Goddio, F. and Masson-Berghoff, A. (2016) *Sunken Cities: Egypt's Lost Worlds*. London and New York: Thames and Hudson.

Johnson, J. (ed.) (1992) *Life in a Multicultural Society: Egypt from Cambyses to Constantine and Beyond*. Chicago: Oriental Institute of the University of Chicago.

Kahn, D. (2008a) Inaros' Rebellion Against Artaxerxes I and the Athenian Disaster in Egypt. *Classical Quarterly* 58: 424–440.

Kahn, D. (2008b) Some Remarks on the Foreign Policy of Psammetichus II in the Levant (595–589 B.C.). *Journal of Egyptian History* 1: 139–157.

Klotz, D. (2006) *Adoration of the Ram: Five Hymns to Amun-Re from Hibis Temple*. New Haven, CT: Yale Egyptological Seminar.

Lipiński, L. (2006) *On the Skirts of Canaan in the Iron Age: Historical and Topographical Researches*. Leuven: Peeters.

Lloyd, A.B. (1972) Triremes and the Saite Navy. *Journal of Egyptian Archaeology* 58: 268–279.

Posener, G. (1936) *La première domination perse en Égypte: recueil d'inscriptions hiéroglyphiques*. Cairo: Institut Français d'Archéologie Orientale.

Radner, K. (2012) After Eltekeh: Royal Hostages from Egypt at the Assyrian Court. In H. Baker, K. Kaniuth and A. Otto (eds) (2012) *Stories of Long Ago. Festschrift für Michael D. Roaf*. Münster: Ugarit Verlag: 471–479.

Ray, J. (2002) *Reflections of Osiris, Lives from Ancient Egypt*. London: Profile.

Ruzicka, S. (2012) *Trouble in the West: Egypt and the Persian Empire, 525–332 BCE*. Oxford: Oxford University Press.

Schmitz, P. (2010) The Phoenician Contingent in the Campaign of Psammetichus II against Kush. *Journal of Egyptian History*: 321–337.

Vittmann, G. (2007) A Question of Names, Titles and Iconography. Kushites in Priestly, Administrative and other Positions from Dynasties 25 to 26. *Der Antike Sudan, Mitteilungen der Sudanarchäologischen Gesellschaft zu Berlin* 18: 139–161.

Welsby, D.A. (1996) *The Kingdom of Kush: The Napatan and Meroitic Empires*. London: British Museum Press.

Index